Beyond Consequentialism

Beyond Consequentialism

Paul Hurley

OXFORD
UNIVERSITY PRESS

OXFORD
UNIVERSITY PRESS

Great Clarendon Street, Oxford OX2 6DP

Oxford University Press is a department of the University of Oxford.
It furthers the University's objective of excellence in research, scholarship,
and education by publishing worldwide in

Oxford New York

Auckland Cape Town Dar es Salaam Hong Kong Karachi
Kuala Lumpur Madrid Melbourne Mexico City Nairobi
New Delhi Shanghai Taipei Toronto

With offices in

Argentina Austria Brazil Chile Czech Republic France Greece
Guatemala Hungary Italy Japan Poland Portugal Singapore
South Korea Switzerland Thailand Turkey Ukraine Vietnam

Oxford is a registered trade mark of Oxford University Press
in the UK and in certain other countries

Published in the United States
by Oxford University Press Inc., New York

British Library Cataloguing in Publication Data
Data available

Library of Congress Cataloging in Publication Data
Data available

Typeset by Laserwords Private Limited, Chennai, India
Printed in Great Britain
on acid-free paper by the
MPG Books Group, Bodmin and King's Lynn

ISBN 978-0-19-955930-5

10 9 8 7 6 5 4 3 2 1

For
My Wife, Mary Braet
and
My Mother, Joy Hurley

Acknowledgments

I am grateful for Kurt Baier's advice to develop the implications of my earlier work for the debate between consequentialists and their critics—he saw the outlines of this book long before I did. A special debt of gratitude is owed as well to David Gauthier, Jean Hampton, and Shelly Kagan for their invaluable role in the early development of many of the arguments presented here. The writings of T. M. Scanlon and Samuel Scheffler have also served as an ongoing source of insight and inspiration. I have benefited from discussions of this material with Stephen Darwall, Fred Schueler, Mark LeBar, Elizabeth Radcliffe, Peter Graham, John Fischer, Corey Brettschneider, Ted Hinchman, Voula Tsounas, Andrews Reath, Alan Nelson, Pierre Keller, Derek Parfit, Michael Meyer, Aaron James, Margaret Gilbert, Hilary Bok, Geoff Sayre-McCord, Amy Kind, Suzanne Obdrzalek, Stephen Davis, Noell Birondo, Peter Kung, Peter Thielke, Ann Davis, Michael Green, and Masahiro Yamada. I am particulary grateful for extensive written and oral comments on substantial portions of the manuscript from Gary Watson, Charles Young, Alex Rajczi, Dion Scott-Kakures, and Mark Lance, and owe an even deeper debt of gratitude to Arthur Ripstein, David Cummiskey, and Rivka Weinberg, who provided invaluable comments and criticisms on the entire manuscript at various crucial stages in its development. I have received helpful feedback on parts of this material from audiences at UC Riverside, Georgetown University, Ohio University, Occidental College, UC Santa Barbara, The University of New Mexico, UC Irvine, and the Claremont Colleges Works in Progress Group. I have also presented portions of this material to many of my classes, and have benefited greatly from many of these discussions. Particular thanks are due to the members of the Philosophy Department at Santa Clara University for inviting me to spend an extremely productive term as a visiting Fagothey Professor.

Additional debts of gratitude are owed to Peter Momtchiloff and Catherine Berry of Oxford University Press for their expertise in overseeing the publication of this book, to Celina Rosas for timely technical assistsance, to Kim Allen for copy editing, to Andrew Hawkey and Cory Davia for proofreading, and to my sons Paul and Joe, who help me keep my feet on the ground when my head is in the clouds. Gratitude is also due to the journal *Ethics* for granting me permission to use revised portions of my essay "Does Consequentialism Make Too Many Demands, or None at All?" (Volume 116, July (2006), pp. 680–706).

Contents

1

Introduction

Morality requires agents to perform the act that promotes the best overall state of affairs—it never permits us to bring about a worse state of affairs when a better one is available. To endorse this claim is to be committed to the paradigmatic version of consequentialism, upon which an action is morally right just in case its performance leads to the best state of affairs.[1] Such moral theories, and variations upon them, can with some plausibility claim a status as the default alternative in contemporary moral philosophy.[2] All roads to a systematic theoretical understanding of our moral practices can seem to lead down slippery slopes to consequentialism. Other approaches can appear upon reflection to smack of post hoc intuition mongering,

[1] This formulation is taken from Tim Scanlon (1998, p. 81). There are almost as many formulations of even the standard form of act consequentialism as there are consequentialists, nor are the differences in these formulations trivial. (See, for example, Shelly Kagan's alternative formulation (1989, p. 8).) But these differences are not relevant to the arguments that follow.

[2] These variations upon standard act consequentialism are usefully categorized by Shelly Kagan, who makes a helpful distinction between foundational consequentialism, which holds that "the ultimate justification for . . . genuine normative factors . . . lies in an appeal to overall good," and factoral consequentialism, which holds that "the goodness of overall consequences is the one and only normative factor with intrinsic moral significance" (1998, p. 213). Kagan's "factoral" consequentialism is sometimes characterized as well as "normative" consequentialism. One could in theory be a foundational consequentialist but not a factoral consequentialist, holding, for example, that although ultimate justification of normative factors appeals to overall states of affairs, such an appeal justifies normative factors other than the goodness of overall states of affairs. One could also in theory be a factoral/normative but not a foundational consequentialist, holding, for example, that although the appeal to the goodness of overall states of affairs is the only relevant normative factor, the ultimate ground for adopting this factor is not itself provided by overall states of affairs. Several recent accounts that reject foundational/philosophical consequentialism but defend normative/factoral consequentialism will be taken up in Section 8.5. Kagan also distinguishes versions of consequentialism by what sorts of things they hold to "be the primary focus of our moral evaluations" (1998, p. 214). Standard alternatives include actions, motives, and rules. Standard act consequentialism takes the proper focal point of direct evaluation to be actions, and embraces both factoral (normative) and foundational (philosophical) consequentialism with respect to the focal point of action. Variations upon such standard act consequentialism that shift the focal point from actions to rules and motives will be taken up in Section 8.4.

or to run afoul of Occam's razor. Beyond philosophy consequentialism is rarely mentioned but widely used. Its pervasive deployment in spheres such as economics, public policy, and jurisprudence is one of the more striking developments of the last century and a half. In public policy, for example, it is now commonplace to rank policies in terms of the better or worse consequences that will result overall from their implementation, often measured in monetary terms of benefits vs. costs.[3] In economics the rational course of action by an agent is taken to be the one that maximizes that agent's own welfare, utility, or preference satisfaction, but the moral course of action is often taken to be that of maximizing overall social welfare, utility, or preference satisfaction.[4] In many areas of contemporary jurisprudence, particularly in the United States, the right strategy is taken to be that which maximizes overall benefit. Markets are taken to be the most effective tools for implementing this consequentialist strategy, hence the role of the laws and the courts is taken to be that of mimicking the market (hence maximizing benefit) in areas in which markets (due to externalities, etc.) fail.[5] Even most of its advocates readily concede that the theory has a host of counter-intuitive implications and conflicts with many of our deeply held moral judgments. Yet efforts to supply such judgments with an underlying rationale can seem to lead ineluctably away from such intuitions and particular judgments and back towards consequentialism.[6]

Much recent work in ethics has consisted of efforts either to mitigate the counter-intuitiveness of generally consequentialist approaches to ethics, or to strike against the fundamental theoretical challenge that consequentialism is taken to provide to considered moral judgments and alternative moral theories. It is the thesis of this book that these discussions of the challenge *of* consequentialism tend to overlook a fundamental challenge *to* consequentialism, an unresolved tension between the theory and many of its most fundamental presuppositions. My project is to demonstrate that the traditional considerations that are taken to drive the challenge *of* consequentialism collapse in the face of this challenge *to* consequentialism. Many others have raised objections to consequentialism, but it

---

[3] See Elizabeth Anderson's discussion of cost–benefit analysis (1993, ch. 9), as well as Amartya Sen (2001) and Henry Richardson (2001).

[4] See, for example, Amartya Sen's characterization of a version of act utilitarianism (1985, p. 175).

[5] See, for example, Richard Posner's account (1981).

[6] For representative discussions of the pressure towards consequentialism that results from theoretical reflection see T. M. Scanlon (1982, pp. 103–28), and Shelly Kagan (1989, chs 1 and 2).

is often open to the consequentialist to respond that such criticisms beg certain of the crucial questions at issue. Critics argue that consequentialism cannot take persons or rights seriously, for example, but consequentialists respond that it is precisely their view that treats each and every person with full and equal seriousness. If rights are to be taken seriously, isn't the right approach to maximize the extent to which they are upheld overall?[7] My approach, by contrast, identifies certain tensions within the consequentialist approach itself. An appreciation of the nature of these tensions grounds the articulation of a fundamental challenge to the theory from within. Plausible steps for meeting this challenge, I will argue, lead us naturally beyond consequentialism; indeed, lead us to certain distinctly non-consequentialist commitments.

The fundamental challenge to consequentialism can be introduced by way of two claims. These claims are typically endorsed not only by advocates of consequentialist moral theories, but by defenders of the standard Aristotelian, Hobbesian, and Kantian alternatives to consequentialism as well. The first claim is that there are some acts that morality prohibits, and others that it requires of us. The second is that we should do what morality requires; we typically have decisive reasons to act in accordance with such moral requirements and prohibitions.[8] The standard alternatives to consequentialism are theories both of the standards set by morality and of the decisive reasons that we have to conform to such standards. In particular, each is a theory of the relationship between reasons and rightness (or "moral" virtues) upon which we have decisive reasons to do what the correct standards for right or virtuous action require of us and to avoid doing what they prohibit. None of these traditional approaches challenges these claims that morality establishes contentful standards of conduct (that morality is contentful) and that we have decisive reasons to do what such standards require (that morality is in this sense rationally authoritative).

---

[7] For classic examples of this sort of criticism and this sort of response see Robert Nozick's criticism (1974, ch. 3) and Samuel Scheffler's response (1982, ch. 4).

[8] I am following Derek Parfit in characterizing reasons to act as "decisive" when such reasons "are stronger than our reasons to act in any of the other possible ways" (2008, ch. 1, sec. 1, quoted with permission of the author). I will also follow Parfit in characterizing reasons as "sufficient" to do something "when these reasons are not weaker than, or outweighed by, our reasons to do anything else." (ibid., ch. 1, sec. 1) Such formulations allow for the possibility that in cases in which we do not have decisive reasons to do any one particular thing, we might have sufficient reasons to do many different things. This spare taxonomy of reasons will suffice for the arguments that are developed in this and the following three chapters, although it will be elaborated in key respects in Chapter 5.

Rather, they are attempts to provide theories of the relationship between what we have reasons to do and what it is right or virtuous to do that supply rationales for both the content that they take moral standards to have and the rational authority of such standards.

Consequentialism is often presented as an alternative in kind to such theories. But this is misleading. Like advocates of these other approaches, standard act consequentialists often appeal to both the claim that morality is contentful and the claim that morality is authoritative. But, unlike these alternatives, consequentialist moral theories are not in the first instance theories of the relationship between reasons to act and right actions. They are instead theories of the relationship between right actions and good overall states of affairs, upon which an action is morally right just in case its performance leads to the best state of affairs. The traditional alternatives are fundamentally theories of the relationship between reasons to act and right (or virtuous) action; consequentialism is fundamentally a theory of the relationship between right action and good states of affairs. Consequentialism thus provide a rationale for the content of morality, but such a rationale can be embraced without taking up any position at all concerning the authoritativeness of such moral standards. Unlike the alternatives, such a theory can be embraced by someone who rejects the claim that moral standards are authoritative. Do the ends justify the means? The consequentialist answer can be deceptively nuanced: their moral standards for right action are only satisfied if an agent acts to promote the best overall state of affairs, but this consequentialist theory of the content of moral standards is agnostic as to whether agents ever have even sufficient (much less decisive) reasons to do what is morally right.

This contrast between consequentialism and the other traditional approaches can be brought into focus with the example of Carl the card-carrying consequentialist. Let us assume that Carl accepts one from among the accounts of practical reason that can be and frequently are espoused by consequentialists, for example that the rational agent has decisive reasons to pursue her own happiness, or the maximal satisfaction of her preferences, or her own well-being, or the effective satisfaction of her plans, projects, and commitments. As a card-carrying consequentialist, he also accepts that the morally right action for him to perform is the action that brings about the best overall state of affairs, for example that maximizes overall happiness or maximizes the overall satisfaction of people's projects and commitments. Carl further accepts the plausible claim that what furthers his own happiness or individual preference satisfaction or the satisfaction of his plans and projects often diverges from what maximizes overall happiness or aggregate preference satisfaction. Carl, while continuing to be a card-carrying consequentialist, draws the obvious conclusion from these commitments: he clearly has decisive reasons *not* to do the right thing in such routine cases. Carl is crystal clear about the action on his part that would be necessary to conform to what he, as a card-carrying consequentialist, recognizes as the correct moral standards. He is equally clear that he routinely has decisive reasons to do what such standards identify as wrong, and should not perform the right action in such cases. Because Harry the Hobbesian and Kate the Kantian espouse theories of the relationship between reasons to act and right actions, theories that purport to provide a rationale for both claims, such a result—that agents routinely have decisive reasons not to do what their theories identify as right—would constitute a devastating objection to their theories. By contrast, Carl can proceed blithely on as a card-carrying consequentialist while embracing such a result. Indeed, he can cite whatever grounds he takes there to be for the truth of his theory of the content of moral standards as providing grounds for rejection of the claim that morality is rationally authoritative. Carl might even conclude that the only reason the authoritativeness of morality has seemed plausible is that we have not recognized the full implications of the truth of consequentialism, and the stark contrast that in fact routinely obtains between what is morally right and wrong (properly, consequentially understood) and what we have decisive or sufficient reasons to do or not to do.[9] This consequence that

---

[9] Carl may adopt a strategy of indirection, holding that the best strategies for achieving his happiness and overall happiness do not aim at these directly, but involve the identification of certain rules of thumb, or perhaps even certain hard and fast rules that he believes will, if followed, lead to his greatest happiness and the greatest happiness overall. (For an insightful discussion of various forms of indirect consequentialism see Eric Wiland (2007, esp. sec. 2).) But Carl will be clear that what he has sufficient or decisive reasons to do will be determined by following the strategies for achieving his own happiness, not those for achieving the greatest overall happiness. In particular, he will have no reason even to take the overall happiness maximizing strategies into account unless doing so can somehow be shown to be relevant to the strategies for securing his own happiness. Absent some implausible congruence between two such sets of strategies, our more indirect Carl will persist in taking himself often to have decisive reasons to do what he recognizes to be morally wrong. Indirect act consequentialist strategies typically distinguish the context of justification from the context of deliberation. But Carl is clear that he is not entitled to presuppose the rational authority of his moral standards, hence that the context of justification diverges from the context of moral evaluation. With this divergence, indirection seems

is blithely accepted by Carl would of course be rejected by virtually all actual consequentialists. To surrender the rational authority of their moral standards as the price for the vindication of their account of the content of such standards would be for them a pyrrhic victory, losing the war as a cost of winning one battle. I will argue in what follows that consequentialism loses both the battle and the war.

This disanalogy between consequentialism and the traditional alternatives receives remarkably little direct attention. In part this is because consequentialists typically invoke the claim that morality is authoritative even when they do not attempt to provide a supplementary rationale for it. Their critics often do not challenge this appeal to the rational authority of moral standards because they share it. It is what they do not share, the consequentialist theory of what moral standards in fact require and prohibit, that becomes the focus of attention. Peter Singer's famous argument for a demanding moral obligation to help the global poor, for example, moves directly from the claim that such action is required to conform to consequentialist moral standards to the claim that we ought to do it: if consequentialist morality requires us to spend ourselves down to our own subsistence to prevent absolute poverty elsewhere, and he believes that it does, then he takes it to be clear, drawing upon the authoritativeness of morality, that we ought to do what morality requires.[10] He offers a consequentialist rationale for the conviction that we are morally required to bring about the best overall consequences, but no rationale is offered for the authoritativeness of moral requirements thus understood. Singer himself concedes that given his account of practical reason there are significant obstacles to providing any such rationale for the authoritativeness of consequentialist moral standards,[11] effectively conceding that he is not clear

---

unlikely to establish the rational authority of moral requirements. Such indirect variations upon standard act consequentialism will be taken up in more detail in Chapter 8.

[10] Singer (1979, pp. 230–1). Singer also draws upon an alleged analogy between his extremely exacting moral requirement to help the global poor, which does not intuitively provide us with decisive reasons, and a moral requirement to rescue a drowning child, which does intuitively provide us with decisive reasons. Once the illicit nature of the move by the consequentialist from moral requirement to decisive reasons becomes apparent, this problematic analogy must be called upon to carry the entire burden of the argument. But once the analogy is separated from any consequentialist claim to the rational authority of moral standards, Singer's analogy threatens to cut in the other direction for the consequentialist, suggesting that rational agents do not have decisive reasons to do what consequentialist morality requires in either case.

[11] Ibid., pp. 320–2.

how he can avoid something along the lines of Carl's argument. Carl will readily accept Singer's argument that it is morally right to spend down to subsistence and wrong to pursue any other course of action, but he will reject any claim that he ought to pursue such a course of action; indeed, he will take himself to have decisive reasons not to do so. Singer's argument fails without an appeal to authoritativeness underwriting the move from the claim that spending ourselves down to subsistence is morally right to the claim that we ought to do so.

The fact that a theory of the relationship between right actions and good overall states of affairs does not without augmentation provide a rationale for the authoritativeness of its moral standards is particularly noteworthy because even many consequentialists grant that we often seem to have sufficient reasons *not* to do what their exacting moral standards require. Such consequentialists allow that if it is right as they claim to bring about the best overall state of affairs, then we often seem to have sufficient reasons not to do what is right, and sometimes seem to have decisive reasons not to do what is right. Indeed, I will demonstrate in what follows that various accounts of practical reason presupposed by standard act consequentialists share certain features that provide obstacles to any reconciliation between the consequentialist theory of the content of moral standards and any commitment to the authority of such moral standards. Taken together, the theories of practical reasons and of moral standards advocated by standard act consequentialists not only do not provide a rationale for the claim that morality is authoritative, they provide a rationale for rejecting the authoritativeness of consequentialist moral standards. Such consequentialists are under tremendous pressure to follow Carl, and abandon the second claim. A dilemma threatens. If theirs is the right account of the content of morality, then it seems that morality cannot have the rational authority that even they commonly take it to have. Consequentialist moral standards are vindicated only by marginalizing the role of morality in practical reason and deliberation. If, however, morality is authoritative, then consequentialism cannot be the correct account of what morality requires and prohibits. Arguments such as Singer's, this suggests, are attempts to eat one's cake while having it too: they appeal to the authoritativeness of morality in the implementation of their theory of the content of morality, but acceptance of their theories of morality and practical reason undermines the legitimacy of just such an appeal. The result is a deep practical schizophrenia.

The problem is not just that consequentialism requires us to be moral saints,[12] it is that it presupposes that we are rationally required to be moral sinners even as it morally requires us to be moral saints.

Over the course of the next three chapters I will clarify the nature of the obstacles to acceptance of these two claims by standard act consequentialists. Armed with this more nuanced understanding of the inability of standard act consequentialists to account for both the content and the authoritativeness of their moral standards, I will turn in Chapter 5 to an examination of the traditional rationales that have been offered in defense of their account of the content of moral standards. I will show that many of these arguments turn on a misappropriation of certain deep intuitions concerning the authoritativeness of moral judgments. The intuition that it is always right to do the best that one can do in the circumstances, what one has decisive reasons to do, is hijacked by the consequentialist and redeployed as an alleged intuition that it is always right to do what brings about the best overall state of affairs, an intuition that appears to support the consequentialist's rationale for his theory of the content of morality. With the illicit nature of this appropriation exposed, many of the traditional rationales offered in support of the consequentialist theory of the content of morality lose much if not all of their apparent force.

One central argument for a consequentialist theory of the content of moral standards, an argument appealing to impartiality, avoids this criticism. It is the project of Chapters 6 and 7 to address this impartiality argument in support of the consequentialist theory of the content of moral standards, and the project of Chapter 8 to demonstrate that the arguments developed in the first seven chapters against standard act consequentialism extend to the most common consequentialist variations upon this standard form of the theory. The argument from impartiality begins with the widely held assumption that morality requires impartiality—the adoption of a standpoint of equal concern for all persons. It asserts that the conception of impartiality deployed in the consequentialist's assessment of better and worse overall *states of affairs* is the fundamental conception of impartiality for moral evaluation of *actions* as well. I will argue in Chapters 6 and 7 that there are profound obstacles to taking the consequentialist's conception of impartiality to be the fundamental moral conception for the evaluation of actions. I will also

---

[12] See Susan Wolf (1982) for the argument that consequentialism requires agents to be moral saints.

demonstrate that one natural response to the inadequacy of consequentialist rationales for the authoritativeness of morality, a response explored by Samuel Scheffler, suggests an alternative conception of impartiality, a conception appropriate in the first instance to the impartial evaluation of actions rather than states of affairs. This alternative conception of impartiality, a conception that plays a central role in many alternatives to consequentialism, avoids the obstacles that confront attempts to take the consequentialist's impersonal conception of impartiality to be the fundamental conception for the moral evaluation of actions. Moreover, an approach that takes this alternative conception of impartiality to be fundamental to morality avoids the obstacles that confront consequentialist theories to establishing the rational authority of moral requirements.

Such an approach, in short, holds out the prospect, closed to the consequentialist, of being incorporated into an account that can provide a plausible rationale for both claims. Non-foundational forms of consequentialism of the sort formulated by David Cummiskey, Brad Hooker, and Derek Parfit, accounts that attempt to ground recognizably consequentialist rules or principles in non-consequentialist foundations, might seem to be resistant to such arguments. Much of Chapter 8 will be spent demonstrating that the arguments developed in Chapters 6 and 7 against standard act consequentialism have purchase upon these non-foundational variants as well.

To summarize: the next three chapters will demonstrate that attempts to establish the authoritativeness of consequentialist moral standards are confronted by profound and debilitating obstacles that provide a fundamental challenge to the plausibility of the theory; Chapters 5–8 will demonstrate that an exploration of the source of these difficulties takes us beyond consequentialism.

2

The Challenge
to Consequentialism: A Troubling
Normative Triad

2.1 Challenges of and to Consequentialism

In this and the next several chapters my focus will be upon the paradigmatic
form of consequentialism, standard act consequentialism.[1] The standard act
consequentialist directly evaluates acts (not rules or motives) as right just
in case they bring about the state of affairs that is evaluated as best
overall from an impersonal standpoint.[2] Moreover, for such a standard
act consequentialist the rationale for the adoption of a consequentialist
normative principle is itself consequentialist, based in the appeal to the

---

[1] More specifically, and deploying a set of distinctions that will be clarified along the way, the
standard form of consequentialism that is our initial focus is direct (not indirect), foundational (as well
as normative/factoral), impersonal/agent-neutral (not evaluator-relative), act (not, e.g. rule or motive)
consequentialism. The challenge that will be developed to standard act consequentialism in these initial
chapters will be extended to other versions of consequentialism in Chapter 8.

[2] Here I adopt the standard characterization of the standpoint from which states of affairs are
impartially evaluated as better and worse overall as the impersonal standpoint. In what follows I will
characterize as "impersonal" and "agent-neutral" reasons that are based in the appeal to the impersonal
value of states of affairs. Non-impersonal reasons, reasons that are not based in the impersonal value of
states of affairs, will be characterized in what follows as "agent-relative" reasons. Thus, if certain reasons
are impartial, general, and universalizable, but not based in the impersonal value of states of affairs,
these reasons will be agent-relative reasons in this sense. The agent-relative/agent-neutral distinction
is drawn in many different ways in the philosophical literature (for a different way of drawing the
distinction, see Christine Korsgaard's "The Reasons We Can Share," in (1996b, sec. II)). The reasons
I characterize in what follows as agent-neutral are identified as agent-neutral on all of these proposals
for drawing the distinction, but many of these distinctions identify certain classes of non-impersonal
reasons in addition as agent-neutral. It is in an effort to avoid the confusion that results from appeal
to these many different ways of drawing the distinction that I will restrict the term "agent-neutral" in
what follows to impersonal reasons, and identify all non-impersonal reasons as "agent-relative".

impersonal value of states of affairs.[3] One reason for this focus on standard act consequentialism is that many of the rationales that apparently provide support for consequentialism support standard act consequentialism, and do not readily extend to many consequentialist variations.[4] Such variants upon standard act consequentialism, moreover, are often beset by distinctive problems that have been pointed out with brutal effectiveness, often by other consequentialists.[5] Another reason is that this proliferation of variants has made consequentialism itself into something of a moving target. It becomes unclear in many cases what is being advocated, and even in some cases whether there is any meaningful sense in which the view defended is still consequentialist. But the most fundamental reason for this initial focus on standard act consequentialism is that despite the many sources of dissatisfaction with this form of the theory, sources reflected in myriad departures from it, the deepest challenges to the standard form of the theory have not yet been clearly articulated. My project in the next several chapters is to articulate these deeper challenges. I will argue in Chapter 8 that these deeper challenges that emerge in our consideration of standard act consequentialism generalize to these other forms of consequentialism. Moreover, I will argue that the tools for moral theory that come into view through developing these deeper challenges to act consequentialism provide the framework for moving beyond consequentialism in any form to an approach that recognizes the promotion of overall states of affairs as playing an important but circumscribed role within a comprehensive moral theory.

We can begin to clarify the nature of the challenge to consequentialism by locating the theory within a triad of claims. The first is the claim that morality is authoritative, that agents typically have decisive reasons to do—are in this sense rationally required to do—what they are morally required to do, and rationally required not to do what they are morally prohibited from doing. Some version of such a claim that rational agents have decisive reasons to do what morality requires, at least typically, and decisive reasons to avoid doing what morality prohibits, is often recognized

---

[3] See David Cummiskey (1996, pp. 7–11), Shelly Kagan (1998, pp. 213–14), T. M. Scanlon (1982, pp. 103–28), and Brad Hooker (2000b, pp. 222–38), for discussions of the distinction between normative/factoral and foundational/philosophical consequentialism.

[4] Many of these rationales are taken up in Chapter 5.

[5] See, for example, the criticisms put forward by Shelly Kagan in his essay "Evaluative Focal Points" (2000) and parts 2 and 3 of Tim Mulgan's *The Demands of Consequentialism* (2001).

as having deep intuitive appeal: if something is morally prohibited, then you shouldn't do it. The utilitarian sympathizer Henry Sidgwick begins *The Methods of Ethics* with this common thought "that wrong conduct is essentially irrational," and the contemporary consequentialist sympathizer Shelly Kagan suggests that one can bracket inquiry into the question as to whether it is ever rational to act immorally because "most of us take ourselves to be quite prepared to act as we morally should, if only we can determine just what it is that morality requires of us."[6] J. J. C. Smart argues that agents are morally required to maximize overall happiness, and takes agents to have decisive reasons to do what such consequentialist morality requires, asserting that "the only reason for performing an action A rather than an alternative action B is that doing A will make mankind . . . happier than will doing B."[7] Non-consequentialists are often more emphatic in their endorsement and defense of some such claim. Stephen Darwall, for example, maintains that such rational authority "captures part of what is felt to be special about moral requirements," and Jay Wallace maintains that "an agent who has serious interest in morality ought to regard compliance with moral principles as a fixed constraint on what may be counted as a good life."[8] I will demonstrate in the next chapter that many of the central debates between consequentialists and their critics presuppose that moral requirements have such rational authority. In particular, pervasive concerns that consequentialism is in particular need of

[6] See Henry Sidgwick (1982, p. 23) and Kagan (1998, p. 11). See also Kagan's discussion of moral requirement and morally decisive reasons (1998, pp. 66–7). For an invocation of the claim by a contractualist critic of consequentialism, see Scanlon (1998, p. 1). A similar claim is identified by Samuel Scheffler as the "claim of overridingness" (1992a, pp. 25–8), by David Brink as the "supremacy thesis" (1997, p. 255), and by Jay Wallace as the "optimality thesis," upon which "someone has most reason to comply with moral demands" (2006, p. 130). Wallace identifies commitment to such a claim as a marker for a "practical conception of ethics" (ibid., pp. 73–5).

[7] Smart (1973, p. 30). I have already shown that although arguments such as Peter Singer's do not explicitly appeal to such a claim, they do implicitly rely upon it. His argument moves from the claim that if the consequentialist moral requirement to assist the global poor is not outweighed by anything of comparable "moral significance," then we ought to do what morality requires. If the claim were only that such an action is required by morality, without any claim about whether or not we have any reason to do what morality requires, then Singer's argument would result only in a set of standards, and not in any rational demands upon agents that they conform to such standards. The argument has the apparent force that it does precisely because it implicitly draws upon the claim that a decisive moral requirement typically provides a rational agent with a decisive reason—with what they ought, simpliciter, to do. If Singer explicitly allowed that on his theory of reasons there is no basis for any presumption that agents rationally ought to perform the action identified by his moral standards as right, it would be clear that his argument fails to establish its intended result.

[8] Darwall (2006 p. 26); Wallace (2006, p. 134).

defense against charges that it is too demanding, confining, and alienating become utterly mysterious unless it is assumed that agents typically have decisive reasons to conform their actions to what is morally prohibited or required.

The second claim is that some practical reasons are fundamentally non-impersonal. We have reasons to pursue courses of action that are not based in the impartial evaluation of states of affairs, reasons that are sometimes sufficient to pursue courses of action that will not bring about the best overall consequences. Such a claim that some reasons are fundamentally non-impersonal, which I will refer to as the non-impersonality of practical reason, is readily endorsed by virtually all alternative theories of the authoritativeness and contentfulness of morality, and is a feature of virtually every theory of practical reason endorsed by consequentialists. Mill inquires into the "sanctions" to which the principle of utility is susceptible precisely because he recognizes that rational agents as he understands them often have good fundamental reasons to pursue their own happiness at the expense of overall happiness, hence that an account must be provided of what is necessary in order to alter these agents and their circumstances such that they typically do have decisive reasons to act to bring about the best overall states of affairs. Absent such circumstances, Mill allows, agents will not have decisive reasons to do what consequentialist moral standards require.[9] Peter Singer endorses a Humean account of practical reason, upon which "reason in action applies only to means, not ends. The ends must be given by our wants and desires."[10] Because these desires are frequently to perform actions that do not result in the best overall states of affairs, the reasons to which they give rise similarly count in favor of actions other than those that would bring about the best overall state of affairs. He agrees with Sidgwick that my concern for my own existence, for example, is fundamentally different from my concern for yours, that this difference is reflected in fundamental non-impersonal reasons, and that for the consequentialist this fact "stands in the way of attempts to show that to act rationally is to act ethically."[11] Samuel Scheffler points out that human beings are "moved by their attachment to particular people, their loyalty to causes, their pursuit of goals, their respect for principles, and their delight in forms of activity . . . the constitution and expression of distinct human

---

[9] But see Millgram (2000).   [10] Singer (1993, p. 320).   [11] Ibid., p. 322.

selves could not take the form that it does if human beings did not treat such a wide and diverse range of considerations as providing them with reasons for action."[12]   At a minimum, accounts of practical reason allow what Derek Parfit characterizes as "stronger reasons to care about our own well-being and the well-being of those we love." Even granting that we also have distinctive impersonal reasons to maximize overall well-being, it seems clear that such non-impersonal and impersonal reasons will often conflict, and that in such cases "we can ask what, all things considered, we have most reason to do."[13] When considerations of our own well-being and the well-being of our loved ones are sufficiently compelling, we will presumably not have decisive reasons to perform the action that best promotes overall well-being, and will have sufficient reasons to act otherwise.

My formulation of this claim adopts the standard characterization of the standpoint from which states of affairs are impartially evaluated as better and worse overall as the impersonal standpoint, and characterizes as impersonal reasons the agent-neutral reasons that appeal to such an impersonal standpoint.[14] On virtually every account of practical reason and deliberation put forward either by consequentialists or their critics, agents have non-impersonal reasons to act, reasons that are not themselves grounded, even indirectly, in appeals to the impersonal value of states of affairs. Advocates of any such theory are committed to the fundamental non-impersonality of practical reason. One form of this claim that some practical reasons are fundamentally non-impersonal is a claim that the plans, projects, interests, and commitments of agents have rational significance independent of whatever rational significance they have in the determination of the

---

[12] Scheffler (2004, p. 237).   [13] Both quotations are from of Parfit (2004, p. 355).
[14] I will follow Shelly Kagan in relying, at least initially, on our intuitive grasp of this distinction, although much will be said by way of refining this intuitive grasp in subsequent chapters. As I suggested in the preceding chapter, agent-neutral reasons will be understood in what follows as reasons based in the appeal to the impersonal value of states of affairs. Because the impersonal value of a state of affairs "gives every agent the same reason to promote it" (Scanlon 1998, p. 80), it provides a reason that is neutral among agents—an agent-neutral reason. Non-impersonal reasons, by contrast, will be understood as any reasons that are not based in the appeal to the impersonal value of states of affairs. All such non-impersonal reasons will be characterized as agent-relative or agent-centered rather than agent-neutral reasons. Such agent-relative reasons may be of varying kinds, including partial reasons to promote states of affairs that are better for the agent in question and impartial reasons to act that are not reasons to promote overall states of affairs. From the impersonal standpoint, any such agent-relative reason to perform or not to perform some action, whether partial or impartial, will appear as a special reason for some particular agent "that does not apply in the same way to others" (ibid., p. 83).

best overall state of affairs, independent significance that manifests itself at the most fundamental level of practical reason.[15] Reasons with such independent rational significance sometimes provide agents with sufficient reasons to act in ways that fail to bring about the best overall state of affairs.

The third claim asserts the consequentialist account of the content of morality, that an action is morally right just in case its performance leads to the best overall state of affairs. Such an act (or acts, in the case of ties) is not merely morally permitted but morally required, and all other acts are morally prohibited. This third member of the triad, the consequentialist account of moral content, is a claim concerning the relationship of distinctively moral evaluations (right/wrong, morally required/morally prohibited) of actions to evaluations of overall states of affairs (better/worse); the second, the non-impersonality of practical reason, is a claim concerning the relationship of certain evaluations of actions and reasons for action (decisive/sufficient/better/worse) to evaluations of states of affairs impersonally considered (better/worse); the first, the authoritativeness of morality, is a claim concerning the relationship between moral evaluations of actions as right/wrong and morally required/morally prohibited and evaluations of actions and reasons for action as sufficient or decisive, better or worse.

These three claims, (1) RAMS: the rational authoritativeness of moral standards (agents have decisive reasons to do what they are morally required to do), (2) NIR: the non-impersonality of practical reason (agents have some fundamentally non-impersonal reasons that sometimes provide them with sufficient reasons not to bring about the best overall state of affairs, and (3) CMS: the consequentialist theory of moral standards, are in considerable tension with each other; acceptance of any two appears to generate obstacles to endorsing the third. If agents have decisive reasons to do what they are morally required to do (RAMS), and they are morally required to bring about the best overall state of affairs (CMS), then they have decisive reasons to bring about the best overall state of affairs. But NIR assures us that whether or not morality is entirely impersonal, reason is not. Agents

---

[15] Samuel Scheffler argues that an agent's own concerns and commitments have moral significance independent of whatever significance they have "in an impersonal ranking of overall states of affairs" (1982, p. 9). I am adopting Scheffler's familiar terminology to make the analogous point about the independent rational significance of such concerns and commitments.

often have sufficient reasons not to bring about the best state of affairs. Similarly, if agents are morally required to bring about the best overall state of affairs (CMS), and they have non-impersonal reasons that are sometimes sufficient to act in ways that do not bring about the best overall state of affairs (NIR), they do not have decisive reasons in such cases to do what they are morally required to do. But this is difficult to reconcile with RAMS, the claim that agents have decisive reasons to do what they are morally required to do. Finally, if agents have decisive reasons to do what they are morally required to do, and to avoid actions that are morally prohibited (RAMS), but they often have sufficient reasons not to bring about the best state of affairs (NIR), then agents cannot be morally required to bring about the best overall state of affairs and morally prohibited from any other course of action. But consequentialism (CMS) holds that this is precisely what morality does require of agents. Peter Railton has captured the tension quite nicely. If the consequentialist's central claim (CMS) is embraced, he argues, a dilemma threatens. Given a plausible account of reason and reasonable expectations of the sort that involves NIR, we must remove "obligation so far from reasonable expectation that we no longer expect most people in our society to come close to carrying out their obligations," thereby giving up on anything in the neighborhood of RAMS and marginalizing morality in the process. If we insist on holding on to RAMS as well as CMS, however, the result will be an account which tells us that we can reasonably expect people to do things that NIR assures us no one could reasonably be expected to do, an account upon which "most people will be amazed at what is expected of them."[16]

It has been suggested by some consequentialists that although moral requirement is impersonal and rational requirement is not, the first member of our triad (RAMS) can nonetheless be satisfied because there either is, or can be, an almost constant congruence between the action required to bring about the best overall state of affairs and decisive reasons to act, for example between the action that will promote my happiness and the action that will promote overall happiness, or between the action that will maximize the satisfaction of my preferences and the action that will maximize overall preference satisfaction. But since Sidgwick such claims

---

[16] These quotations are both from Peter Railton's essay "How Thinking About Character and Utilitarianism Might Lead to Rethinking the Character of Utilitarianism" (2003, p. 238).

of congruence have been recognized, even by most consequentialists themselves, as highly dubious.[17]

Alternatively, many contemporary consequentialists have been led by the tension among the three members of this triad to abandon standard act consequentialism (CMS) in favor of indirect, non-foundational, and other forms of consequentialism. Although such variants bring a host of new difficulties in their wake, they are taken to hold out the prospect of closing the yawning gap that confronts standard act consequentialism between what agents have sufficient or decisive reasons to do and what act consequentialist morality requires. But I will present a series of arguments in Chapters 4–7 that undermine the plausibility of an appeal to a foundational role for the consequentialist's impersonal conception of impartiality in moral evaluation. These arguments demonstrating that the impersonal conception of impartiality cannot play such a foundational role will also allow us to extend the arguments against standard act consequentialism to indirect variants and variants that focus upon rules rather than acts. They will also reveal the structural features of an alternative conception of impartiality, an interpersonal conception, that can plausibly be called upon to play just such a foundational moral role. I will demonstrate in Chapter 8 that the availability of such a plausible alternative conception of impartiality presents significant challenges to arguments by Brad Hooker, David Cummiskey, and Derek Parfit that consequentialist norms can be grounded in non-consequentialist foundations.

2.2 Elaboration of the Normative Triad: Preview of Chapter 3

I have up to this point provided only the briefest sketch of the tensions among these claims that will be explored and developed throughout the

---

[17] I suggest in the next chapter that Mill himself is plausibly understood as pursuing this congruence strategy. See Sidgwick (1981, pp. 499–501) for his rejection of this aspect of Mill's argument. For a contemporary discussion of such prospects for congruence, see Scheffler (1992). See, in particular, his arguments that any morality that is to aspire even to a "potential congruence" (ibid., p. 4) with the point of view of the individual agent must be a moderate morality that is difficult to reconcile with consequentialism. Even the potential for congruence requires that "the most demanding moral theories are mistaken" (ibid., p. 6). If consequentialist standards lack rational authority, it becomes unclear what reasons there are to establish such a congruence if it is lacking, or to maintain such a congruence if it has somehow been established.

next several chapters. But even this brief sketch might be taken to show that no triad of claims is necessary to generate a challenge to consequentialism because NIR and CMS alone prove sufficient. The two claims put together suggest that agents often have sufficient reasons to ignore what morality requires and do what morality prohibits. If morality prohibits some course of action, however, isn't it the case that we have decisive reasons not to perform that action—that we are rationally required, not just morally required, not to perform it? As T. M. Scanlon and countless others have pointed out, "the fact that a certain action would be morally wrong seems to provide a powerful reason not to do it, one that is, at least normally, decisive against any competing considerations."[18] NIR, however, suggests that we often fail to have decisive reasons to perform the action that consequentialist moral standards identify as right.

It is one of the striking features of consequentialist moral theory, however, that it not only invites, but in some of its formulations appears to presuppose a radically different understanding of moral requirement and prohibition, rightness and wrongness, an understanding which is agnostic with respect to any commitment to RAMS. As we saw in the first section, this is because consequentialism, unlike, for example, traditional Hobbesian and Kantian alternatives, is not a theory of the rational authority of its moral standards.[19] These alternatives, by contrast, are theories of the rational authority of a certain set of moral standards. Hobbesian moral theories, for example, identify moral standards as rational constraints that rational persons typically have decisive reasons to adopt.[20] Their accounts of the rational authority of rightness are constitutive components of their accounts of standards for right action themselves. A similar point can be made about traditional Kantian alternatives.

Consequentialism, by contrast, is a theory of the relationship not of rightness of actions to goodness (sufficiency and decisiveness) of reasons for acting, but of the rightness of actions to the goodness of overall states of affairs. It can be, and frequently has been, augmented with accounts of the rational authority, or lack thereof, of such standards

---

[18] See Scanlon (1998, p. 1). Although some version of this claim is commonly presupposed or explicitly invoked as a platitude, it has been challenged. See Joshua Gert's *Brute Rationality* (2004) for the articulation of an account that challenges this claim.

[19] This point will be developed and clarified in the next chapter.

[20] See Hobbes's *Leviathan* (1994). For a contemporary Hobbesian approach, see David Gauthier (1986).

for right action. But no such account is a constitutive component of consequentialism, and the theory can be, and has been, wedded to radically different accounts of the rational authority, or lack thereof, of its moral requirements and prohibitions. Other traditional alternatives present, as a constituent component of the theories themselves, accounts that provide a rationale for the intuitive claim that moral requirements have rational authority. Consequentialists often draw upon this claim, but no such rationale for it is a component of consequentialism. This opens theoretical space within consequentialism for an account of moral requirement and prohibition shorn of any claims to rational authority. The example of Carl has already demonstrated that a consequentialist can maintain, for example, that an agent has decisive reasons to promote her own happiness, that the best state of affairs is that which brings about the greatest overall happiness, and that agents are always morally required to bring about the best overall state of affairs (and prohibited from doing anything else). But such a consequentialist can also insist, seemingly with great plausibility, that the agent's own happiness and overall happiness frequently fail to coincide, and that in such cases the rational agent has decisive reasons not to bring about the best overall consequences, hence not to do what morality on her view requires. The right action is the action that conforms to the standards of morality, and wrong actions fail to conform to such standards, but there is no claim on such a version of consequentialism that the agent typically has decisive reasons to conform her actions to such standards. An advocate of a consequentialist moral theory can thus with perfect consistency allow that agents typically (even always!) have decisive reasons not to perform the action identified by the theory as morally required. Only with the addition of RAMS, a commitment to the rational authority of moral requirements and prohibitions, does the threatened tension among claims arise, but only with the addition of RAMS is consequentialism a theory that makes rational demands upon agents to do what morality requires and avoid what morality prohibits.

Traditional Kantians and Hobbesians accept some form of the first two members of our triad. On such theories agents sometimes have sufficient reasons not to bring about the best overall consequences and sometimes have decisive reasons not to bring about the best overall consequences. These commitments cannot readily be reconciled to CMS, hence it is no surprise that advocates of such theories reject such a consequentialist theory of moral standards. Consequentialists, by contrast, take there to be a powerful set of considerations in support of this third member of the triad. Surely it is always right to do what is best? Consequentialism can seem to be merely the obvious interpretation of such a powerful general intuition. Similarly, prudence may seem to require that I do what is best for me, but isn't it also clear that morality appeals to what is best simpliciter? This is just what consequentialism does. Again, everyone recognizes that consideration of the resulting states of affairs is relevant to the determination of what's best, but what else besides such results could be relevant? How could it ever be right to bring about worse results?[21] In addition, the rational response to value would seem to be its promotion. Consequentialism is the theory that requires rational agents to promote valuable states of affairs, hence that captures what seems to be the rational response to value.[22] Finally, morality requires impartiality, and consequentialism secures such impartiality by linking rightness and wrongness of action to the impartial ranking of overall states of affairs as better and worse.

In light of such independent considerations offered in support of CMS, the strength of other alternatives—that they are committed by their acceptance of both RAMS and NIR to the rejection of CMS—can come to seem a weakness. By contrast, the strength of consequentialism, the apparently powerful independent considerations that support CMS, highlights its central weakness—a difficulty with reconciling such a claim to the other independently appealing members of our triad, members consequentialists themselves often presuppose in the articulation and advocacy of their theory of moral standards. Indeed, I will argue in Chapter 4 that standard consequentialist accounts presuppose the independent rational significance of non-impersonal reasons (NIR) in the process of generating the moral requirements that they take to have rational authority. In presupposing such fundamental non-impersonal reasons, however, any claim to the rational authority of consequentialist moral standards is undermined in the very articulation of such standards.

Many of the most powerful and persistent objections to consequentialism can productively be understood as invoking the tension in this triad to

---

[21] Philippa Foot formulates the pull towards consequentialism in this way in "Utilitarianism and the Virtues" (1988, pp. 224–42).

[22] Such a line of argument is developed by Phillip Pettit in his "Consequentialism" (1992, pp. 230–40).

justify rejection of one particular member, CMS itself. Consequentialism, such objectors maintain, is too extreme—too demanding, too confining, too alienating—to provide a plausible alternative moral theory.[23] These extremism arguments invoke different aspects of the problem that, by RAMS and CMS, we have decisive reasons always to bring about the best overall state of affairs, but rational agents frequently appear to have sufficient reasons not to bring about the best overall state of affairs (NIR), hence to do what consequentialism identifies as wrong. If RAMS is presupposed, CMS leads us to the conclusion that we have decisive reasons to do many things that we have perfectly good reasons—sufficient or even decisive—not to do (by NIR). Presupposing RAMS, CMS makes rational demands upon us that are unreasonable (by NIR), alienates us from ends that we have good and sufficient reasons (by NIR) to undertake and maintain, and confines us (at least de facto) to considerations of only certain reasons and courses of action that are often in fact not decisive in light of all relevant reasons (by NIR). We have sufficient reasons in many situations not to bring about the best overall outcome, we have decisive reasons to avoid wrongdoing, hence a moral theory that identifies as wrong any action that fails to bring about the best overall consequences is unacceptable. The real difficulty is not that rational agents are alienated *by* consequentialist morality from their plans, projects, and commitments, but that rational agents are alienated *from* such a consequentialist morality by the good reasons each has to honor her commitments and pursue her plans and projects. Consequentialism ratchets up the level of sacrifice that is necessary for agents to satisfy its standards, but inadvertently ratchets down the rational demands upon agents to make such sacrifices. The difficulty is that NIR and CMS taken together appear to open up a yawning chasm between reason and morality even as consequentialists help themselves to some form of RAMS to close this gap. This is the fundamental structure underlying demandingness, alienation, confinement, and integrity arguments against consequentialism, and I believe that these arguments are ultimately compelling. Much of the remainder of this book will be engaged in clearing away misconceptions,

---

[23] See Liam Murphy (2000), and Hurley, "Does Consequentialism Make Too Many Demands, Or None at All?" (2006), for discussions of the alleged demandingness of consequentialism. Samuel Scheffler (1992a) provides a lucid discussion of the confinement challenge, Bernard Williams (1973) and Peter Railton (1986) provide illuminating discussions of the charge that consequentialism is too alienating.

often shared by both consequentialists and their critics, that stand in the way of an appreciation of the nature and full force of arguments that share this basic structure.

I have suggested that the extreme demandingness, alienation, and confinement arguments against consequentialism can all productively be understood as variations upon the challenge captured by the triad of claims laid out above. Samuel Scheffler's central argument against consequentialism can also be profitably understood as an instance of this type.[24] Scheffler recognizes the independent rational significance of considerations that arise from each agent's own point of view, rational significance that is independent of whatever significance such considerations have from the impersonal standpoint. Such recognition of the independent rational significance of the agent's point of view, such that her projects and commitments can properly be given weight by the agent disproportionate to any impersonal weight that they have, provides a rationale for NIR. A philosopher who accepts NIR has two options. The first is to maintain that although such non-impersonal reasons have independent rational significance, they have no independent moral significance. On this option only impersonal considerations are relevant to the determination of what it is right and wrong to do, but *pace* RAMS it is often reasonable, given the independent rational significance of the person's point of view, to do what is morally wrong. This is to recognize that commitment to RAMS and CMS together is difficult to reconcile with NIR, and to reject RAMS, the rational authoritativeness of morality. The consequence is the threatened marginalization of morality.

Alternatively, some form of RAMS can be treated as an adequacy condition on an acceptable moral theory.[25] Such a commitment to RAMS leads one who recognizes the independent rational significance of the person's point of view (thereby embracing NIR) to recognize its independent moral significance as well. If agents rarely have sufficient reasons to act immorally (RAMS), but often have sufficient reasons not to bring about the best overall state of affairs (NIR), it cannot be morally wrong, as consequentialism maintains, to fail to bring about the best overall state of affairs

---

[24] This argument is laid out in the first three chapters of Scheffler (1982).

[25] Although Scheffler expresses qualified skepticism about the strong claim that "it can *never* be rational knowingly to do what morality forbids" (1992a, p. 7, emphasis mine), he allows that some weaker form of this claim, a version of our claim 1, is a component of our pre-philosophical understanding of the relationship between reason and morality. Moreover, he offers a qualified defense of such a weaker version of this claim in later chapters.

in all such situations. This second option concludes that non-impersonal reasons must have an independent moral significance that consequentialism is unable to recognize. Recognition of non-impersonal reasons as having independent rational significance (NIR) naturally leads advocates of some form of RAMS to recognition of the independent moral significance of such non-impersonal considerations as well. Because consequentialism cannot recognize any moral significance of such non-impersonal reasons that is independent of their impersonal moral significance, it is consequentialism (CMS) which is the member of the triad that Scheffler is prepared to reject.

Scheffler points to the independent moral significance of the agent's own point of view to ground his rejection of CMS. But he does not take such non-impersonal reasons to be, like impersonal considerations, distinctively moral considerations. Although the relevant non-impersonal reasons weigh against the relevant moral considerations, hence are independently morally significant in the moral assessment of right and wrong, they do not weigh as countervailing moral considerations—they do not, for example, generate moral requirements, as impersonal moral considerations do, when they are of sufficient weight. Rather, their independent rational significance is reflected in an independent moral significance that consequentialism cannot recognize.[26] The core argument thus can productively be understood as maintaining that some versions of both NIR and RAMS are plausible, and concluding that these claims provide a rationale for recognizing the independent moral significance of non-impersonal reasons, hence for the rejection of CMS, the consequentialist theory of the content of moral standards.

Ultimately, my suggestion will be that although consequentialists reject a consequentialist theory of *rational* requirement, upon which an agent has decisive reasons to perform some action just in case its performance leads to the best state of affairs, and explicitly defend only a consequentialist theory of *moral* requirement (CMS), they often rely in practice upon RAMS to smuggle in just such a theory of consequentialist rational requirement, de facto if not de jure. Indeed, concerns by both defenders and critics of consequentialism regarding its excessive alienation, confinement, and demandingness only make sense within the context of a commitment to RAMS. If the right action brings about the best state of affairs overall

---

[26] I have benefited from discussions with Alex Rajczi on this point.

(and all others are morally prohibited), and we typically have decisive reasons to do what morality requires and avoid what it prohibits, then we typically have decisive reasons to bring about the best overall state of affairs, and other courses of action will typically be irrational as well as immoral—we are after all rationally required, not just morally required, to bring about the best overall consequences. Consequentialism as a theory of rational requirement is thrown out the front door only to be smuggled in through the side window by presupposing RAMS. I will attempt to expose the illicit nature of this smuggling operation in various forms over the course of the next three chapters, but we have already seen one influential example in the work of Peter Singer. Singer defends a consequentialist account of moral requirement, concedes that his account of reason and morality allows that agents may well often have sufficient reasons not to do what his consequentialist morality requires, yet concludes from the premise that prevention of global poverty is morally required that the agent "ought" to prevent global poverty. Clearly this "ought" invokes the rational authority of moral requirements in an effort to establish the conclusion that morality makes far more demands upon rational agents than we ordinarily think. But equally clearly Singer's commitment to NIR and CMS undermines the legitimacy of any appeal on his part to such rational authority for moral requirements as he understands them. Ordinary morality may well intuitively have such rational authority, but for precisely that reason consequentialist morality intuitively does not have such rational authority in the cases that Singer is at pains to highlight—cases in which ordinary and consequentialist moralities diverge dramatically. Moreover, because Singer's account of practical reason commits him to NIR, it generates significant obstacles to any effort to demonstrate that contrary to intuition consequentialist morality does have such rational authority. The conclusion invited by such a position would appear rather to be that although consequentialist moral standards are more exacting to satisfy, the theory provides no grounds for concluding that we should try to satisfy them—no grounds, that is, for the conclusion that we ought to do what such moral standards identify as right.

In the next chapter I will demonstrate that the debates between consequentialists and their critics regarding the central challenges that have traditionally been offered against the theory, challenges that focus upon its extremely demanding, confining, and alienating nature, turn on acceptance

by both parties to the dispute of some form of RAMS. But consequentialism, in contrast with Kantian and Hobbesian alternatives, is not a theory
of the rational authoritativeness of its moral requirements (although it can,
of course, be augmented to produce such a theory); indeed, the accounts of
practical reason advocated by consequentialists typically support NIR, the
claim that agents often have sufficient reasons not to bring about the best
overall consequences. Coupled with CMS, this suggests that agents often
have sufficient reasons not to do what morality requires.

The consequentialist can embrace an account of practical reason and
deliberation that supports NIR, but such an account, coupled with CMS,
threatens the marginalization of her moral standards for rational agents. Such
standards threaten to become merely one among other sets of standards
for action that rational agents may or may not have any reasons to take
into account, and cease to be what moral standards, including, typically,
consequentialist moral standards, purport to be—a set of standards that are
distinctive in large part due to the rational authority that they have for
agents. Alternatively, she can insist upon the rational authority of her moral
standards (RAMS), but then owes us an account of practical reasons and
deliberation upon which agents do not have good non-impersonal reasons
to act at the foundational level, or upon which, if they do, such reasons
somehow can be reconciled to the rational authority of impersonal moral
requirements.

2.3 A Williams-Inspired Diagnosis: Preview of Chapter 4

The task of the first three chapters is to introduce a fundamental challenge
to consequentialism, but the purpose of the fourth chapter is to sharpen
and refine this challenge in ways that provide the tools to undermine the
traditional challenge *of* consequentialism. Bernard Williams' path breaking
critique of consequentialism provides many of the materials needed to
sharpen this challenge. My Williams-inspired diagnosis proposes that the
very structure of standard act consequentialism presupposes an account of
practical reason and deliberation that is in tremendous tension with appeals
to the rational authority of its moral standards; indeed, that the alienation,
loss of integrity, demandingness, and confinement of consequentialism are

inevitable consequences of the tendency by both consequentialists and their critics to presuppose RAMS while at the same time presupposing, in the very determination of the overall value of states of affairs from the impersonal standpoint, an account of practical reason and deliberation upon which agents often have good reasons not to bring about the best overall state of affairs (NIR). Williams demonstrates that standard act consequentialism presupposes that agents have a range of non-impersonal reasons; indeed, that the best overall outcome is achieved in large part by maximizing the extent to which agents can effectively act upon such non-impersonal reasons. Yet such accounts, he argues, also appeal to some form of RAMS to provide a second account of practical reason and deliberation that cannot be reconciled to the first, an account upon which the "agent as utilitarian" always has decisive reasons to do what impersonal morality requires.

I take Williams' diagnosis to reveal a systematic equivocation that allows the consequentialist to treat the impersonal standpoint as a standpoint of moral rather than rational requirement de jure while treating it as the standpoint of rational requirement de facto. Such consequentialist accounts cannot account for the rational authority of their moral requirements because they presuppose an account of practical reason and deliberation that precludes such rational authority in the very determination of the best overall state of affairs. If impersonal value sets the standard for right action, any claim to the rational authority of such a standard is threatened by the account of practical reason and deliberation that is presupposed in the articulation of that very standard. This suggests that the standpoint of moral requirement cannot be fundamentally impersonal if moral requirements have rational authority.

It may be thought that movement by recent consequentialists beyond the traditional narrow monistic account of value to an account that can recognize the significance of a plurality of intrinsic values in the evaluation of states of affairs, including rights and respect for persons as ends in themselves, for example, along with happiness or well-being, can avoid Williams' criticisms. But Williams' diagnosis, I argue, suggests that such a move inadvertently exacerbates the problem confronting more traditional forms of act consequentialism. Impersonal recognition of such intrinsic non-impersonal moral values undermines not only the claim that consequentialist moral requirements have rational authority, but the claim, central to any form of foundational consequentialism, that the impersonal standpoint is the foundational moral standpoint. The result is a second strategy for sharpening the challenge to consequentialism, a strategy that will be developed in Chapter 6. In the remainder of Chapter 4 I argue that certain misleading parallels between theoretical and practical reasoning have also fueled the consequentialist's appeal to the impersonal standpoint as a de facto standpoint of rational requirement, and not just a standpoint of moral requirement. Exposing these misleading parallels allows for refinement and clarification of the challenge of consequentialism in order that the challenge to consequentialism can effectively be brought to bear upon it.

2.4 Deflating the Challenge of Consequentialism: Preview of Chapters 5–8

Although considerable work is necessary to bring the central challenge to consequentialism into focus, the general outline of the challenge of consequentialism to its opponents has been clear—these opponents must reject CMS, but consequentialists put forward what they take to be powerful independent considerations in support of CMS. The question to be taken up in Chapters 5 and 6 is whether development of the foregoing challenge *to* consequentialism provides the tools for a more effective response to the alleged challenge *of* consequentialism, particularly to the traditional considerations that have been taken to provide powerful and independent support for CMS.

I will demonstrate in Chapter 5 that many of the traditional grounds offered in support of such a consequentialist theory of the content of moral standards collapse in the face of the resources generated through the preceding refinement of the challenge to consequentialism. These traditional considerations draw upon certain powerful general intuitions concerning the relationship between rightness and goodness. I will argue, however, that these are most plausibly understood as intuitions concerning the relationship between moral rightness/wrongness of actions and the goodness/badness of actions as revealed through practical reasons and deliberation—between what it is right and wrong to do and what agents have better or worse, decisive or sufficient, reasons to do. Many of the standard rationales for consequentialism, I will argue, misappropriate these intuitions concerning the relationship between rightness and goodness as properties of actions, and treat them as contours of the relationship between rightness as a property of actions and goodness as a property of overall states of affairs. Such a misappropriation, once allowed, leads inevitably to consequentialism, even as it precludes truly satisfactory accounts of the relationship of goodness as a property of overall states of affairs both to right actions and to good and bad actions. With these traditional sources of support for consequentialism revealed as illusory, considerable pressure is brought to bear upon consequentialism itself. It emerges as the obvious member of our triad to be rejected in order to avoid the tension among them.

By the end of this fifth chapter one traditional source of support for consequentialism remains. Morality is impartial. If impersonality is the fundamental conception of impartiality relevant to moral evaluation, then morality must be fundamentally impersonal. I will demonstrate in Chapter 6 that development of the second Williams-inspired strategy for sharpening the challenge to consequentialism undermines the apparent force of this impartiality rationale for consequentialism. Recent developments of consequentialism have rendered it more susceptible to this second strategy. In particular, advocates of consequentialism have argued, quite persuasively, against a monistic construal of the theory upon which the impersonal standpoint is adopted toward a single intrinsic value, such as happiness or pleasure or welfare maximization.[27] Rather, they argue that the impersonal standpoint is appropriately adopted towards many sources of intrinsic value—not merely happiness and well-being but in addition such values as rights, autonomy, friendship, and/or respect for persons as ends in themselves. But it is this very argument for the broadening of the values towards which the impersonal standpoint is appropriately adopted that narrows the role of such a standpoint within an account of right action. If rights, for example, are recognized as intrinsic moral values towards which it is appropriate to adopt the overall impersonal standpoint, this is to recognize the appropriateness of adopting the impersonal standpoint towards distinctively moral values; indeed, towards non-impersonal moral values. To recognize the intrinsic value of rights is to recognize the legitimacy of non-impersonal constraints upon the pursuit of impersonal

---

[27] See Railton (1988) for an explicit rejection of monism, and Nozick (1974, pp. 28ff.) for an early suggestion that among the values that can be viewed impersonally are rights themselves. I take up such a "consequentialism of rights" in Chapter 6.

goals and of one's own plans and projects.[28] It is also to presuppose that such non-impersonal values have a non-impersonal rationale, or at least that they do not need such a rationale in order for their intrinsic value to be recognized. But this is to presuppose what ordinary morality suggests—that impersonal evaluations of states of affairs do not exhaust the moral considerations that are relevant to the determination of right actions, and that the relevant impersonal moral considerations, properly understood, presuppose the relevance of other fundamental non-impersonal moral considerations with non-impersonal rationales. To acknowledge that the impersonal standpoint takes into account non-impersonal moral values in its determination of the best overall state of affairs, and in this sense "comprehends" or "considers" all such values, is not to recognize that it is a comprehensive moral standpoint, but to acknowledge implicitly that it is not—that it is a standpoint for the articulation of only some among other fundamental moral considerations.[29] When all of the relevant fundamental moral considerations that such an approach presupposes to be relevant are taken into account, non-impersonal as well as impersonal, no grounds are provided for expecting that the right action will always be the action that brings about the best state of affairs impersonally considered.

I will close Chapter 6 by demonstrating that Scheffler's justly influential argument that there is no rationale for non-impersonal rights can be turned on its head within the framework of the challenge to consequentialism, revealing the outlines of just such a rationale. This rationale, in turn, further disarms the impartiality rationale for consequentialism. The impartiality rationale draws upon the widely held conviction that the standpoint for moral evaluation of actions as right and wrong must be an impartial standpoint—a standpoint of equal concern for persons. Because the impersonal standpoint is an impartial standpoint, albeit a standpoint in the first

---

[28] Here I am indebted to F. M. Kamm's discussion of rights in *Morality, Mortality* (1996, esp. p. 263).

[29] An analogy with higher and lower-order desires is relevant here. There is a sense in which higher-order desires comprehend lower-order desires within their content, but as Gary Watson has argued (2004a, pp. 13–32), they are not for that reason more comprehensive motives; indeed, this sense presupposes that such a higher-order desire is merely one of the agent's motives among others, including the lower-order desires that are its object. So too there is a sense in which the higher-order moral reasons that are articulated through appeal to the impersonal standpoint comprehend all of the lower-order moral reasons that make up their content, but it is a sense which presupposes that impersonal moral reasons are not comprehensive moral reasons. This analogy between higher-order desires and higher-order moral reasons will be developed in Chapters 4 and 6.

instance for evaluating overall states of affairs rather than actions, it can seem to be the default candidate for the moral evaluation of actions as well. But we have already seen that even consequentialists grant that rational agents have fundamentally non-impersonal reasons, reasons the rational significance of which is independent of whatever impersonal rational significance they have. If the conception of impartiality fundamental to morality is impersonality, then when such non-impersonal reasons have sufficient force morality will lack rational authority. Such a challenge to the rational authority of moral standards can be met if, as Scheffler proposes, each rational agent recognizes the independent moral significance of her own non-impersonal reasons. But such recognition by each agent only of the independent moral significance of her own non-impersonal reasons violates the requirement of equal concern that is the hallmark of impartiality. Recognition of the independent moral significance of fundamentally non-impersonal reasons is necessary for morality to have rational authority, but only if each rational agent recognizes the independent moral significance of the non-impersonal reasons of each such rational agent will morality maintain its impartiality. This line of argument provides powerful support for the recognition that a fundamental role is played in the moral evaluation of actions by an alternative to the impersonal conception of impartiality, an interpersonal conception of impartiality. Kantian, Hobbesian, and many contractualist accounts, among others, appeal to just such an interpersonal conception of impartiality to play a fundamental role in the moral evaluation of actions. My arguments demonstrate that the tensions within a consequentialist approach are properly seen as driving it to recognition of the fundamental role of this alternative conception of impartiality, and that standard arguments against recognizing a fundamental role for the interpersonal conception of impartiality collapse in the face of the challenge to consequentialism. Consideration of Scheffler's arguments thus allows us to bring into view a distinct conception of the impartiality that is involved in the evaluation of actions as right and wrong, an interpersonal conception that differs markedly from the impartiality as impersonality appropriate for the evaluation of overall states of affairs as better or worse. There is a distinct conception of impartiality appropriate for the evaluation of actions as right and wrong just as there is a distinct conception of impartiality appropriate for evaluating overall states of affairs as better or worse. Each involves a form of equal concern for persons; moreover, impartial determinations of better and worse overall states of affairs are relevant to impartial determinations of right and wrong actions. But they are merely some among other relevant considerations, and it will sometimes be the case that taking into account equally each person's plans, projects, and interests in the impartial evaluation of actions will generate moral prohibitions against acting to bring about the best overall consequences.

My central project in Chapter 6 is thus to demonstrate that a proper framing of the challenge to consequentialism allows us to put Williams' diagnosis of the shortcomings of consequentialism in a new and more productive light. Properly framed, this diagnosis sharpens the challenge to consequentialism, and establishes by the end of Chapter 6 that the arguments that sharpen the challenge undermine the force of the traditional considerations that have been taken by both consequentialists and their critics to provide independent support for the third member of the triad, the consequentialist account of moral standards itself. With this undermining of traditional considerations that are taken to provide independent support for CMS, the traditional challenge of consequentialism loses its force in the face of the challenge to consequentialism, and the member of the triad to be surrendered is CMS, the act consequentialist theory of the content of moral standards. Indeed, the apparent force of the consequentialist challenge can be seen as drawing upon a systematic misappropriation of central features of the relationship between rightness and goodness as properties of actions, and their deployment as purported features of the relationship between right action and good overall states of affairs.

I will demonstrate in Chapter 7 that an account of morality structured by the interpersonal conception of impartiality can avoid the obstacles that doom efforts by consequentialists to establish the rational authority of their impersonally structured moral requirements. Intuitively, ordinary moral requirements have rational authority, and certain moral restrictions upon acting to bring about the best overall state of affairs and moral permissions not to bring about the best overall state of affairs (agent-centered restrictions and agent-centered options) are integral components of ordinary morality. Consequentialism has difficulty accounting for either these restrictions or these permissions, but the alternative interpersonal conception of impartiality readily suggests rationales for both. Hence, it provides the framework for a moral theory that does generate the sorts of moral restrictions and permissions integral to the ordinary morality that intuitively satisfies RAMS. Whereas the claim that consequentialist moral requirements have rational authority is contrary to intuition, the rational authority of the moral requirements that emerge from this alternative conception of impartiality dovetails, at least in outline, with these broadly held ordinary moral intuitions. In addition, I will demonstrate that the second-personal reasons that Stephen Darwall has recently argued are central features of the practical reasoning and deliberation of typical rational agents, reasons that are tied to a distinctive practical authority to make a demand or claim on another, presuppose just such a distinctive interpersonal conception of impartiality in the moral evaluation of actions.[30] Finally, I will take up certain alleged analogies between the theoretical and practical spheres that have been endorsed even by critics of consequentialism such as Thomas Nagel, analogies that threaten to undermine any fundamental role for the interpersonal conception of impartiality in the evaluation of actions as right and wrong and good or bad. I will demonstrate that it is the claims concerning alleged analogies themselves that are misguided. Indeed, there is a plausible way of drawing out the relevant analogies and disanalogies between theoretical and practical reason that supports rather than undermines both the claim that our alternative conception of impartiality as interpersonality is the fundamental standpoint of impartial practical evaluation, and the claim that such interpersonal evaluation of actions has rational authority.

The argument in the first seven chapters focuses upon what I have characterized as the standard version of consequentialism, foundational/normative impersonal direct act consequentialism. The move to other versions of consequentialism, versions that focus only indirectly upon acts, or focus upon rules rather than acts, or adopt a non-impersonal evaluation of overall states of affairs, or ground normative consequentialism in non-consequentialist foundations, is often motivated by attempts to avoid problems with standard act consequentialism. I will demonstrate in Chapter 8, however, that the fundamental challenge to standard act consequentialism developed in earlier chapters extends to such nonstandard variants as well. I will show that a change in focal point from acts to rules or motives will not avoid the challenge to consequentialism, because the challenge to the claim that morality is in the business of maximizing the

---

[30] The argument is sketched in the first two chapters of Darwall (2006).

value of states of affairs is equally effective against any form of foundational consequentialism regardless of focal point. Attempts to ground normative consequentialism on a non-consequentialist foundation are also unlikely to succeed, I argue, because the alternative conception of impartiality that has emerged in Chapters 6 and 7 for the moral evaluation of actions as right or wrong precludes consequentialism at the normative as well as the foundational level. A departure from agent-neutral (impersonal) evaluation of states of affairs also won't avoid these arguments, because resources developed in Chapter 5 will allow us to see that such moves away from agent-neutral evaluation of states of affairs are most plausibly understood not as moves within consequentialism, but away from consequentialism and towards alternative moral theories. The goal of this final chapter is thus to suggest that the challenge to consequentialism, once fully articulated, undermines not only standard act consequentialism, but standard variations upon it as well.

2.5 Summary

Chapter 2 has outlined the challenge to consequentialism, Chapter 3 will magnify and refine this challenge through the lens of the demandingness objection, and Chapter 4 will harness Williams' analysis to sharpen the challenge in two distinct ways. With these resources in hand, Chapter 5 will demonstrate that many of the most prevalent arguments in support of consequentialism rely upon a systematic misinterpretation of general intuitions concerning rightness and goodness. Chapter 6 takes up the second direction for sharpening the challenge to consequentialism, demonstrating that on the most plausible understanding of the values to be taken up in the impersonal evaluation of states of affairs, the consequentialist's claim that the impersonal standpoint is the fundamental standpoint for the moral evaluation of actions is undermined. In addition, this argument provides the resources to undermine a rationale for consequentialism that is grounded in appeal to the impartiality of the impersonal standpoint. It is shown that a reinterpretation of one standard argument that there is no rationale for agent-centered restrictions instead provides an attractive rationale for such restrictions. This rationale suggests that although the impersonal conception of impartiality is appropriate for the impartial evaluation of overall states of affairs, it is not the conception of impartiality that is appropriate for the impartial evaluation of actions; moreover, it provides the outlines of the conception of impartiality, an interpersonal conception, that is appropriate for the impartial evaluation of actions as right and wrong.

Chapter 7 provides grounds for optimism that this alternative interpersonal conception of the impartiality that is relevant to the evaluation of actions as right and wrong, in contrast with the impersonal conception, can be reconciled with the other two members of our triad, in particular with the rational authority of moral requirements. Chapter 8 demonstrates that the challenge to standard act consequentialism, a challenge that undermines the rationale for (hence the challenge of) foundational act consequentialism, also undermines traditional rationales for variants upon standard act consequentialism. The next stage in my argument is a development and refinement of the triad, and the challenge to standard consequentialism that it reveals. This task will be undertaken in the next chapter by focusing upon the debate between consequentialists and their critics concerning the alleged extremely demanding and confining nature of consequentialist moral theories.

3

The Demandingness Objection: Too Demanding, or Not Demanding at All?

3.1 Too Demanding, or Not Demanding at All?

Consequentialism has, since its inception, faced persistent challenges of excess: it is, critics charge, too demanding, too confining, and too alienating to offer a plausible alternative moral theory.[1] Defenders typically concede that consequentialist moral theory is indeed extremely demanding, confining, and alienating, but deploy a range of defenses against such charges. Some look for partners in guilt, arguing, for example, that typical alternatives are no less extreme in relevant respects. Others, while conceding that the theory is extreme, argue that it is less extreme than might be thought; indeed, that it is not implausibly extreme. Still others bite the bullet, allowing that the theory is counter-intuitively extreme along some or all of these dimensions, but maintaining that we are nonetheless driven to embrace these counter-intuitive results by theoretical reflection.[2]

In what follows I will argue that the deeper challenge confronting consequentialism is not one of excess but of defect, in particular of defects

---

[1] Much of the material in this chapter is drawn from my "Does Consequentialism Make Too Many Demands, or None at All?" (2006).

[2] For a recent example of the partners in guilt strategy see Elizabeth Ashford (2003, p. 273). Her strategy is to allow that consequentialism comes across as "unreasonably demanding," but that "contractualist moral obligations . . . are just as demanding as utilitarian obligations" (ibid., p. 273). For three quite different arguments that consequentialism, properly understood, is less extreme than it may initially appear, see Liam Murphy (2000), Peter Railton (1988), and Tim Mulgan (2001). For an unapologetic example of the bullet-biting strategy, see Shelly Kagan's argument that although a consequentialist view "strikes us as outrageously extreme in its demands . . . it is nonetheless true" (1989, p. 2).

along precisely these dimensions upon which it is taken to be excessive. Developing a line of thought introduced in Chapter 1, I will argue that consequentialism, as it is typically presented, is a theory of exacting moral standards but not of decisive reasons for agents to conform to these standards. As a result, this theory of exacting moral standards can, with perfect consistency, be incorporated within an overall account upon which there are few if any rational demands upon agents to heed such standards. I will argue, moreover, that these challenges of defect confronting consequentialism are far more formidable than the traditional challenges of excess. The charges of excess array intuitions and considered judgments against the apparent theoretical strength of consequentialism. The charges of defect expose serious theoretical lacunae in consequentialism, undermining this apparent theoretical strength. In the next section I will distinguish two different types of moral theories, theories of moral standards and theories of moral reasons. I will demonstrate that consequentialism per se is best understood as a theory of the former sort. In Sections 3 and 4 I will distinguish theories of moral standards that can plausibly appeal to our ordinary conviction that we have decisive reasons to avoid wrongdoing from others that run foul of this ordinary conviction. I will demonstrate that consequentialism is a theory of moral standards of this latter sort. These arguments will establish that for the theory of consequentialist moral standards to provide rational agents with decisive reasons to avoid what it identifies as moral wrongdoing, it must be augmented with an account of practical reasons and deliberation upon which rational agents typically have decisive reasons to conform their actions to such standards. The final two sections will explore the prospects for augmenting consequentialism such that the result is not simply a theory of exacting standards, but a theory of consequentialist moral reasons, a theory upon which there are decisive reasons for agents to meet these exacting moral standards.

3.2 Theories of Moral Standards vs. Theories of Moral Reasons

The extreme demandingness objection is not that consequentialism makes demands—any plausible moral theory must account for this. Nor is the objection that consequentialism sometimes makes extreme demands. Again, this is a feature it will share with other moral theories. The objection is rather that the demands that it makes strike us as so extreme that consequentialism cannot be a plausible moral theory. As Liam Murphy points out, the traditional version of consequentialism "requires us to keep benefiting others until the point where further efforts would burden us as much as they would help the others." Although such a requirement "has the virtue of simplicity," he continues, "the demands it makes strike just about everyone as absurd—as we say, a principle that makes such demands 'just couldn't be right'."[3] Shelly Kagan suggests that the problem is that "to live in accordance with such demands would drastically alter my life. In a sense, neither my time, nor my goods, nor my plans would be my own. . . . The claim is deeply counterintuitive."[4]

In this section I will argue that the central challenge to consequentialism is not the extreme nature of the demands that it makes but its inability, without augmentation, to make any rational demands at all. Moreover, I will argue that this lacuna in the theory follows from certain readily recognized features of the theory in contrast with standard alternatives. This contrast can be highlighted by distinguishing theories of two different sorts. The first sort, which I will characterize as theories of moral reasons, are theories of the relationship between practical reason and morality, according to which agents typically have decisive reasons, as each theory understands such reasons, to avoid wrongdoing, as each understands moral wrongdoing. These are theories of the authoritativeness as well as the content of moral standards. Such theories are comprised not only of an account of moral standards, but in addition of a distinctive account of (1) practical reason, and (2) the decisive reasons agents typically have to avoid wrongdoing. They are theories, in short, that include rationales for the rational authority of their moral requirements (RAMS). Traditional Hobbesian and Kantian theories are examples of such theories of moral reasons. For the traditional Hobbesian, it is rational for the agent to pursue her own preservation, interest, utility, and/or preference maximization. The Hobbesian's distinctive account of decisive reasons to avoid wrongdoing arises from seeing moral standards as a set of rationally justified constraints upon the reasons we have for acting: We ought, rationally, to conform to moral standards of right and wrong action, properly understood, because they are

---

[3] Murphy (2000, p. 6).   [4] Kagan (1989, p. 2).

rationally justified constraints upon what we ought, rationally, to do.[5] The highly circumscribed account of moral standards that results is determined by the limited nature of such rationally justified constraints. Tradition-al Kantians offer an alternative account of practical reason that includes pure practical reasons, and an alternative account of moral standards for right/wrong action as dictates of pure practical reason. The distinctiveness of these categorical rational "oughts" also purportedly explains the status of such moral standards as decisive reasons to avoid wrongdoing.[6] In each case an account of practical reasons, an account of moral standards for action, and an account of decisive reasons to conform to these moral standards are all constituent components of the relevant theory. Such theories of moral reasons thus put forward not just an account of the content of moral standards but an affirmative answer to the question of why agents should perform the actions identified by these standards as morally required.

Theories of the second sort are theories not of moral standards as reasons, but of moral standards alone. To be an advocate of such a theory, one need only adopt the distinctive account of moral standards that it offers. These are theories of the content of moral standards, but not of the authoritativeness (RAMS) or lack thereof of such standards. Advocates of such a theory of moral standards alone can augment it with very different accounts of practical reason, and of the reasons agents have, if any, to avoid moral wrongdoing. If the augmentation is one upon which agents typically have decisive reasons to avoid wrongdoing, then the result is an alternative theory of moral reasons in the above sense. But to be an advocate of such a theory of moral standards, it is sufficient that one embrace the distinctive theory of moral standards on offer, regardless of the account of practical reason with which one augments it, and regardless of whether or not one takes there to be decisive reasons to act in accordance with such moral standards.

Consequentialism, as the theory is commonly formulated, is typically offered as a theory of this latter sort—a theory of moral standards alone.

---

[5] See, for example, David Gauthier's contemporary Hobbesian account (1986), and discussions of Hobbes' own moral theory by Stephen Darwall (1998, ch. 10) and Christine Korsgaard (1996a, pp. 21–7.)

[6] I use the qualifier "traditional" here to distinguish such accounts from more recent "neo-Kantian" alternatives that avoid the adoption of central aspects of Kant's account of practical reason. Such neo-Kantian alternatives will be discussed in Section 3.3. Developments of various aspects of such traditional Kantian accounts can be found in Barbara Herman (1993) and Onora O'Neill (1989).

It is not a theory of the relationship between practical reason and moral standards, but of the relationship between rightness of actions and goodness of states of affairs—between moral standards for action and evaluation of overall consequences. Specifically, it is the theory that an action is morally right just in case it brings about the best overall state of affairs; all other actions are morally prohibited.[7] Our ordinary moral judgments involve appeals to impartial moral considerations such as rights that prohibit us in certain cases from undertaking what would in this consequentialist sense be the right course of action. Consequentialist theories of moral standards, by contrast, limit the considerations relevant to the determination of standards for right action, as we have seen, to what Derek Parfit has characterized as "outcome-given" impartial considerations,[8] considerations based in the appeal to better and worse overall states of affairs. Appeals to rights can only supply such outcome-given impartial considerations to the extent that rights violations are taken to contribute to the badness of overall states of affairs, such that it is a better resulting state of affairs if fewer or less serious violations of rights occur.

A moral theory that accepts this distinctive account of the relationship between right action and the best state of affairs, upon which agents are morally required to bring about the best overall state of affairs and all other actions are morally prohibited, is consequentialist, regardless of its account of the relationship between practical reason and rightness/wrongness; indeed, regardless of whether it includes an account of this relationship at all. Such

[7] Thus Mill characterizes utilitarian consequentialism as the view that "actions are right in proportion as they tend to promote happiness; wrong as they tend to produce the reverse happiness" (2001, p. 7). J. J. C. Smart characterizes it as the view that "the rightness or wrongness of an action depends only on the goodness or badness of its consequences" (1973, p. 4). Alan Donagan (1977, p. 189) and Railton (1988, p. 108), respectively, characterize consequentialism as the theory that "actions are right if and only if their consequences are better than those of any other actions that could be done instead," and that assesses "rightness in terms of contribution to the good." In each case consequentialism is presented as the theory that endorses a distinctive relationship between standards for the rightness of action and standards for the evaluation of overall consequences.

[8] Derek Parfit (2004, p. 355). Such a restriction to "outcome-given" considerations, however, leaves important questions at the margins unresolved. For John Rawls, a view upon which distributive considerations are held to be relevant is not a consequentialist view (1971, p. 25). For Parfit it can be (2004, pp. 358–9). I take this to indicate a substantive disagreement concerning whether such distributional considerations can properly be understood as among the impartial outcome-given considerations to which a consequentialist account of moral standards is typically taken to be restricted. Rawls takes it to be the case that such distributional considerations are properly understood as appeals to impartial considerations which, like standard appeals to rights, are not in the relevant sense outcome-given. Parfit holds that such distributional concerns can be among the relevant outcome-given impartial considerations. See, in addition, Kagan's discussion of distributional considerations (1998, ch. 2).

theories of moral standards alone are in a different and more circumscribed business than theories of moral reasons. The tendency to overlook this distinction has important consequences for the debates among advocates of such theories. In particular, the assumptions that consequentialism is extremely alienating, demanding, and confining are only plausible if the consequentialist theory of moral standards is credited with being something that (without augmentation) it is not—a theory of its moral standards as reasons. Only if the theory of moral standards (CMS) is augmented with a rationale for the claim that such standards have rational authority (RAMS), a rationale that is no part of the theory itself, do the standard concerns about the demanding, confining, and alienating nature of such a theory even arise. An example will clarify this point. Consider a particular, and particularly economic, version of consequentialism, upon which the right action to perform maximizes overall utility or welfare.[9] Such a consequentialist theory provides us with moral standards for action, as do Hobbesian and Kantian alternatives. Let us grant, moreover, that it would be far more demanding for an agent to conform her actions to such consequentialist standards for right actions than it would be for an agent to conform her actions to Kantian and Hobbesian standards:[10] it would, for example, be significantly more disruptive to her plans, projects, and relationships to conform her actions to consequentialist standards. Consequentialism, then, is at the extreme end of this continuum, the continuum of more or less exacting moral standards.

But traditional Kantian and Hobbesian moral theories not only establish more or less exacting standards; they are theories of their standards as reasons—of the decisive reasons agents have to avoid what they identify as wrongdoing. That is, they are theories of the rational authority of their standards for rational agents (RAMS) such that agents typically have decisive reasons to avoid what is morally prohibited and do what is morally required. This suggests a second continuum, not of relatively exacting

---

[9] See, e.g., the version of utilitarianism articulated by John Harsanyi in "Ethics in Terms of Hypothetical Imperatives" (1976), and Amartya Sen's characterization of such a version of act utilitarianism (1985, p. 175).

[10] It will become apparent, however, that the difficulty I am raising for consequentialist moral theory is not avoided by a demonstration that its standards are less exacting than might be thought. A consequentialist theory with less exacting standards must still be augmented in order for the result to be a theory that makes rational demands upon agents to conform their actions to its (less exacting) standards.

moral standards, but of the relative strength of the rational demands that different theories make upon agents to make sacrifices in order to avoid wrongdoing. I will refer to this second continuum as the continuum of more or less demanding reasons to act morally. Traditional Kantian and Hobbesian theories of moral reasons are theories of an isomorphism between the continuum of exacting moral standards and the continuum of demanding reasons to act morally. Because they offer a rationale for the rational authority of their moral standards, such theories provide reasons for conforming to their standards: what they morally prohibit, the agent has decisive reasons not to do. By contrast, our economic consequentialism, because it is not a theory of moral reasons, cannot even be located upon this second continuum, the continuum that gauges the relative strengths of the rational demands upon rational agents to avoid moral wrongdoing. It must first be augmented by an account of practical reason before it can be located upon this continuum. Moreover, the augmenting account of practical reasons must establish the rational authority of its moral standards if it is to be located on the demanding end of this second continuum.

To see why this second continuum, the continuum of more or less demanding reasons to act morally, is crucial to the debate concerning demandingness, consider one standard proposal for augmenting economic consequentialism with an account of practical reason such that the resulting theory can occupy a position on the continuum of more or less demanding reasons to act morally. On this proposal economic consequentialist standards for morally evaluating states of affairs and actions are augmented with the standard economic account of practical reason, upon which the rational action maximizes the agent's own utility or welfare. On the resulting theory of rightness/wrongness and practical reason, the right action to perform will maximize overall utility (all others are morally prohibited), while the action that it is reasonable for an agent to perform will maximize her own utility. If it turns out that only rarely does the action that maximizes overall utility also maximize a particular agent's utility, such a consequentialist will rarely have decisive reasons to avoid what her own exacting moral standards identify as moral wrongdoing.[11] Moreover, she will frequently

---

[11] Even when it is reasonable to conform to impersonal moral standards on such an account, morality need not be in the relevant sense demanding and alienating. In such cases the standards set by morality and the action that will maximize the agent's utility may simply coincide. The agent, in pursuing his own utility, is conforming to moral standards.

have decisive reasons to do what is morally wrong. She will rarely have decisive reasons to act rightly, and will frequently have decisive reasons to do what is morally wrong. Such a theory of practical reasons, when wedded to a consequentialist moral theory, supports NIR, the second member of our triad, but undermines RAMS.

Economic consequentialism, augmented with an economic account of reason, can with perfect consistency occupy both the extremely exacting end of the continuum of more or less exacting moral standards, and the opposite extreme of the continuum of more or less demanding reasons to act morally. The overall theory of reasons and moral standards is one upon which its standards are excessive by comparison with other theories, but the rational demands for moral sacrifice that it makes upon rational agents are relatively deficient, since it provides agents with decisive reasons in typical cases to ignore such exacting standards in pursuit of their own utility. The theory is consequentialist because it embraces the defining feature of consequentialism, the distinctive relationship between moral standards for action and overall value of consequences. But it is not in the relevant sense demanding at all. Although conformity to its moral standards would require extreme sacrifices, an agent would rarely have decisive reasons to make such sacrifices and would often have decisive reasons not to. The aforementioned theories of moral reasons, by contrast, are theories of the rational authority of their moral standards for agents.

The point of this example is not to privilege in any way this version of consequentialism, but to highlight the fact that consequentialism, as it is commonly presented, is only a theory of moral standards, not of moral reasons—a theory of CMS, not of RAMS. Like traditional Hobbesian and Kantian theories, it sets moral standards. But unlike them, it is not a theory of the rational authority of such standards. To play this latter role it would have to be augmented by an account of practical reason, and an account of why there are decisive reasons, thus understood, to avoid actions that such exacting moral standards identify as wrong. We have seen that with certain augmenting accounts of reason, such as individual utility maximization, the resulting theory of moral standards plus reasons makes few rational demands upon agents. Such an economic consequentialist identifies the actions that bring about the best consequences, and labels such actions as the right actions, but can with perfect consistency maintain that agents rarely if ever have any reasons to take such facts about moral rightness/wrongness into account in the determination of what they have reason to do. On such a theory rational agents are not alienated *by* morality but *from* morality. Consequentialists and their critics often take consequentialism to be the most demanding moral theory—not just to put forward extremely exacting standards but to make rational demands upon agents to act in conformity with such standards. But this is to presuppose what unaugmented consequentialism does not itself offer—a theory not just of moral standards but of moral reasons, and in particular of an isomorphism between its exacting standards for moral wrongdoing and corresponding demands upon rational agents.

On one common reading, Mill himself avoids such an unwarranted presupposition, offering a consequentialist theory of moral reasons, not simply of moral standards. On this reading Mill's theory maintains both that the individual's happiness is the ultimate end of reason and that aggregate happiness sets the proper moral standards. One component of this broader theory, of which moral standards are only one part, is an account upon which appropriately trained agents in a society such as ours typically have decisive reasons, as the theory understands such reasons, to conform their actions to the standards of morality, as the theory understands such standards, hence to avoid acting in ways such standards prohibit.[12] Mill's overall theory, then, augments the consequentialist theory of moral standards with (1) an account of practical reasons, upon which (2) agents typically have decisive reasons to avoid wrongdoing. The result is an example of a theory that provides an alternative in kind to traditional Kantian and Hobbesian theories, including accounts of practical reason, rightness/wrongness, and the decisive reasons agents typically have to avoid wrongdoing. This is a theory that can be placed upon both the continuum of exacting moral standards and the continuum of more or less demanding reasons to act morally.

Without undue distortion Mill's solution can be recast in the parlance of contemporary consequentialism: the demands of practical reason are determined from the agent's own personal standpoint; the standards of

---

[12] Happiness, Mill argues, is both "the end of human action" and "the standard of morality" (2001, p. 12). But it is an agent's own happiness that is the end of human action, and the general happiness that sets the standard of morality. The Chapter 2 argument on sanctions, in turn, attempts to establish that properly trained agents in an advanced society will typically have reasons to conform their actions to utlilitarian consequentialist moral standards. See Korsgaard (1996a, pp. 78–84), and Elijah Millgram (2000), for quite different readings of Mill's argument that nonetheless share these general features.

morality from the impartial, impersonal standpoint. In his case, the personal standpoint is taken to be a partial standpoint that aims at the agent's own happiness, while impersonal standards are set by aggregate happiness. To demonstrate the rational authority of moral standards, for Mill, is to show that there is the requisite sort of linkage between the impersonal and the personal standpoints such that the properly trained agent has decisive reasons, from the personal standpoint of his own happiness, to conform his actions to moral standards of rightness determined from the impersonal standpoint of aggregate happiness. If this linkage can be established, then the agent will typically have decisive reasons to avoid what is morally prohibited.

Here, then, is a consequentialist theory of moral reasons that is as demanding as its standards are exacting. But it is a theory of moral reasons which even many consequentialists, following Sidgwick, take to fail in its central task.[13] They agree with many non-consequentialist critics of Mill that if good reasons are exhausted by personal reasons thus understood, it is simply implausible to expect that such an account will establish the requisite linkage between consequentialist moral standards and decisive reasons. Rather, rational agents will often have decisive reasons to act in ways prohibited by consequentialist moral standards. Extreme moral standards will not make extreme demands upon us on such a theory; indeed, agents will often have decisive reasons not to act in accord with morality. I will not pause here to rehearse these criticisms. It suffices for my purposes to show that if the end of reason is taken to be the agent's own happiness, even many consequentialists will allow that the resulting theory may not be nearly as demanding as even moderately demanding alternative theories. Indeed, it may make few if any rational demands upon agents to conform their actions to its exacting moral standards.

Nor does Sidgwick's own account of practical reason hold much promise for augmenting a consequentialist theory of moral standards such that the result is in our sense a consequentialist theory of moral reasons. Sidgwick takes there to be a dualism of practical reason such that, although it is

---

[13] Henry Sidgwick rejects this aspect of Mill's argument (1981, pp. 499–501). Kagan allows that if rationality aims at my own happiness or well-being, "it seems much more plausible to deny that the rational point of view and the moral point of view must coincide" (1998, p. 42). For a detailed criticism of Mill's attempt to demonstrate that agents in a culture such as ours will typically have good reasons, as he understands them, to conform their actions to utilitarian moral standards, see Millgram (2000, esp. secs VII–IX). See also Samuel Scheffler's discussion (1992a).

always "reasonable" for an individual to bring about overall happiness, it is "no less reasonable for an individual to take his own happiness as his ultimate end."[14] In cases of conflict, although the agent has sufficient reasons on such an account to do what consequentialist moral standards require, she also has sufficient reasons to do what consequentialist moral standards prohibit. An account of consequentialist moral standards for right and wrong action augmented with such an account of reason would allow that agents have sufficient reasons to act in ways consequentialist moral standards prohibit whenever promotion of the agent's own happiness and promotion of overall happiness diverge. Indeed, only in cases in which individual and overall happiness converge will an agent have decisive reasons not to perform actions prohibited by such moral standards.

As the foregoing discussion of Mill makes clear, this point about the absence of demands is not a point about the motivational externalist commitments of many consequentialists.[15] Indeed, Mill offers an externalist solution that would, if plausible, provide a theory of moral reasons upon which agents typically have decisive reasons to act as required by exacting consequentialist moral standards. The difficulty is not with the externalism of the solution, but with the failure of this externalist account, even by most consequentialists' lights, to provide agents with decisive reasons to avoid what the theory identifies as moral wrongdoing. Kantians offer a distinctive family of internalist accounts of the relationship of practical reason to moral standards such that agents have decisive reasons to avoid wrongdoing. Hobbesians are sometimes understood as offering a distinctive family of externalist accounts of the relationship of practical reasons to moral standards, such that agents typically do have decisive reasons to avoid wrongdoing.[16] My point is that any such account, whether externalist like

---

[14] Sidgwick (1981, p. 404, n.1). See also his "Concluding Chapter," and discussions of Sidgwick's account by Parfit (1984, pp. 461–3), and David Phillips (1998). I am grateful to David Phillips for help clarifying my discussion of Sidgwick's views at various points.

[15] The externalism/internalism distinction that I invoke here turns on the acceptance or rejection of what has been characterized by Darwall as judgment internalism (1995, p. 40), and by Michael Smith as the "practicality requirement" (1994, p. 61). Roughly, this is the view that there is a (perhaps defeasible) conceptual ("internal") connection between moral judgment and motivation to act such than an agent who sincerely makes such a judgment will, if rational, be motivated to act accordingly. Although most consequentialists reject internalism, the theory does not require such a rejection. Indeed, R. M. Hare (1981) and David Cummiskey (1996, pp. 162ff.) are avowed consequentialists who also embrace forms of internalism.

[16] Darwall (1998, ch. 10).

the Hobbesian or internalist like the Kantian, is itself, in effect, external to consequentialism as this theory is typically presented. Indeed, this is precisely why certain proposals for augmenting the consequentialist theory of moral standards with accounts of practical reason and deliberation result in internalist theories, while others result in externalist theories. As a theory of exacting moral standards, consequentialism incorporates no account of reasons, and a fortiori no account of decisive reasons to act morally. For it to be a theory of such rational demands, the consequentialist theory of moral standards must be incorporated within a broader theory, whether internalist or externalist, upon which agents have decisive reasons (albeit only "typically" in the externalist case) to avoid wrongdoing.

The consequentialist thus has a compelling and surprising response to the traditional extreme demandingness objection. The traditional complaint that consequentialism is extremely demanding, properly understood, simply misses its mark. Theories of moral reasons make demands, some of them extreme. But both the consequentialist and the critics who worry that a consequentialist theory of moral standards makes extreme demands upon agents conflate theories of moral standards, which can only be placed on the continuum of exacting standards, with theories of moral reasons, which have locations as well on the continuum of demanding reasons to act morally. Moreover, such consequentialists and their critics take the consequentialist theory of moral standards somehow to commit its advocate to taking its extreme location on the first continuum to be reflected by an extreme location on the second. But we have seen that the consequentialist theory of moral standards, which maintains only that the right action brings about the best consequences, requires no such commitment, and is agnostic as a theory with respect to the relationship between these two continua. Its standards for right/wrong action, although they would be exacting to satisfy, could just as easily be a component of a theory that makes few if any rational demands upon agents to make the sacrifices that conformity with such exacting moral standards would require. That the theory as such makes no demands whatsoever, however, will hardly be welcomed by most consequentialists as a satisfying defense against its alleged excessive demandingness.

3.3 Why the Intuition that Moral Requirements Have Rational Authority Is No Help

But is it legitimate to expect the consequentialist to provide a theoretical rationale for the assumption that underlies her concerns about excessive demandingness, alienation, and confinement, the assumption that agents have decisive reasons to conform to her exacting moral standards?[17] Might it not be sufficient, in the absence of such a rationale, simply to appeal to our ordinary conviction that we typically have decisive reasons to avoid moral wrongdoing? Other moral theories, including some neo-Kantian and contractualist theories, appear to rely upon some such ordinary conviction to establish the prima facie demandingness of their moral standards. Might not the consequentialist do the same? In this section I will argue that the consequentialist theory of moral standards cannot plausibly help itself to this ordinary conviction. Indeed, such an ordinary conviction serves only to highlight additional problems for any consequentialist assumption that its exacting moral standards are mirrored by corresponding rational demands upon agents.

Consequentialists take themselves to provide a compelling theory of moral standards (CMS). Let us grant that we ordinarily take ourselves to have decisive reasons to avoid moral wrongdoing, that is, that RAMS is intuitively plausible. If the consequentialist can plausibly wed her (purportedly) superior theory of moral standards to this intuitive link between moral standards and reasons, the result is an account upon which agents have decisive reasons not to do what is prohibited by the consequentialist's exacting standards. The difficulty with any such line of argument, however, is that RAMS is itself bound up with our ordinary convictions concerning reasonableness and wrongness. If entire classes of ordinary judgments concerning moral wrongness are jettisoned, as they are by the consequentialist, the intuitive appeal of RAMS itself is undermined. It is what ordinary, more "moderate" morality identifies as wrong that we take ourselves to have decisive reasons to avoid. But it is widely acknowledged by both consequentialists and their critics that the ordinary morality reflected in our everyday moral judgments frequently permits agents not to bring about the

---

[17] I am indebted to David Cummiskey for assistance in clarifying the central issues at stake in the arguments of this section.

best consequences, and in other cases prohibits them from bringing about the best consequences.[18] These features of ordinary morality are typically characterized as agent-centered options or permissions and agent-centered restrictions or constraints. Ordinary morality, then, allows that we often have sufficient moral reasons to act in ways that fail to bring about the best overall consequences. But the theory of consequentialist moral standards identifies such actions as morally wrong. Intuitively, it is often by our ordinary, everyday lights both reasonable and moral to act in ways that consequentialist moral standards identify as morally wrong. We may well ordinarily have decisive reasons to avoid ordinary moral wrongdoing. But for this very reason we often appear to have at least sufficient reasons to do what consequentialism identifies as wrong.

Many other theories of moral standards retain and explicate central features of ordinary morality such as permissions and restrictions.[19] They can be plausibly understood as supplying rationales for the central features of the ordinary moral standards that our ordinary morality suggests do typically provide decisive reasons to avoid wrongdoing. Hence they can draw upon the intuitive appeal of RAMS. The consequentialist account of moral standards, by contrast, rejects these central features of ordinary morality, and offers in their place moral standards that rule out entire classes of what we ordinarily take ourselves either not to have decisive moral reasons to do or to have decisive moral reasons to avoid. The intuitive rational authoritativeness of ordinary moral requirements thus works against any attempt to establish the rational authoritativeness of their own moral requirements.

Consequentialists often hold that there is no plausible rationale for the restrictions that constitute a central feature of ordinary morality and no plausible rationale for according any moral relevance to the agent's own plans, projects, and interests beyond their role in the determination of the best overall states of affairs.[20] But even if, for the sake of argument,

---

[18] For examples of the standard concession by both consequentialists and their critics that permissions and restrictions are intuitively plausible, see Scheffler (1982, pp. 103–4) and F. M. Kamm (1996, p.143) concerning restrictions, and Kagan's discussion of permissions (1989, ch. 1).

[19] Kamm (1982, esp. chs 8–10) and T. M. Scanlon (1998) offer theories of moral standards that provide rationales for the intuitive restrictions and permissions that are central features of ordinary morality.

[20] Scheffler, for example, argues that there is no plausible rationale for restrictions (1982, ch. 4); Kagan doubts that there are plausible rationales for either restrictions or permissions, but the bulk of his

such controversial claims are granted, no presumption results that agents have decisive reasons to conform their actions to consequentialist moral standards. The ordinary morality that intuitively satisfies RAMS, providing us with decisive reasons to avoid wrongdoing, takes each agent's plans and interests to have rational significance that is not captured from the impersonal standpoint. But it takes this independent rational significance to be reflected as well in the independent moral significance of such plans and interests in the determination of right and wrong action, moral signifi-cance that is not exhausted from the impersonal standpoint. If, *pace* ordinary morality, the moral significance of the agent's plans and interests is exhausted from the impersonal standpoint, it in no way follows that their rational sig-nificance is also exhausted from such a standpoint, only that morality is not "properly" understood as reflecting this independent rational significance in its determination of right and wrong actions. If, as consequentialism sug-gests, the independent rational significance of such plans and interests is not reflected within morality, should we not expect the rational significance of such considerations instead to weigh against whatever rational significance consequentialist moral standards might have? Since such non-impersonal reasons often appear to provide us with at least sufficient reasons not to bring about the best overall consequences (NIR), they would seem often to provide us with sufficient reasons to do what consequentialist standards identify as wrong (thereby violating RAMS).[21] The very non-impersonal rationally significant factors that intuitively moderate ordinary moral stan-dards would seem in the case of consequentialism to moderate whatever reasons there are for rational agents not to do what its moral standards prohibit. With the rejection of central features of our ordinary standards for wrongness, the consequentialist cannot plausibly appeal to our ordinary conviction that we have decisive reasons to avoid wrongdoing to establish the demandingness of his own moral standards. Instead, he must provide a

argument is directed against purported rationales for permissions (1989, esp. chs 1 and 5). In Chapter 6 I will demonstrate that there is such a plausible rationale for moral resitrctions upon bringing about the best overall state of affairs.

[21] See Scheffler (1982) for his characterization of the personal point of view as having independent moral significance. Scheffler may seem to deflect the threat to a consequentialist theory of moral reasons outlined here by outlining a theory of moral standards that reincorporates non-impersonal consideration of the agent's plans, projects, commitments, and interests. This alternative theory of moral standards is made possible by the presentation of a rationale for recognizing the independent moral significance of the personal point of view. His view will be taken up in detail in the second half of Chapter 6.

theory of moral reasons, not just of moral standards, and this requires the augmentation of the consequentialist account of moral standards with the relevant components of an account of practical reason, and in particular of the typically decisive reasons agents have not to do what such standards identify as wrong (RAMS).

3.4 Kagan and Standpoint-Relative Reasons

There is one highly circumscribed sense in which a consequentialist theory of moral standards can be understood as offering an account of moral reasons, and even of decisive moral reasons, without any augmentation of its theory of moral standards. It is worthwhile to consider this circumscribed sense, if only to make clear why it does not obviate the need to provide a true theory of moral reasons. The guiding insight here is supplied by Shelly Kagan. Crucial to his account is a characterization of a moral theory such as consequentialism as involving claims about "what people should do from the moral point of view." These should not be confused "with claims about what people should do from the legal point of view. Nor, of course, should they be confused with claims about what people should do from the aesthetic point of view, or the economic point of view, or the patriotic point of view . . ."[22] Each is a determination of what there are decisive reasons to do relative to a particular standpoint or point of view. They should not be confused with each other, but nor should these reasons from various standpoints be confused with what people should do simpliciter, and the demands, simpliciter, that reasons make upon us. On such views, there can be decisive reasons from the patriotic, economic, or moral standpoint for an agent to act in some particular way without her having decisive reasons to act that way. There may, for example, be decisive economic reasons to end a life, but also decisive reasons simpliciter to discount the economic standpoint entirely in such a case. Consequentialist moral standards, then, provide reasons that are decisive relative to the impersonal standpoint. From such a standpoint, the moral relevance of a harm that an agent will do, for example, is exhausted by viewing it as one among other harms and benefits that will happen.

---

[22] Kagan (1998, p. 10).

Such a characterization of consequentialist moral standards allows a consequentialist who has not yet provided a theory of the rational authority of its moral standards to talk without begging the question of moral reasons, not merely moral standards. But although this shows us how an account of moral standards can be understood as providing an account of decisive moral reasons, it also clarifies the nature of the gap between a theory of decisive moral reasons thus understood, and a theory of decisive moral reasons simpliciter. Consequentialist moral standards provide reasons relative to a standpoint. But without an account of any reasons we might have to take into account such standpoint relative reasons, we are no closer to a consequentialist theory of moral reasons. Kagan has articulated an account of moral reasons relative to a standpoint, but not an account of such relative reasons as reasons simpliciter. In short, he has not articulated an alternative account of consequentialist moral standards as (decisive) reasons. About this point Kagan is at points refreshingly clear. He allows that such a theory only proposes an account of "how people ought to act, morally speaking," and must be augmented with an answer to "the crucially important—but nonetheless distinct—question of the degree to which rationality endorses the demands of morality."[23] An action is wrong, on this view, if there are decisive moral reasons not to do it, but such reasons are decisive only relative to the impersonal standpoint. Such reasons that are relative to a standpoint that itself has an indeterminate relationship to the agent's reasons are not thereby shown to be a subset of the agent's reasons, any more than a claim that is reasonable relative to

<hr />

[23] Ibid., p. 11. See also Kagan (1989, p. 66). One could of course challenge the legitimacy of this question of the degree to which reasons that are decisive only relative to various standpoints provide agents with non-relative reasons. In particular, one could maintain that the only reasons agents have are reasons relative to such standpoints. (See David Copp (1997) for a defense of such a view.) Whatever the merits of such a view of practical reason, augmentation of the consequentialist theory of moral standards by such a view seems unlikely to establish that such exacting standards make extreme rational demands upon agents. Such a view can allow that standpoint relative consequentialist moral standards are extremely exacting—the agent has reasons that are decisive relative to the moral standpoint to act in ways that she would experience as extremely demanding and confining (far more demanding and confining than ordinary morality). But the view also allows that agents have decisive reasons relative to other standpoints, e.g. the prudential, economic, and patriotic standpoints. These will often provide agents with decisive standpoint relative reasons to perform actions they have decisive moral reasons not to perform; indeed, Copp's account presupposes that there are such conflicting standpoint relative decisive reasons. The agent will in such cases have decisive standpoint relative reasons to undertake multiple and conflicting courses of action, including morally prohibited courses of action. There would simply be no answer on such an account concerning which of these courses of action an agent has decisive reasons simpliciter to undertake or avoid.

a set of premises is shown to be a reasonable claim. Only if the premises are themselves taken by the agent to be reasonable does she actually have reasons to accept the conclusion, and to see the argument as demanding her assent to the conclusion. Similarly, only to the extent that an agent has reasons to take into account considerations from the impersonal standpoint do reasons relative to that standpoint become reasons for him. What is left indeterminate by such a consequentialist account of moral reasons, then, is precisely whether, and to what extent, moral reasons, thus understood, are reasons for the agent at all.

Such a consequentialist moral theory allows that moral reasons as it understands them might be relativized to a standpoint that has nothing to do with the agent's reasons, or, even if the agent does have reasons to take into account reasons that are relativized to this standpoint, she may have other reasons that systematically outweigh whatever reasons these reasons-from-a-standpoint provide. Thus Kagan allows, with characteristic candor, that on such a theory "there may be reasons which have weight from the moral standpoint but which are not genuine reasons for action for some individuals."[24] Consequentialist moral standards are supplied by what an agent would have reason to do from an impersonal standpoint. But such an account must still be augmented with an account of what agents have reasons to do, and of why they have decisive reasons not to do what they have decisive reasons not to do from an impersonal standpoint, in order for its exacting standards to make corresponding rational demands upon agents.

After acknowledging the "logical possibility" of a gap, Kagan proceeds to treat such decisive moral reasons as providing the agent with decisive reasons:

the suggestion that a morally decisive reason must outweigh the opposing reasons is an extremely plausible one. It is certainly hard to see how a reason for reacting in a given way could be decisive if it was itself outweighed by more powerful reasons that supported reacting in some other way. . . . So let us assume that a necessary condition for being a morally decisive reason is that the reason override the opposing reasons.[25]

[24] Kagan (1989, p. 66).
[25] Ibid., p. 67. In *Normative Ethics* he appeals to the ordinary moral intuition that moral requirements have rational authority: "most of us take ourselves to be quite prepared to act as we morally should, if only we can determine just what it is that morality asks us" (1998, p. 11). But we have already seen in

Although Kagan suggests that it is "hard to see how a reason for reacting in a given way could be decisive if it is itself outweighed by more powerful reasons," this is precisely what his take on the consequentialist theory of moral standards makes it all too easy to see in the case of decisive moral reasons. A moral reason, on such an account, is decisive relative to the impersonal standpoint. But many such reasons that are decisive from a standpoint, for example the aesthetic, patriotic, or economic standpoint, fail to be decisive reasons simpliciter. Why expect anything else of reasons that are decisive from the impersonal standpoint? The consequentialist theory of moral standards appears designed precisely to undermine, not to draw upon, the plausibility of the claim that morally decisive reasons, in the highly circumscribed sense it supports, are decisive reasons.[26] The only decisiveness established on such a theory is decisiveness relative to a standpoint, and decisive standpoint relative reasons are routinely outweighed by other reasons (when they have weight as reasons at all).

Traditional Hobbesian and Kantian approaches offer theories of moral reasons that attempt to establish decisive reasons for agents to act morally. More intuitionistic Kantian and contractarian theories of moral standards explicate central features of ordinary morality, hence can with some plausibility rely upon the intuition that ordinary moral reasons, when decisive, provide decisive reasons simpliciter. The consequentialist theory of moral standards is not a theory of decisive reasons to act morally. Moreover, because it rejects central features of ordinary morality, it cannot rely on the ordinary moral intuition that moral reasons, when decisive, provide decisive reasons simpliciter. Indeed, decisive consequentialist moral reasons frequently fail, intuitively, to provide decisive reasons simpliciter.

---

the previous section that such an appeal to the intuitive link between ordinary morality and decisive reasons is not available for a theory that rejects wholesale many of the ordinary moral commitments that intuitively give rise to such reasons.

[26] Kagan rightly points out, in his discussion of subjective reasons (1989, p. 335, n. 1), that to give such priority to plans and projects when they conflict with morally decisive reasons is to act in a way that is morally forbidden, and that agents are taken to have decisive reasons not to do what is morally forbidden upon more moderate theories. My point, however, is that the consequentialist cannot help himself to this aspect of moderate morality. Although moderate moral standards do, intuitively, provide decisive reasons to avoid wrongdoing, the consequentialist swaps out this moderate morality for an alternative, and there is no intuition that agents have decisive reasons to avoid the actions it identifies as wrong; indeed, quite the contrary: we often appear to have justification to do what consequentialist morality "forbids".

Although the standards put forward by the theory morally prohibit a great deal, our ordinary judgments suggest that agents frequently have at least sufficient reasons to act contrary to such consequentialist moral prohibitions.

As with demandingness, so too with confinement. The difficulty identified by the objection that consequentialism is unacceptably confining is that consequentialist moral standards always, except in cases of ties, dictate some particular course of action as the required action to perform.[27] If consequentialist standards of rightness and wrongness always provide decisive reasons, then an agent always, except in the case of ties, has decisive reasons to pursue the course of action that brings about the best overall state of affairs. She is confined within the impersonal standpoint and the unique (save in the case of ties) course of action it dictates. In particular, she is unable to take into account other apparently relevant reasons, for example non-impersonal considerations concerning her own plans and projects, and the claims that others have upon her.

But this makes it clear that any confinement by consequentialism only results if the consequentialist's exacting moral standards are reflected in corresponding rational demands upon agents. The unaugmented theory of consequentialist moral standards, insofar as it is a theory of reasons at all, is a theory only of reasons relative to a standpoint. It leaves unanswered whether or not agents have reasons to take into account such standpoint-relative reasons. Even granting that an agent has in this sense morally decisive reasons to perform a particular action in every case, it does not follow for the consequentialist that his moral theory is confining at all. Indeed, it places no constraints upon the reasons that an agent should take into account: it is not, without augmentation, a theory of moral reasons that confine us. To assume that consequentialism confines is to presuppose what consequentialism, without augmentation, does not provide: an account of reasons and of why, contrary to intuition, the relevant impersonal considerations are decisive reasons. It is to presuppose, in short, that the consequentialist theory of moral standards is a theory of typically decisive reasons to act morally.

[27] Murphy (2000, p. 26), citing Scheffler (1992a, p. 98), characterizes a theory as confining "to the extent that it narrows the range of permissible options for action." For development of these arguments concerning confinement see Hurley (2003).

3.5 Can Consequentialist Moral Requirements have Rational Authority?

The argument presented so far has sought to establish that the most fundamental challenge to consequentialism regarding demandingness and confinement is just the opposite of what is often thought. Consequentialism is a theory of moral standards. Intuitively, rational agents do not have good reasons to avoid many of the actions identified by such standards as morally wrong. Such a theory must be incorporated into a broader theory that includes an account of reasons, and of the relationship between consequentialist moral standards and reasons, before it can be part of a theory of demanding moral reasons (and not just exacting moral standards). This section explores the prospects for developing such a consequentialist theory of demanding moral reasons.

We have seen that certain non-impersonal considerations, in particular consideration of an agent's own individual well-being, are widely recognized as grounding good reasons for acting. Certain impersonal considerations, considerations from the standpoint of overall happiness, well-being, etc., are widely recognized as among the considerations relevant to the determination of appropriate moral standards. It is a source of the apparent theoretical simplicity and explanatory power of the classical consequentialist approaches of Bentham and Mill that they can be read as taking good reasons and appropriate moral standards to be exhausted by such impersonal considerations of what is best overall and such partial considerations of what is best for the agent. Reason and morality are collapsed into these considerations that any plausible theory must seemingly recognize as relevant. Other alternatives appeal to considerations that seem by comparison contentious, considerations that must defend themselves from Occam's razor in the face of the theoretical parsimony of classical consequentialism.

Such theoretical parsimony comes at a cost, however. To maintain such parsimony, any augmentation of the consequentialist theory of moral standards to produce a theory of demanding moral reasons must restrict itself to such partial and impersonal considerations. Otherwise, what is kicked out the front door in the name of theoretical simplicity and explanatory power is covertly smuggled in through the side window. There appear to be two main options for a consequentialism that retains this theoretical parsimony. The first and most straightforward option takes the relevant partial considerations, understood as considerations of what is better or worse for the agent, to set the goals of reason, while the relevant impersonal considerations set the standards of morality. Such partial considerations certainly do seem to provide relevant reasons. But we have already seen that even many consequentialists accept some form of Sidgwick's argument that an account identifying fundamental reasons entirely with such partial considerations will not provide rational agents with decisive reasons to act morally. The challenge confronting any approach that takes such partial considerations to exhaust an agent's reasons is that it will be difficult to provide a plausible theory upon which rational agents typically have decisive reasons to conform their actions to the consequentialist's exacting moral standards.

A less obvious strategy that nonetheless maintains the classical consequentialist's theoretical parsimony is to identify the relevant impersonal considerations themselves not only as establishing the standards of morality but also as setting the ends of reason properly understood. That some sort of principle promoting overall well-being is at least among the relevant reasons for action is widely acknowledged. Moreover, such an account, upon which considerations of consistency or universality might be thought to lead agents to the recognition of impersonal moral standards as the standards of reason, will likely result in an account of decisive reasons to conform to consequentialist moral standards. For such an approach, however, the apparent independent rational significance of an agent's own personal plans and interests proves an embarrassment. Indeed, if the viability of a consequentialist theory of moral reasons requires its advocate to demonstrate that impersonal value supplies the ultimate end of reason, consequentialism seems to face an uphill task. Sidgwick certainly entertains the possibility that promotion of the impersonal good is *the* ultimate end of reason, and cites others with sympathy for such a position, but ultimately takes the dualism of practical reason to stand in the way of accepting such a view.[28] Derek Parfit seems right in suggesting that a century after Sidgwick such questions of rightness and reasonableness, for the consequentialist, "seem further apart."[29] Stipulation that impersonal considerations provide the ultimate

---

[28] Sidgwick (1981, pp. 498ff.). Parfit labels such a view "rationalist utilitarianism" (2004, p. 310).
[29] Parfit (1984, p. 129).

ends of reasons may well result in a view upon which consequentialist moral standards provide decisive reasons. But stipulation cannot take the place of argument.

Partial considerations, understood as considerations of what is better or worse for the agent, may provide a plausible candidate for the class of good reasons simpliciter, but challenges confront any attempt to show that agents typically have decisive reasons to conform to consequentialist moral standards on such an approach. An account of impersonal considerations as themselves providing the ultimate ends of reason will support such decisiveness, but is problematic as an account of good reasons. To produce a plausible account of consequentialist moral standards as (decisive) reasons, the best strategy may be to abandon theoretical parsimony.[30] Such a consequentialist must concede that neither the set of relevant partial considerations nor the set of relevant impersonal considerations constitutes the set of good reasons. But abandonment of theoretical parsimony allows him to appeal to a more robust account of practical reason and to argue that on such an account certain impersonal considerations typically do provide agents with decisive reasons to act.

Such an account cannot emerge, as Thomas Nagel has pointed out, if apparently relevant partial and impersonal considerations "are simply left to fight it out or reach some kind of individual accommodation within each person."[31] Rather, an account of reasons is necessary that establishes the proper relationship among impersonal reasons, partial reasons, and any other relevant reasons as one upon which the relevant impersonal reasons are typically decisive. In Nagel's words, such an account must explain why impersonal reasons are "dominant, at the most basic level of justification, whenever they conflict with more personal values."[32] The

---

[30] Sidgwick's dualist account, as we have seen, also seems ill-suited to the task of establishing the rational authority of consequentialist moral requirements. Sidgwick's account of practical reason will be taken up again in Section 8.5.

[31] Thomas Nagel (1991, p. 15).

[32] Ibid., p. 15. It may be thought that Nagel himself inadvertently provides the outlines of such an account of rational requirements, and of the relationships of the personal and impersonal standpoints to reason. Nagel points out that we can abstract away from our own personal points of view to an impersonal point of view, and that we come to realize, in so doing, that some things have impersonal value (e.g. 1991, pp. 10–20). But these aspects of Nagel's account can be endorsed upon most moral theories, including Kantian moral theories. Support for consequentialism as a theory of extreme demands is only forthcoming if it is established, in addition, both that impersonal value exhausts moral value, and that this moral requirement to promote overall value effectively functions as a categorical requirement of reason simpliciter, properly understood. Nagel himself certainly takes such additional

crucial component of such a theory of moral reasons (not merely of standards) will be an account of good reasons simpliciter that can provide a rationale for the counterintuitive claim that the relevant impersonal considerations typically provide decisive reasons.

In these respects such a consequentialist theory of moral reasons would be no different structurally than its rivals. The difference would no longer be the relative theoretical simplicity of the consequentialist alternative, but its insistence that moral standards will be generated entirely from the impersonal standpoint, and that rational agents will typically have decisive reasons to conform their actions to such standards. Here, however, intuition is not on the consequentialist's side, nor does consequentialism, properly understood, provide the grounds with which it has often been credited for discounting intuition. Our common sense morality, for example, includes reasons not to act in accord with such impersonal considerations, non-impersonal reasons of autonomy, rights, fairness, special obligations, etc. that are not among the agent's own partial considerations (indeed, such reasons also constrain pursuit of the agent's own well-being). Consequentialists previously could have cited the comparative theoretical parsimony of their view as grounds for discounting such reasons, since they are neither partial nor impersonal reasons. But such a response is no longer available to a consequentialist taking this approach. Such reasons are neither impersonal nor partial. But such a consequentialist now must recognize that neither the partial nor the impersonal standpoint is the standpoint of reason, and that reasons articulated both impersonally and partially play certain appropriate roles in a practical rational evaluation of actions properly understood. What these appropriate roles are awaits an articulation of an account of practical reason and deliberation. Intuitively, good non-impersonal moral reasons that prohibit bringing about the best overall state of affairs also play a prominent role in practical reason. Kantian and Hobbesian approaches attempt to provide accounts of practical reason that specify what these moral but not impersonal reasons are, how they are related to reason simpliciter, and why they often provide decisive reasons not to act in pursuit of impersonal ends. Our consequentialist must insist, contrary to intuition and now (with the abandonment of theoretical parsimony) in the absence of any supporting rationale, that the

claims to be indefensible (e.g. 1991, pp. 14–17). For his more recent (and very different) arguments against such claims see Nagel (2002, pp. 31–52).

moral subset of the set of reasons is generated entirely from the impersonal standpoint. To provide a theory of consequentialist moral standards as rational demands, the consequentialist taking this approach must provide an account of reasons and demonstrate that it is plausible in light of such an account to continue to take impersonal considerations both to exhaust relevant moral considerations, and to provide decisive reasons simpliciter.

3.6 Rejecting Rational Authority, Marginalizing Morality

The argument up to this point has proceeded within the context of the assumption that the first member of our triad (RAMS) sets an adequacy condition on an acceptable moral theory; any plausible theory of moral standards must be such that rational agents typically have decisive reasons to avoid what these standards identify as cases of wrongdoing. Indeed, traditional concerns about the extremely demanding, confining, and alienating nature of consequentialism only arise within the context of the conviction that the consequentialist theory of moral standards can somehow be augmented to satisfy RAMS. If this assumption were abandoned, there would be no reason to expect that consequentialism would result in comparatively extreme rational demands to make moral sacrifices at all.

It is open to an advocate of the consequentialist theory of moral standards, however, to reject this assumption and allow that, once both practical reason and moral wrongness are "properly" understood, rational agents may often have decisive reasons to do what is wrong. Such an approach may even seem to be invited by augmentations of the consequentialist theory of moral standards such as the economic theory sketched in Section 3.2. The moral standards may be exacting on such a theory, but what is mistaken, on this approach, is the ordinary expectation that agents typically have decisive reasons to conform their actions to the standards set by morality. Moral standards only tell us the impact of our actions on overall utility. The rational agent may have occasion to utilize this information in the pursuit of his own utility, but he may rarely if ever have decisive reasons to perform the action that has the maximal beneficial impact on overall utility (what is right), or to avoid actions that have far less beneficial impact on overall utility (what is wrong).

Such an approach, however, only wins this strategic battle by losing the war so many consequentialists have taken themselves to be fighting. A central aim of many consequentialists has been to demonstrate that we should be doing more than moderate morality requires of us. But the approach in question lowers the bar of rational demands to act morally even as it raises the bar of moral standards. More fundamentally, such a strategy appears to concede what philosophers from Friedrich Nietzsche to Bernard Williams have argued,[33] that morality itself is a far more "peculiar institution" than we have realized, and ethics, understood as the inquiry into what one has sufficient and decisive reasons to do, may have far less to do with the standards set by morality once the latter are properly understood. If we accept that morality, properly understood, provides merely one among other sets of standards, and that this set of standards lacks the distinctive relationship that has been claimed for it to our reasons for acting, then morality is shifted toward the margins in meaningful inquiry into what rational agents such as ourselves have reasons to do. This would be a pyrrhic victory for the consequentialist, vindicating his account of moral standards only by marginalizing the role of such standards in practical reason and deliberation.[34]

I have argued in this chapter that arguments concerned with the extremely demanding and confining nature of consequentialism often

---

[33] See Nietzsche's *On The Genealogy of Morals* (1967), and Bernard Williams (1985, ch. 10). The characterization of morality as a "peculiar institution" is taken from Williams.

[34] But not all consequentialists will consider this victory empty. Alastair Norcross has recently argued (2006), in an essay building upon earlier work with Frances Howard-Snyder (Norcross and Howard-Snyder 1993), that the standard approach, upon which consequentialism is put forward not just as providing an account of moral reason, but as providing an account of "the significance each of us gives to such moral reasons relative to other reasons," amounts to a misinterpretation by consequentialists of their own theory. He grants that agents have better moral reasons to do what it is morally better to do, and that it is morally better to do what brings about a better overall outcome. His consequentialist, like Kagan's, can recognize that she always has decisive moral reasons to bring about the best overall consequences. But whereas Kagan takes it to be the case that agents have decisive reasons to do what they have such decisive moral reasons to do, Norcross is skeptical that this is the case, and skeptical that it is the business of consequentialist moral theory, properly understood, even to inquire into the extent to which this is or is not the case. Consequentialism is only a theory of moral standards, of what agents have decisive moral reasons to do, and should be judged as such. The question of what demands such moral reasons make upon us relative to other reasons "is not something which can be settled by a moral theory." Acting as we have decisive consequentialist moral reasons to act would be extremely demanding and confining. But whereas Hobbesian and Kantian alternatives are theories of the decisive reasons agents have to conform to their less exacting moral standards, consequentialism is not a theory of decisive reasons to conform to its exacting standards. Its reputation for extreme demandingness, he suggests, comes from a failure to appreciate this fact by both its advocates and its critics.

presuppose either that consequentialism, as standardly formulated, is a theory of its moral standards as decisive reasons, which it is not, or that it can help itself to the intuitive link between ordinary moral standards and decisive reasons, which it cannot. Rather, CMS stands in need of augmentation if it is to be a theory of moral standards that agents have decisive reasons to satisfy—a theory that can maintain a commitment to RAMS as well. Without some such augmentation, consequentialism is not a theoretically simpler alternative theory of more demanding and confining moral reasons but a bare theory of moral standards. Such a theory, however exacting its standards, does not yet make rational demands upon agents at all. Indeed, although advocates and critics of this theory alike typically presuppose that it is a theory of the rational authority of its moral standards, the accounts of practical reason and deliberation typically advocated by consequentialists instead support NIR, hence undermine any such commitment to RAMS. If there is such a deep tension at the core of consequentialism, an obvious question is why it has not been the focus of more debate. In the next chapter I will argue that Bernard Williams provides the tools for a diagnosis of this tendency to overlook this challenge to consequentialism. Moreover, I will argue that his integrity objection provides a far more profound challenge to consequentialism than is commonly recognized. Development of Williams' tools will set the stage for arguments in Chapters 5 and 6 that a full appreciation of these challenges to consequentialism undermines the traditional considerations that are taken to provide such powerful support for the challenge of consequentialism.

4

Harnessing Williams to Sharpen the Challenge to Consequentialism

4.1 Introduction

In Chapter 2 I located the act consequentialist theory of moral standards within a triad of claims that are typically endorsed by consequentialists, and showed the difficulties that confront any effort to reconcile CMS to the other independently plausible members of this triad. In Chapter 3 I argued that consequentialists typically appeal to another member of the triad, the rational authority of moral standards (RAMS); indeed, that the traditional debate between consequentialists and their critics becomes unmoored unless it is understood as operating within the context of this assumption. But consequentialism is a theory of moral standards alone, a theory that provides no rationale for RAMS. If, contrary to intuition, consequentialism does provide the right account of moral standards, it becomes unclear what rational demands such moral standards make upon rational agents. To provide a rationale for their rational authority, CMS must be augmented with an account of rational agency upon which such moral standards have rational authority. We have seen that the obstacles to providing such an account are considerable. There would thus appear to be serious lacunae at the core of any consequentialism that purports to be a theory of moral reasons.

In this chapter I will argue that Bernard Williams' classic critique of Smart's act utilitarian consequentialism provides resources for sharpening this challenge. On the reading of Williams articulated in this chapter, the alienation, loss of integrity, extreme demandingness, and confinement of consequentialism are consequences of the tendency by both consequentialists and their critics to presuppose the rational authority of moral standards (RAMS), while at the same time presupposing in the very articulation of their moral standards accounts of practical reason and deliberation upon which agents often have sufficient reasons, and in some cases even sufficient moral reasons, not to bring about the best overall state of affairs (NIR).[1] I will suggest that Williams' arguments allow us to sharpen the challenge to consequentialism in two ways. The first is this demonstration that standard versions of the theory presuppose NIR in their very articulation of the best overall consequences. CMS need not be augmented with NIR to create the tension with RAMS, but only because CMS presupposes NIR in its very articulation. The second is that on the most intuitively plausible approach to articulating impersonal standards, the consequentialist claim that the impersonal standpoint is the standpoint for moral evaluation of actions as right or wrong is straightforwardly undermined: CMS cannot in such cases be reconciled with its own presuppositions. These two intensifications of the challenge to consequentialism will be developed in Sections 4.3 and 4.4 respectively, after some initial stage setting in the next section. The chapter will close with an examination of certain misleading parallels between the theoretical and practical spheres that have been taken to support the challenge of consequentialism, grounds that cease to be persuasive within the context of Williams' diagnosis. Chapter 5 will take up traditional rationales for CMS, and demonstrate that our challenge to consequentialism, honed by way of the Williams diagnosis, provides the resources to undermine these traditional rationales.

4.2 A Consequentialist Theory of Rational Requirement?

Consequentialists and their critics alike agree that in our everyday reasoning and deliberation we appear to take into account reasons of various sorts,

[1] There are of course consequentialist alternatives that deny the rational authority of its moral standards, and there are alternatives that reject the account of practical reason and deliberation that supports the second claim of the triad, e.g. upon which impersonal value is taken to be the ultimate source of rational as well as moral justification. But we have seen in the previous chapter that the costs to consequentialism of such strategies are high. The first threatens to marginalize, perhaps even entirely, the role of moral standards in the practical reason and deliberation of rational agents (see the arguments in Section 3.6). The second requires consequentialists to commit to a counter-intuitive account of practical reason and deliberation that even most consequentialists recognize to be implausible (see Section 3.5).

many of them non-impersonal reasons to pursue our own happiness, interests, plans, and projects out of proportion to whatever claims they make upon us from the impersonal standpoint. Moreover, they allow that among these reasons appear to be moral reasons, and that many of these apparently good moral reasons, for example reasons not to violate the rights of others, have significance that also is not captured (at least not directly) from the impersonal standpoint. From such an impersonal standpoint rights violations that the agent in question commits have relevance only as some among the rights violations that will be committed overall. In her own practical reasoning and deliberation, by contrast, recognition of the intrinsic value of rights is recognition of distinctive non-impersonal reasons for her to refrain from committing such rights violations, just as recognition of the distinctive value for her of her own happiness is recognition of distinctive non-impersonal reasons to pursue her own happiness.

The consequentialist will of course resist many aspects of this picture of everyday practical reason and deliberation. She will insist that reflection reveals certain of them either to be illusory or to be grounded indirectly in appeal to the best overall state of affairs. What I want to emphasize at this point, however, is not the aspects of everyday practical reason and deliberation that consequentialism might reject, but those features of such an account that the theory typically presupposes. As a first step, it will be useful to consider the initial prospects for a theory of practical reason and deliberation that directly supplants everyday practical reasoning about what we have better and worse reasons to do with an account upon which the only reasons are those based in consideration of the impersonal value of resulting states of affairs. This is not consequentialism, the moral theory according to which agents are morally required to bring about the best overall state of affairs, but a theory of practical reason and deliberation according to which agents are *rationally* rather than *morally* required to perform the action that brings about the best overall state of affairs—upon which such impersonal reasons are always decisive. This is a theory not merely of consequentialist morality—of right action—but of consequentialist rational agency—of rational action. It would hold that agents always have decisive reasons to perform the action that brings about the best overall state of affairs. The myriad apparently good reasons of everyday practical reason would give way on such a theory, at least at the foundational level, to reasons that appeal to better and worse things that can happen overall. Such an account would straightforwardly deny the second member of our triad (NIR), maintaining that an agent has decisive reasons to act just in case the action promotes the best overall state of affairs.

Such a theory of practical reason and deliberation, a theory of consequentialist rational requirement, would of course be strikingly counter-intuitive. It is noteworthy that it is also typically taken to be a nonstarter by non-consequentialist and consequentialist moral theorists alike. Bentham, Mill, and Sidgwick, along with preference theoretic consequentialists, explicitly reject such a theory of rational requirement, and most contemporary consequentialists are explicitly or implicitly committed to its rejection. It is not plausible even to such consequentialists because it seems so clear that at the very least each agent also has has fundamentally non-impersonal reasons to promote her own happiness, interests, and/or well-being; reasons that at least potentially conflict with whatever reasons agents might have to pursue the best overall state of affairs. Such non-impersonal reasons must be taken into account alongside whatever relevant impersonal-involving reasons agents have. One course of action may promote her interests more effectively, while another more effectively promotes more interests overall. The presence of non-impersonal reasons at the foundational level suggests that at least in certain cases agents will have sufficient reasons to pursue courses of action other than those suggested by the relevant impersonal considerations taken alone (NIR). Consequentialists, then, typically embrace a consequentialist theory of moral requirement but not a consequentialist theory of rational requirement. The disagreement with their critics concerns the plausibility of the former, not the implausibility of the latter.

The difficulty, however, is that consequentialists who are committed to moral authoritativeness (RAMS) are committed to just such an implausible account of consequentialist rational requirement de facto if not de jure. Agents are morally required to bring about the best overall state of affairs (CMS), have decisive reasons to do what they are morally required to do (RAMS), hence have decisive reasons to bring about the best overall state of affairs. It is not only a moral requirement on such a theory to bring about the best overall state of affairs, the agent is rationally required (has decisive reasons) to do so. De facto if not de jure, the impersonal standpoint is the standpoint of practical reason and deliberation for consequentialists committed to RAMS and CMS. Consequentialism is introduced as a theory of moral requirement and not as a theory of rational requirement. But because it always morally requires the agent to bring about the best overall state of affairs, and morally prohibits her from doing anything else, it becomes, with an appeal to RAMS, a theory of rational requirement as well, at least de facto. The theory both explicitly is not, and by implication is, a theory of rational requirement. This feature of a consequentialism that accepts RAMS, that it appears both to reject and to accept a consequentialist theory of rational (not just moral) requirement, sets the stage for a full appreciation of the implications of Bernard Williams' arguments.

4.3 A Williams Inspired Diagnosis: Higher and Lower-order Projects

I have already pointed out that many consequentialists explicitly reject an account of practical reason and deliberation upon which rational agents are rationally required, not just morally required, to bring about the best overall state of affairs. They allow that rational agents have good non-impersonal reasons at the foundational level, reasons that seem to be sufficient in many cases for acting in ways that do not bring about the best overall consequences. This is already enough to pose a serious challenge to any attempt at reconciling the theory with the rational authority of its moral standards. But there is a line of thought running through Williams' early writings on consequentialism that suggests an argument for a stronger result—not simply that consequentialists typically recognize such good non-impersonal ends and reasons, but that at least the standard forms of utilitarian consequentialism that he considers *presuppose* in their very account of impersonal evaluation of states of affairs that rational agents have good non-impersonal reasons at the foundational level even as they presuppose that rational agents have decisive reasons to pursue impersonal value as their ultimate end.[2] Indeed, the psychological

---

[2] Williams later offers arguments that he takes to apply against an entire range of moral theories, including consequentialism (see, e.g., 1981, pp. 1–19). These general arguments are in many respects a significant departure from the distinctive criticism of consequentialism that he develops in *Utilitarianism: For and Against* (1973), and lose much of the force of this earlier criticism. For this reason I will focus primarily on the early argument formulated specifically against consequentialism. I suspect that an initial tendency by interpreters (myself included) to read the later, more generalized argument back into the

fragmentation, alienation, and loss of integrity identified by Williams and his interpreters as costs of consequentialism are, on this view, properly diagnosed as symptoms of this more fundamental problem—that standard forms of consequentialism presuppose accounts of practical reason and deliberation that are in tremendous tension with the rational authority (which they also often presuppose) of moral requirements.[3] It is this more fundamental problem, I will argue, that is at the core of Williams' claim that "utilitarianism . . . cannot coherently describe the relation between a man's projects and his actions."[4]

Williams' argument takes up the traditional form of utilitarian consequentialism advocated by J. J. C. Smart, and demonstrates that in its very articulation of moral standards such an account presupposes an account of practical reason and deliberation. He demonstrates that although this account of practical reason and deliberation can plausibly be seen as giving rise to rankings of better and worse overall states of affairs such that rational agents have reasons to promote these states of affairs, the very articulation of such impersonal-involving reasons presupposes that they are at most some reasons among others. Moreover, in precisely the cases upon which consequentialists and their critics focus, cases in which conformity to consequentialist moral standards would appear to alienate rational agents from their most fundamental plans and projects, such rational agents will have decisive reasons to act contrary to consequentialist moral standards—to perform actions identified by the consequentialist as wrong. If such determinations of better and worse states of affairs set the standards for right and wrong action, but only provide some reasons among others for an agent to act, reasons that fail to be decisive when acting upon them would result in alienation, the rational agent will frequently have sufficient reasons to do what is morally prohibited. The problem isn't that morality alienates rational agents from their deepest projects and commitments, it is that reason as consequentialists such as Smart understand it alienates agents from consequentialist standards for moral conduct. Rational agents are alienated by reason from consequentialist moral standards on the very account

earlier argument tends to obscure central features of the criticism of act consequentialism contained in this earlier work.

[3] See Ashford (2003, pp. 422ff.) on the charge of psychological fragmentation, and Scheffler (1982, ch. 1) and Railton (1988) on the charges of alienation and loss of integrity.

[4] Williams (1973, p. 100).

of practical reason and deliberation that is presupposed by consequentialists in the articulation of such standards.

There are resources in Williams' discussion to explain the tendency by consequentialists to conflate their account of moral standards, properly understood as merely articulating some reasons among others, with an account of such standards as providing ultimate reasons that comprehend all others. I will present these resources, and finish this section by considering the extent to which Williams' criticism generalizes beyond the act utilitarian version of consequentialism articulated by Smart to other consequentialist accounts that invoke very different accounts of practical reason and deliberation. My suggestion will be that aspects of Williams' argument generalize quite broadly, and provide the core of a general diagnosis both of why the account of practical reason presupposed by consequentialists in the very articulation of their moral standards undermines the rational authoritativeness of such standards, and of why this problematic aspect of consequentialist accounts is systematically obscured from view.

Williams takes himself to share with act consequentialists such as Smart and Singer an account of practical reason and deliberation upon which an agent's practical reasons are controlled by his desires, broadly construed to include his most central plans, projects, and commitments: "*his* actions and *his* decisions have to be seen as the actions and decisions which flow from the projects and attitudes with which he is most closely identified."[5] It is through appeal to these attitudes and commitments, and what they are attitudes and commitments towards, that an agent determines the best course of action available to him. My reasons, and the decisions to which they give rise insofar as I am rational, flow from my attitudes, projects, and commitments; your reasons flow from your attitudes, projects, and commitments. Such attitudes and commitments are "dispositions not simply of action, but of belief and judgment; and they are expressed precisely in ascribing intrinsic and not instrumental value to various activities and relations such as truth-telling, loyalty, and so on."[6] A "grounded decision," then, will be based upon reasons that flow from a thorough understanding of such plans, projects, and commitments.[7] To say that the course of action decided upon is one the agent has sufficient or even decisive reasons to

---

[5] Ibid., p. 116. In subsequent writings Williams will label this set of desires, broadly construed to include the agent's plans, projects, and commitments, her subjective motivation set.

[6] Williams (1995, p. 164).   [7] Williams (1973, p. 118).

pursue is, on such an account, to say that it is grounded in this way. For example, you are committed to your friends and I to mine. The reason that flows from your commitments, what you will take to be the best course of action available to you, will be to stick by your friends; the reason that flows from my commitments will support sticking by my friends.[8] How do such claims relate to the traditional utilitarian focus on happiness? Williams points out that "happiness . . . requires being involved in, or at least content with, something else."[9] It is this "something else" that he characterizes in terms of the agent's plans, projects, and commitments: "If such commitments are worth while, then pursuing the projects that flow from them, and realizing some of these projects, will make the person for whom they are worth while happy."[10] Happiness results from realizing the worthwhile projects and plans and honoring the commitments that comprise the subject's motivational set. The first step in Williams' account, then, is his suggestion that rational agents have plans, projects, and commitments, a subjective motivational set, from which their reasons for action flow (insofar as they are rational) through sound deliberative routes.

I will now introduce a second step that Williams does not explicitly introduce at any point in his argument. Making it explicit, however, clarifies the nature of subsequent steps. This step points out that any agent can readily adopt a 3rd person observer's standpoint towards the plans and projects that she and other agents have and the reasons for action to which they give rise. Moreover, she can attempt to determine, from such a 3rd person observer's standpoint, what outcomes will allow for the maximal realization of everyone's plans and projects overall. The agent can rank potential outcomes from such an observer's standpoint according to the degree that each state of affairs allows agents to successfully realize their projects and honor their commitments overall.

It is crucial to note that by itself a 3rd person observer's standpoint, when adopted towards oneself as well as others, is not itself a source of practical reasons, much less a standpoint of practical reason and deliberation, for any agent.[11] It is instead an observer's standpoint towards all the projects

---

[8] Williams is notoriously a reasons internalist. But nothing in the argument that follows turns on his commitment to reasons internalism. This point will be taken up directly later in this section.

[9] Williams (1973, p. 112).   [10] Ibid., p. 113.

[11] Note, however, that the 3rd person standpoint may also serve as a standpoint for the evaluation of the reasons that another agent has. From the 3rd person standpoint we can both observe which projects

and commitments and the reasons flowing from them that persons have. Because it is a standpoint towards the projects of rational agents and the reasons to which they give rise, and not a standpoint from which any rational agent reasons and deliberates, the occupant of this standpoint, qua occupant of this standpoint, has no reasons. Taken by itself, the observer's 3rd person standpoint is not an independent source of reasons that can even be in tension with the reasons that flow from the projects and commitments of each rational agent. It is an observer's standpoint towards the practical reasons I and others have, not a standpoint of practical reason.

From such a 3rd person observer's standpoint your reasons for sticking by your friends are no different than my reasons for sticking by mine. It does not distinguish among the projects I have reasons to pursue and those of others—each is a set of projects it is observed that someone has reasons to pursue. I have reasons to stick by my friends, but from the 3rd person observer's standpoint mine are just another set of reasons a rational agent has to stick by his friends. Such a 3rd person observer's standpoint towards the plans, projects, and commitments of agents presupposes the 1st person practical reasoning and deliberation of the various agents towards which it is adopted. Indeed, it is precisely the plans, projects, and commitments that come into view from the standpoint of each rational agent, and the reasons to which they give rise, that are the material for observation from such a 3rd person standpoint.

A rational agent with a completely self-interested subjective motivational set could readily produce such a ranking of potential states of affairs from such an observer's standpoint according to the degree to which each maximizes the realization by agents of their plans and projects overall. But because such a ranking will likely not be relevant to the projects and plans that our self-interested agent will have reasons to pursue, there is no sense in which these empirical rankings of outcomes as higher or lower will correlate with any rankings by such an agent as better and worse. It is the agent's projects and commitments that control her reasons. Only if such 3rd person rankings of states of affairs are relevant to the reasons that flow from the agent's projects and commitments will they play any role in the practical reasoning of such an agent.

and ends the agent arrives at through rational deliberation and assess the rationality of the deliberation involved in arriving at these ends. For a detailed treatment of the interaction of the 1st and 3rd person perspectives in both the theoretical and practical spheres see Richard Moran (2001).

How, then, is such a non-evaluative empirical ranking transformed into an impersonal evaluation of states of affairs as better or worse? Williams' answer to this question provides the third step in his account. In particular, he provides an account of how impersonal moral evaluation can develop out of applications of this 3rd person, observer's standpoint in the pursuit of a certain distinctive project or commitment that rational agents may have. Among the worthwhile projects of agents there may be a "higher-order project of maximizing desirable outcomes,"[12] a project of a rational agent that is concerned with the projects of all agents. In order to carry out such a higher-order project, such a rational agent must harness the 3rd person, observer's standpoint described above first to observe what the lower-order projects and commitments of other rational agents are, and then to determine empirically which states of affairs will more or less effectively maximize the overall pursuit of their projects and honoring of their commitments. Because among the agent's projects is this "second-order utilitarian project of maximally satisfying the first-order projects,"[13] the rational agent with such a project has a reason to pursue such maximal satisfaction of lower-order projects. As a result, the states of affairs arranged on the scale of greater or less effective realization of the lower-order projects of rational agents will be viewed by the agent with such a higher-order project as in the relevant respect better or worse: "desirable outcomes are going to consist, in part, of the maximally harmonious realization of these projects."[14]

Without some such higher-order project, adoption of this 3rd person observer's standpoint towards the projects of rational agents yields only a non-evaluative ranking. But when this non-evaluative ranking of the states of affairs that promote the maximization of lower-order projects and commitments is augmented with a higher-order project to promote such states of affairs, the states of affairs ranked on such a scale will come to be viewed not just as ranked higher, but, in virtue of being ranked higher, as in the relevant sense better or worse states of affairs. Moreover, the agent with such a higher-order project will not only evaluate higher ranked outcomes as better, but will have a reason to bring about states of affairs thus ranked; indeed, more reason to bring about states of affairs that are ranked as better.

It is only when coupled with a project such as this higher-order project of maximizing the realization of the plans, projects, and commitments of

---

[12] Williams (1973, p. 114).   [13] Ibid., p. 112.   [14] Ibid., p. 110.

rational agents, only, that is, when such a project of impartial benevolence is coupled to the 3rd person observer's standpoint, that rankings of states of affairs from a 3rd person observer's standpoint as satisfying more or fewer projects overall become impersonal evaluations of these outcomes as better and worse. Traditional consequentialism (CMS) holds that the right action is the action that brings about the best available state of affairs as determined by such a ranking. Upon such a theory, which claims that the right action brings about the best overall state of affairs as determined by such a ranking, the 3rd person standpoint for ranking states of affairs is the moral standpoint, and the higher-order project in light of which the empirical rankings become evaluations is the moral project.

Williams suggests that for the traditional consequentialist such a higher-order project could be at most one project among others, hence that whatever reasons flow from such a higher-order project are themselves only some of the agent's reasons among others. Evaluation from the 3rd person standpoint in the pursuit of such a higher-order project, he argues, presupposes that "there must be other more basic or lower-order projects which he and others have," and the best outcomes from the 3rd person standpoint "are going to consist, in part, of the maximally harmonious realization of those projects."[15] Without such basic plans and projects any such higher-order project appealing to the 3rd person observer's standpoint "would have nothing to work on, and would be vacuous."[16] Such "basic" or "first-order" projects will, Williams suggests, be of various unsurprising kinds: "desires for things for oneself, one's family, one's friends . . . and in more relaxed circumstances, objects of taste." But they can also include "projects connected with . . . some cause . . . or . . . which flow from some more general disposition towards human conduct and character, such as hatred of injustice, or of cruelty, or of killing."[17] It is largely these basic, first-order commitments and projects of such rational agents that provide the content for the higher-order project. Thus, for Sidgwick, Williams argues, "we are required to be concerned with the very same thing that each of those persons has to be concerned with . . . in his own case, so it will

---

[15] Williams (1995, p. 162).

[16] Both quotations are taken from Williams (1973, p. 110). See also Williams (1981, p. 51): "there is no coherent view of human welfare itself which is independent of such issues as what people care for, in non-utilitarian spirit."

[17] Williams (1973, pp. 110–11).

precisely be something like each person's objective or rationally organized set of preferences that will become the raw material of the additive sum of the universal good."[18]

If among the rational agent's myriad plans, commitments, and projects are certain higher-order projects that involve 3rd personal assessments of overall states of affairs, then such 3rd personal considerations will to that extent be integrated within the reasons of such rational agents. From the standpoint of such an agent, these impersonal-involving projects and commitments will merely be some projects among others, much as a higher-order desire or volition is only one desire or volition among others.[19] Notice also that to take this higher-order project to be the foundational project would simply be to stipulate a consequentialist account of rational requirement, and we have seen in the previous section that even most consequentialists themselves reject such an alternative as implausible. The higher-order project, then, presupposes that rational agents have certain basic lower-order projects along with any such higher-order projects towards projects. As a higher-order project, it in one sense comprehends all other projects by its very nature as a project about these other projects. But in the practical reasoning of agents such a higher-order project is but one project among others that is a source of but some of the agent's reasons among others.

Williams' point seems to allow that some particular anomalous rational agent could have as the sole project that she pursues the higher-order project of maximally realizing agents' projects overall. The point is rather that this cannot be the ultimate project of every rational agent, otherwise no rational agent would have any contentful project to secure. The higher-order project of bringing about the maximal harmonious realization of agents' projects will only have content if among the projects and commitments of some rational agents are certain lower-order projects and commitments that can provide the content for this higher-order impersonal project. Our anomalous agent might nonetheless have as her only project this higher-order impersonal project. But such a necessarily anomalous agent would not experience alienation or loss of integrity in the pursuit of this consequentialist project, because the higher-order impersonal

---

[18] Williams (1995, p. 162).

[19] A point made forcefully by Gary Watson: "since second-order volitions are themselves simply desires, to add them to the context of conflict is just to increase the number of contenders; it is not to give a special place to any of those in contention" (2004a, p. 28).

consequentialist project simply is the overarching project of such a rational agent. Nor would acting to bring about the best overall state of affairs undermine her integrity, because in her anomalous case these actions, and her reasons to perform them, flow from her most fundamental projects and commitments.

Nor would typical rational agents, for whom this higher-order project is merely one among others, experience morality as in any way alienating. But in their case the reason is quite different. For such typical rational agents the 3rd person observer's standpoint is at most involved in articulating one of their projects—albeit a higher-order project—among the other projects that such agents have. The reason that flows from such a higher-order project, a reason to promote the highest impersonally ranked state of affairs, will for them compete with other reasons that flow from their other plans, projects, and commitments. If the action that promotes this best overall state of affairs is identified as the morally right action, and all others are wrong, the result would appear to be an account upon which agents have sufficient or decisive reasons to perform actions identified by such a moral theory as morally wrong whenever the reasons that flow from their lower-order plans and projects are sufficient or decisive, all things considered. If moral standards support one course of action, but it conflicts with another course of action dictated by lower-order projects that are more deeply grounded in the agent's commitments, the account suggests that such a rationally integrated agent will have decisive reasons to pursue his lower-order commitments, in the process performing an action that the consequentialist identifies as morally wrong. Consequentialist rightness provides only one reason among others for such a typical agent, since it reflects only one (albeit higher-order) project among other projects. If these other lower-order projects and commitments are more central to the agent's subjective motivational set, the agent will have decisive reasons to pursue her lower-order projects rather than her higher-order project, but this is to have decisive reasons to do what consequentialist morality prohibits. The rational agent would not in such cases be alienated by consequentialist morality, but from consequentialist morality. Conformity to consequentialist moral standards in such cases would be profoundly alienating, but on the account of practical reason presupposed by the consequentialist in the very articulation of these standards such conformity would make no sense—it would be to act contrary to decisive reasons to do what is wrong.

Consider, for example, how such an account applies to Williams' famous George example. George has a deep commitment that gives rise to a central lower-order project of not producing chemical or biological weapons (WMD). Let us assume that he also has another project, a higher-order project to promote agents' lower-order projects overall. The first project will be furthered by refusing to do WMD research; the second, let us assume, will be furthered in George's case by doing WMD research (poorly!). George thus has two projects which give rise to reasons to pursue conflicting courses of action; the second is the consequentialist moral project. Which of the two it will make sense for him to pursue will presumably depend upon the centrality of these respective projects—how deeply each is grounded in his fundamental commitments. If it is the lower-order project that is more central to George's subjective motivational set, as Williams suggests, George will have decisive reasons to pursue it rather than his higher-order project in this case. But this is just to say, for the consequentialist, that he will have decisive reasons to do what is morally wrong. Acting in pursuit of the higher-order project would undermine his very integrity as a rational agent, but on such an account of moral standards George would appear to have decisive reasons to maintain the integrity of his rational agency and act immorally. Moreover, the account of moral standards presupposes, in its very articulation of such moral prohibitions, that George has such decisive reasons to do what morality prohibits. If, for another agent, it is the higher-order project that is more firmly grounded in her commitments, then she will have decisive reasons to do what is morally right, and will act with integrity in so doing.

Indeed, consequentialism would appear to be the perfect theory for avoiding alienation from a rational agent's own deepest projects and commitments at the hands of morality. For rational agents the higher-order project of maximizing the satisfaction of projects overall, the consequentialist moral project, is but one project among others, one source of reasons among others. When these other lower-order projects are sufficiently deep and central to the agent's subjective motivational set, the rational agent will have sufficient reasons not to act in conformity with moral standards, hence to avoid the alienation and loss of integrity that would otherwise result from abandonment of such deep commitments and conformity to moral standards.

For typical rational agents the standpoint of a 3rd person impersonal evaluation of states of affairs is involved at most in articulating certain of her projects among others. If such a standpoint plays only this limited role, there is as yet no basis for claims to alienation, loss of integrity, or psychological fragmentation at the hands of morality; indeed, quite the contrary. The challenge, as we have seen in the previous chapter, would appear instead to be whether, and to what extent, moral standards, as the consequentialist understands them, make rational demands upon agents at all. The answer to this question will depend upon whether or not the rational agent has the relevant sort of higher-order project at all, and if so, how central it is to her subjective motivational set relative to her other lower-order plans, projects, and commitments. Thus, when the utilitarian moral standpoint is developed naturally out of the 1st person standpoints of rational agents, the threat of alienation of the rational agent *from* morality appears to be far more pressing than the threat of alienation *by* morality. The threat to consequentialism is to the rational authority of its moral standards, not one of alienation and disintegration at the hands of such standards. The structure of traditional consequentialism, as it is rendered explicit by Williams' account, suggests that although acting in accordance with consequentialist morality would often alienate agents from their deepest commitments, the agent will always have decisive reasons not to act contrary to her deepest commitments. Such commitments, ex hypothesi, are more central to her plans and projects than is her higher-order project, hence she will have decisive reasons to maintain these commitments rather than to do what consequentialist moral standards identify as right. Such an agent, in acting as an integrated rational agent, will be alienated from what consequentialist morality requires: it is the understanding of morality as authoritative that appears to be surrendered on such an account of morality as merely one (albeit higher-order) project or commitment among others.

4.4 What Lies Beneath the Alienation and Integrity Objections

But what if the consequentialist persists, in the face of these countervailing considerations, in appealing to just such an assumption that its moral requirements are authoritative (RAMS)? The fourth step in Williams' account is his contention that consequentialists such as Smart do in fact persist in making this assumption that morality is authoritative. Such consequentialists, he argues, persist in the normal conviction that the "point of the question what acts are right, relates to the situation of deciding to do them."[20] Williams' account has shown that Smart's consequentialism presupposes that moral standards for right and wrong action merely identify the course of action that most effectively realizes one of the agent's projects, a higher-order project that is at most one among others the rational agent has reasons to pursue. But he also points out that at the same time the theory puts forward as the standpoint of rational agency that of the "agent as utilitarian," from which the agent "is committed only to . . . his higher-order project of maximizing desirable outcomes."[21] For such an agent as utilitarian, with only this overarching higher-order project, all reasons are grounded in the 3rd person observer's standpoint. When I reason from this standpoint of the agent as utilitarian I "must be just as much responsible for things that I allow . . . as I am for things that I . . . bring about. Those things also must enter my *deliberations*, as a responsible moral *agent*, on the same footing"(emphasis mine).[22]

Such a standpoint of practical reason and deliberation involves the adoption of a 3rd person observer's standpoint towards the various lower-order projects that each agent is revealed to have reasons to pursue from her respective standpoint of rational agency. But pursuit of the higher-order project toward these projects is itself put forward as the overarching project of the rational "agent as utilitarian." To occupy this second standpoint as a standpoint for practical reason and deliberation does require the agent to "step aside from his own . . . decision and acknowledge the decision which utilitarian calculation requires."[23] Although the account presupposes that a rational agent appropriately takes into account the various projects, whether lower- or higher-order, that he has good reasons to pursue, it also claims that his deliberations as a "utilitarian agent" are entirely "a function of all the satisfactions which he can affect from where he is."[24] Williams' diagnosis suggests that the theory (1) presupposes 1st person standpoints of non-impersonal rational agency from which agents have myriad projects and commitments that give rise to reasons, (2) adopts a 3rd

---

[20] Williams (1973, p. 128).   [21] Ibid., p. 114.   [22] Ibid., p. 95.
[23] Ibid., p. 116.   [24] Ibid., p. 115.

person, observer's standpoint towards these lower-order projects that are revealed from such 1st person standpoints and the reasons to which they give rise, (3) appeals to a higher-order project to promote such lower-order projects to rank resulting states of affairs from better to worse (since such higher ranked outcomes more effectively further this higher-order project), then (4) puts forward a second standpoint of rational agency, that of the agent as utilitarian, a standpoint with a single ultimate project—the higher-order project of impersonal maximization of the overall realization of the lower-order projects that rational agents have reasons to pursue. It is this last step, step 4, that engenders profound alienation and loss of integrity, transforming consequentialism from perhaps the most alienation free theory of moral standards to the most profoundly alienating theory of moral reasons.

The consequentialist who takes this final step appeals to RAMS, the conviction that responsible rational agents have decisive reasons to do what is right. It is always right, for the consequentialist, to pursue in the most effective way possible the higher-order project by bringing about the best overall state of affairs, and wrong to do anything else. Hence, the agent always has decisive reasons to bring about the best outcome as dictated by this higher-order project, and decisive reasons not to do anything else. As a result the higher-order project towards the projects we have good reasons to adopt and pursue comes to be treated as the sole project that we always have decisive reasons to pursue.

The account is left with two rational standpoints, each of which purports to be comprehensive. One is the 1st person standpoint of the rational agent, which takes into account myriad plans and projects, both lower- and higher-order; the other is the standpoint of the agent as utilitarian, with the single overarching higher-order project of maximally realizing the projects of agents. It is this invocation of two conflicting rational standpoints that engenders the profound feeling of alienation Williams identifies. Alienation results because a higher-order project that presupposes the existence of lower-order projects, and stands alongside these lower-order projects as one among others that are more or less central to the agent's practical reason and deliberation, is also put forward, through appeal to RAMS, as a project that comprehends all others and always provides the rational agent with decisive reasons to act. Integrated into the agent's rational standpoint, the moral project is but one among others, a project which frequently appears—as in the George example—to be less central for the agent than his other projects. The consequentialist thus appears to be committed in George's case to the position that George has decisive reasons to pursue his lower-order project rather than his higher-order project—to do what the consequentialist identifies as morally prohibited. But appeal to RAMS dis-integrates this higher-order project from its place as one project among others that grounds one reason among others, putting it forward as the ultimate project that always provides decisive reasons for action. George's most central project involves a commitment not to develop weapons of mass destruction. On the account of rational agency presupposed by the consequentialist, it is this project that provides George with decisive reasons to act in the circumstances. But if George is a consequentialist who accepts RAMS, then his central project, the project that he will always have decisive reasons to pursue, will be to bring about the best overall state of affairs. The theory proposes that George has decisive reasons, qua rational agent, to pursue his lower-order project even as it presupposes that he has decisive reasons, qua agent as utilitarian, to pursue the consequentialist's higher-order project. In George's case, utilitarian consequentialism articulates its account of moral standards in such a way that it presupposes both that George has decisive reasons to do what such standards identify as wrong (because his lower-order project is more fundamental, more centrally integrated into his set of projects and commitments than is his higher-order project) and that he has decisive reasons to what such standards identify as right (because moral requirements are treated as rationally authoritative).

The reason that the rational demands upon the "agent as utilitarian" are experienced as alienating is that they are put forward as rational demands that the agent not do what the theory seems to allow that agents often have sufficient or even decisive reasons to do. Moreover, these demands are from a standpoint that presupposes such reasons in the articulation of its moral standards even as it denies them standing as reasons in its application of those moral standards. The reason the theory is an attack on the agent's integrity is that the reasons that consequentialists presuppose an agent has to follow through with her lower-order projects and commitments lose their standing as reasons from the standpoint of the agent as utilitarian, who takes the higher-order project to provide the only ultimate reason for action. By acting in pursuit of the higher-order project she will systematically thwart the pursuit of plans and projects that the utilitarian consequentialist presupposes agents have, projects that often appear to be more central for her as an integrated rational agent. But:

It is absurd to demand of such a man, when the sums come in from the utility network which the projects of others have in part determined, that he should just step aside from his own project and decision and acknowledge the decision which utilitarian calculation requires.[25]

Williams' point is that traditional consequentialism requires the agent to make two different all things considered rational evaluations in each case. From the 1st person standpoint of the rational agent, the impersonal standpoint plays a role in articulating one among the projects that a rational agent has reasons to pursue. What the agent will have sufficient or decisive reasons to pursue will be a function of the relative depth of the commitments and centrality of the projects in her motivational set. From the standpoint of the agent as utilitarian, one project among others itself becomes the standpoint of rational evaluation. The agent as utilitarian takes herself always to have decisive reasons to act in pursuit of this higher-order project; other projects and commitments figure in this second rational evaluation not as sources of alternative reasons, but as the object of the single ultimate higher-order reason. This second rational evaluation from the standpoint of the agent as utilitarian is put forward as supplanting the 1st person standpoint of the rational agent, but at the same time it presupposes in its very articulation the legitimacy of the very standpoint of rational agency that it purports to supplant. As a result the theory alienates an agent "in a real sense from his actions and the source of his actions in his own convictions . . . but this is to neglect the extent to which *his* actions and *his* decisions have to be seen as the actions and decisions that flow from the projects and attitudes with which he is most closely identified."[26] As Williams argues, "my life, my action is quite irreducibly mine, and to require that it is at best a *derivative* conclusion that it should be lived from the perspective that happens to be mine is an extraordinary misunderstanding. Yet it is that idea that is implicitly contained in the model of the point of view of the universe."[27] The point of the Williams inspired diagnosis is that consequentialism both presupposes that I am the rational agent whose life and actions are "quite irreducibly mine," and at the same time takes

---

[25] Williams (1973, p. 116).   [26] Ibid., pp. 116–17.   [27] Williams (1995, p. 170).

me to be the rational agent for whom one of my higher-order projects is *the* ultimate project, hence for whom my projects and commitments are merely some among others, such that any reasons to live my life from "within" can be at best derivative. The agent as utilitarian dismisses in its application the first-person standpoint of integrated rational agency that the theory presupposes in its very articulation of its moral standards. This is why it is "in the most literal sense, an attack on his integrity."[28]

The consequentialist presupposes that morality as the consequentialist understands it is but one (albeit higher-order) project among others, hence that it is merely one source of competing reasons among others. But it is transformed, through appeal to RAMS, into the project which subsumes all others. What explains the tendency by consequentialists to invoke this assumption in the face of the obvious structural obstacles for doing so? Part of the answer surely resides in the independent plausibility of RAMS, the conviction that moral requirements have rational authority. But as we have already seen, the very structure of traditional consequentialism is difficult to reconcile with this assumption. This structure presupposes that the moral project is just one among other projects that rational agents have good reasons to pursue. Williams' examples are of cases in which these lower-order projects provide such rational agents with reasons that weigh against, and in some cases are decisive with respect to, whatever reasons they have to pursue a higher-order project on projects—the consequentialist's moral project. Alternative moral theories, theories of moral reasons, offer rationales for the claim that agents have decisive reasons to conform to their moral standards. But Smart's utilitarianism provides no such rationale; indeed, it invokes an account of practical reason and deliberation upon which the reasons agents have to conform to consequentialist moral standards are but some reasons among others. Intuitively, such other reasons are often sufficient for the agent to be justified in not bringing about the best overall outcome, hence in doing what the consequentialist identifies as wrong. Indeed, we have seen that consequentialists typically accept NIR, allowing that there are fundamentally non-impersonal reasons, and that such non-impersonal reasons sometimes provide agents with sufficient reasons not to bring about the best overall outcome. Consequentialism maintains that the right action brings about the best overall outcome, but not that the

---

[28] Williams (1973, p. 117).

rational action brings about the best overall outcome. When these fail to coincide, the rational agent will have sufficient reasons to act in ways the consequentialist identifies as wrong.

An additional contributing factor appears to be the higher-order nature of the consequentialist moral project, its status as a project that comprehends all other projects in its content. But here Gary Watson's remarks on higher-order desires are relevant. Watson points out that although there is a sense in which higher-order desires comprehend certain lower-order desires this is not, as is sometimes assumed, a sense that allows them somehow to subsume the motivating force of those desires. Higher-order desires, although they are desires concerning desires, "are themselves simply desires, to add them to the context of conflict is just to increase the number of contenders; it is not to give a special place to any of those in contention."[29] As higher-order desires they comprehend lower-order desires in their content, but they are not for this reason more comprehensive or authentic motives. Similarly, higher-order projects are themselves simply projects that the rational deliberator has good reasons to pursue. To add them to the set of the rational agent's projects is just to add to the reasons such a rational agent must take into account, it is not to give a special place to any of the reasons that are in contention. Higher-order projects comprehend lower-order projects as their object, but they do not for this reason provide more comprehensive or authentic reasons.

I have lower-order reasons from my standpoint of practical reason and deliberation, reasons to cultivate friendships, achieve excellence in my chosen field, etc.—to pursue the projects that I value as a rational agent. From my standpoint as a practical reasoner and deliberator I also have higher-order reasons to maximize the extent to which agents accomplish what they have good reasons to do, higher-order projects that I value along with the first-order projects. These are projects to maximally promote the realization of the lower-order projects that I and other agents have reasons to pursue. Pursuit of this higher-order project requires the adoption of an impersonal standpoint from which I can evaluate states of affairs as better or worse overall insofar as they effectively further or thwart my higher-order project. Such a higher-order project concerning projects comprehends all other lower-order projects that rational agents have good reasons to pursue.

[29] Watson (2004a, p. 28).

But Watson's remarks concerning higher-order desires allow us to see that although higher-order projects in this sense comprehend other lower-order projects as their object, they do so in a way which presupposes that they are not comprehensive projects, projects that provide comprehensive reasons for rational agents. Rather, such higher-order projects are, ex hypothesi, just some among the other projects that I value from my standpoint as a practical reasoner and deliberator. If I make the mistake of viewing such higher-order projects not as some projects among others, but as comprehensive projects that provide the agent with comprehensive reasons, then the impersonal standpoint adopted for the purposes of articulating certain higher-order reasons comes mistakenly to be viewed as the standpoint of practical reason and deliberation, the standpoint from which the comprehensive project for a rational agent is properly articulated. But just as a higher-order desire is but one competing source of motivation among others, such a higher-order project is but one competing project among others, projects that often appear to provide rational agents with conflicting reasons.

Williams' suggestion is that the structure of traditional consequentialism is one that should invite the conclusion that the moral project is at most one project among others that rational agents have reasons to pursue, a structure that threatens to marginalize morality by alienating rational agents from moral standards as rationally authoritative. But consequentialists often persist in the assumption that moral requirements have rational authority, and that the higher-order moral project, in comprehending all other projects, at the same time subsumes all lower-order reasons the agent might have within this higher-order project. This is a deep tension within consequentialism, and my suggestion is that Williams' argument is profitably read as attempting to highlight this tension within the theory itself as traditionally understood.

The theory's own presuppositions suggest that it does not make sense in such cases to do what is right, understood as acting on the reason to pursue our higher-order project, in preference to what is wrong, understood as acting on our reasons to pursue our most deeply held commitments and our most central projects. When the theory then presumes that reason demands compliance with its moral standards for right and wrong action, the tension is not with intuitions external to the theory, but with its own presuppositions. This is the "incoherence" in traditional consequentialism that is at the heart of Williams' critique. It is not a true demonstration of incoherence, because it is possible that the agent's projects and circumstances are so configured that no discord between the reasons that arise from these higher- and lower-order projects arises.[30] But the point of Williams' examples is precisely to point out that in practice such discord between the standpoint of the rational agent and the standpoint of the "agent as utilitarian" routinely occurs, and in such cases the theory tells us that we have decisive reasons to do, as a rational agent acting with integrity, what it also presumes that we, as utilitarian agents, have decisive reasons not to do. We cannot help but feel that so acting will undermine our very status as integrated rational agents, hence our ability to act with integrity, because the theory itself presupposes that this is the case.

It will be helpful at this point to locate this largely Williams-inspired diagnosis within our original triad of claims. The consequentialist theory of moral standards (CMS), wedded to appeal to the rational authority of morality (RAMS), results in consequentialist agents who always have decisive reasons to bring about the best overall state of affairs as determined from a 3rd person impersonal standpoint. Appeal to RAMS results in agents whose practical reason and deliberation will always result in a rational requirement to bring about the best overall state of affairs. Such an agent has lower-order projects that provide her with lower-order, non-impersonal reasons to act, reasons that often appear sufficient to act in ways that do not bring about the best overall state of affairs (NIR). She then adopts a 3rd person observer's standpoint towards the ends and actions she has reasons to pursue, adopts an overarching higher-order project that evaluates states of affairs from this 3rd person standpoint, and, if she is a consequentialist, takes the right action to be the action that furthers this project, hence (via appeal to RAMS) takes rational agents to have decisive reasons to bring about the best states of affairs as determined from this 3rd person standpoint. The very articulation of CMS by the consequentialist presupposes NIR, and these are difficult to reconcile with RAMS. But advocates of CMS typically presuppose RAMS, which rules out NIR. If the role of RAMS in consequentialism is left off stage, and we have seen why

---

[30] It could be the case, e.g., that although the reasons in support of the moral project are merely some reasons among others to support one project among others, they virtually always outweigh all other reasons, leading to a de facto congruence of the moral and rational requirements. It could also be the case that the two standpoints in certain circumstances could through social and psychological engineering be made to align in certain agents, such that the course of action that leads to the realization of the moral projects will almost always be the course of action that leads to the realization of all of the agent's projects taken together.

it is tempting to do so, the consequentialist gets to eat her cake and have it too, deploying de facto an account of practical reason as consequentialist *rational* requirement while at the same time presupposing an account of practical reason upon which the agent often has sufficient reasons to violate consequentialist moral standards. The consequentialist is under pressure to abandon either the claim that the impersonal standpoint is the standpoint of moral requirement (CMS), or the claim that moral requirements have rational authority (RAMS).

Williams' challenge, as I have presented it, is to a traditional version of utilitarian consequentialism, one which he takes to presuppose a distinctly internalist account of practical reason and deliberation. But how broadly does it generalize to other forms of consequentialism, forms that may involve very different accounts of practical reason and deliberation? It would seem that the answer is: quite broadly. The Williams diagnosis appears to apply with equal force, for example, whether the agent's pursuit of her plans and projects is understood eudaimonistically, as in Smart's case, or, for example, preference theoretically. More significantly, aspects of the challenge readily transpose from Williams' own reasons internalist account to a reasons externalist account.[31] For Williams the plans, projects, and commitments that make up an agent's subjective motivational set control the agent's reasons. Very roughly, if there is a sound deliberative route from this subjective motivational set (whatever its content) to some course of action, the agent has a reason to perform such an action. The 3rd person observer's standpoint that such an agent can take up towards his reasons and those of others is not itself a source of reasons, on such a view, except insofar as it is involved in the elaboration and articulation of one or more of the projects in the subjective motivational set of the particular agent in question. Impersonal evaluation only becomes a source of rational demands insofar as it is relevant to one of the projects that a rational agent has, and the strength of these demands is a function of the relative centrality for an agent of the project(s) in question.

On a reasons externalist account,[32] by contrast, the 3rd person observer's standpoint is a standpoint towards the reasons that agents in fact have whether or not there is a sound deliberative route to those reasons from

---

[31] See "Internal and External Reasons" (Williams 1981).
[32] Such as that articulated by John McDowell (e.g. 1995, pp. 68–85).

the current set of the agent's plans, projects, and commitments. But such a standpoint will be relevant to the agent's reasons, thus externally understood, only if among the reasons the agent in fact has are reasons that involve the adoption of such a standpoint for their articulation. Thus, a reasons externalist may well take each agent in fact to have good reasons to stand by his or her friends. From an observer's standpoint my reasons to stand by my friends are just another set of reasons one agent has to stand by his friends. But this observation by itself provides me with no additional reasons. Only if, among the other reasons I and other agents in fact have, are good higher-order reasons to maximize the extent to which agents succeed in achieving the ends and projects that they in fact have good reasons to pursue will agents have, in addition to a good reason to stick by their own friends, good reasons, for example, to maximize the extent to which people stick by their friends. Such a good reason will involve the 3rd person standpoint for its articulation, and can compete with the aforementioned reasons that agents have to stick by their own friends. Acting in accordance with some of these reasons will often interfere with others, and which action it makes more sense to pursue will depend upon which of the relevant reasons are in fact decisive in the circumstances. Thus Scanlon has argued that a person "who values friendship will take herself to have reasons, first and foremost, to do those things that are involved in being a good friend: to be loyal . . . to spend time with her friends, and so on."[33] In addition to such lower-order reasons, Scanlon suggests, a person who values friendship will also have higher-order reasons that involve "holding that it is good that friendship should occur and that friendship is therefore 'to be promoted'."[34] But these good higher-order reasons presuppose that rational agents have such good lower-order reasons; indeed, they are reasons to promote states of affairs upon which rational agents have the opportunity to act on such good lower-order reasons—to be loyal, etc. to their friends. Scanlon takes it to be clear; moreover, that it is the lower-order reasons "that are most central to friendship," and that "when conflicts occur these reasons take priority over the reasons we have to promote friendship."[35] Higher-order reasons to promote friendship are reasons to promote the extent to which rational agents can act on the good lower-order reasons that they have to be good friends, and a person who

---

[33] Scanlon (1998, p. 88).   [34] Ibid., p. 89.   [35] Ibid., p. 89.

appropriately values friendship will stick by her friends in typical cases in which such higher- and lower-order reasons are in conflict.

Of course it is open to a reasons externalist consequentialist to maintain both that each agent does in fact have such higher-order reasons to promote the overall realization of what agents in fact have lower-order reasons to value, and, *pace* Scanlon, that such higher-order reasons are always decisive in conflicts with such lower-order reasons. But the burden would appear to fall squarely upon the advocate of any such account to demonstrate that although such higher-order reasons presuppose that agents have other lower-order reasons, they are always decisive with respect to such reasons in cases of conflict. This burden is all the more pressing because intuitively, we often appear to have sufficient reasons to act in accordance with such lower-order reasons in such cases of conflict. Moreover, virtually every account of practical reason, whether internalist or externalist, accepts NIR—that fundamental non-impersonal reasons are sometimes sufficient reasons for agents not to bring about the best overall outcome—to do what the consequentialist identifies as wrong. But to accept NIR is precisely to accept that whatever higher-order reasons we have are not always decisive with respect to our lower-order reasons.

More fundamentally, aspects of Williams' argument readily generalize because its central point is that the impersonal standpoint is a higher-order standpoint that is taken up towards the lower-order non-impersonal reasons of rational agents. Such lower-order reasons, he suggests, reveal much of what agents value, and higher-order reasons reveal additional values of rational agents, values that presuppose the independent and potentially conflicting values reflected in these lower-order reasons. Only if such a rational agent has a reason to bring about the higher ranked states of affairs and prevent the worse ranked states of affairs will the fact that some outcome maximizes satisfaction of agent's lower-order reasons provide her with reasons for acting. But if the impersonal standpoint is a higher-order standpoint that is taken up towards the lower-order reasons of agents, then by assumption whatever reasons such an agent has to promote overall outcomes will be at most some reasons among others. This is just to say, however, that any reason to do what the consequentialist identifies as morally right will simply be one higher-order reason among other (often conflicting) lower-order reasons. As Williams' examples suggest, such reasons often appear to fail to be decisive within the context of an agent's other reasons. On any consequentialism that fits this general structure, whether eudaimonistic or preference theoretic, monistic or pluralistic, or wedded to reasons externalism or reasons internalism, the central threat is that the integrated rational agent who accepts CMS will be alienated by reason from moral standards.

I can determine what you take yourself to have reasons to want and to do by observing you from a 3rd person standpoint, taking into account what your interests are, what you want, what and who you are committed to, and what your deepest projects are.[36] I can also adopt such a 3rd person standpoint towards myself. But my primary mode of access to my commitments, plans, wants, and projects is from my own 1st person standpoint of practical reason and deliberation, not from a 3rd person observer's standpoint.[37] Mine is not just another set of commitments that I observe that happens to be mine, it is the one set among all others that I have good reasons to uphold and pursue through action. I have the commitments, desires, and projects I do because I take myself to have reasons for having them. Impersonal observation of such commitments and desires presupposes the first person deliberative reflection "whose conclusion is some desire."[38] To say that some state of affairs is the best thing that can happen overall, on such a diagnosis, is to say that it is the state of affairs that most effectively allows people to achieve what they have lower-order reasons to pursue, and to presuppose that the agents making such an assessment recognize that they have higher-order reasons to promote such overall outcomes. To say that some action is best is to say that, taking into account all of her higher- and lower-order reasons, the agent in question has decisive reasons to perform this action rather than any other. There is no conflict, then, in saying that although one state of affairs is best overall (it most effectively furthers the agent's higher-order reasons), it is best to do (the agent has decisive reasons taking all higher- and lower-order reasons into account) something other than promote the better overall outcome. You have reasons to stick by your friends, I have reasons to stick by mine, and your sticking by your friends is no better a

---

[36] I may of course also take each rational agent, qua rational agent, to have certain reasons to have certain fundamental projects and undertake certain commitments.

[37] This line of argument was originally developed before an encounter with Richard Moran's *Authority and Estrangement* (2001), but its subsequent development has benefited from engagement with his arguments.

[38] Moran (2001, p. 162).

thing to happen, from a 3rd person observer's standpoint, than my sticking by mine. But ex hypothesi my reasons are for sticking by my friends, and your reasons are for sticking by yours. My lower-order reasons not to abandon my friends are not grounded in the appeal to the impersonal badness of friend abandonment happening. Rather, any such impersonal assessment is a reflection of the good lower-order reasons each of us has to stick by our friends.[39] When such lower-order and higher-order reasons conflict, agents often appear to have lower-order reasons to stick by their friends that are decisive with respect to whatever higher-order reasons they have to minimize the friend abandonment that will happen overall. Although minimizing friend abandonment will bring about the best thing that can happen overall, such a rational agent will have decisive reasons not to abandon her friends.

In Chapter 3 we saw that consequentialism, properly understood as a theory of moral standards, makes no rational demands upon agents. Williams' diagnosis suggests that impersonal evaluations do provide reasons for agents, but do so precisely because—and to the extent that—such evaluations of states of affairs can be given a rationale based in certain of the higher-order reasons that it is rational for such agents to have. In short, what accounts for the role for the impersonal standpoint in practical reason is a rationale that locates the relevance of any appeals to impersonal value in certain higher-order reasons that rational agents have to facilitate the pursuit of lower-order reasons.[40]

On this diagnosis the appeal of traditional consequentialism is based upon a mistake, an understandable tendency to move from the insight that certain higher-order reasons must be articulated through appeal to a standpoint that comprehends the lower-order reasons of each agent to the conclusion that evaluation from such an impersonal standpoint provides rational agents with comprehensive higher-order reasons. A shared commitment to RAMS obscures the mistaken nature of such a move, but Williams' diagnosis challenges the legitimacy of the appeal by traditional consequentialists to RAMS. Moreover, it reveals the mistake involved in conflating the sense in

---

[39] Scanlon (1998, pp. 88–100).

[40] This is precisely the opposite of what is often claimed by consequentialists—that the only relevant reasons are those that can be given a "value-based" rationale, understood as a rationale based in the appeal to value of outcomes either from an observer's impersonal standpoint or from the agent's own partial standpoint.

which such a higher–order reason and the 3rd person standpoint to which it must have recourse does comprehend other reasons with another sense in which such a higher–order reason does not comprehend other reasons; indeed, in which it presupposes that such a higher–order reason is but one among other reasons that a rational agent appropriately takes into account, a reason that often fails to be decisive.

4.5 The Second Sharpening of the Challenge to Consequentialism

The first Williams-inspired sharpening of the challenge to consequentialism built upon his demonstration that the theory presupposes that rational agents have good non-impersonal reasons to pursue lower-order projects. Insofar as the impersonal standpoint makes any demands upon such a rational agent, such demands result from commitment to a higher-order project. Such a higher-order project, however, is but one among the agent's projects, and, appropriating Watson's remark about higher-order desires, to add such a project "is just to increase the number of contenders; it is not to give a special place to any of those in contention."[41] The apparent demandingness of consequentialism results precisely from presupposing the "special place" that moral requirements are taken to have, but it is just such a special place that consequentialism itself calls in to question in the identification of morality with the impersonal evaluative standpoint. We have seen that the central features of Williams' diagnosis generalize beyond the particular form of act consequentialism he criticizes and the particular account of practical reasons that it presupposes.

The second Williams inspired sharpening of the challenge to consequentialism builds upon his suggestion that among agents' lower-order projects, the projects that any higher-order project on projects will properly take into account in ranking states of affairs as better and worse, are certain distinctively moral lower-order projects. Recall Williams' point that among the lower-order projects we encounter are often "projects which flow from some more general dispositions toward human conduct and character, such as a hatred of injustice, or of cruelty, or of killing,"[42] and that

---

[41] Watson (2004a, p. 28).   [42] Williams (1973, p. 111).

the attitudes and commitments that ground such projects are "expressed precisely in ascribing intrinsic and not instrumental value to various activities and relations such as truth-telling, loyalty, and so on."[43] These are lower-order commitments that are moral commitments, and distinctively non-impersonal moral commitments. "The vital question," Williams suggests, "is . . . whether . . . similar projects are to count among the projects whose satisfaction is to be included in the maximizing sum." He takes the answer obviously to be "yes." If the higher-order project maximizes happiness by maximizing the satisfaction of lower-order projects, surely it will simply skew the result if certain distinctively moral lower-order projects are excluded. To say "no," Williams argues, is to "eliminate any desire at all which was not blankly and in the most straightforward sense egoistic."[44] Here Williams finds copious support from many contemporary consequentialists themselves, who argue that impersonal evaluation appropriately considers not merely the non-moral commitments and ends of rational deliberators, but in addition their moral commitments to, for example, avoiding lying, treating others fairly, and respecting the autonomy and rights of others. They agree with Williams' assessment that the classical view would implausibly commit the rational agent to "the one second-order project" of "maximizing satisfaction of frankly egoistic first-order projects."[45]

If rational agents have first-order reasons not only to promote their own happiness, but to avoid violating the rights of others and to respect their autonomy, to oppose injustice, to avoid lying, and to remain loyal, then the 3rd person determination of better and worse overall states of affairs will take into account not only the extent to which happiness is achieved overall, but the extent to which such rights violations are minimized and such respect for autonomy is maximized. If among our first-order commitments, for example, is a commitment to the intrinsic value of rights, then, as Frances Kamm has argued, such a commitment provides each of us with, at the very

---

[43] Williams (1995, p. 164).
[44] Williams (1973, p. 111). As we have seen, Williams himself suggests that there are difficulties with attempting to take into account the higher-order, impersonal projects of other agents from the impersonal standpoint. But the projects, commitments, and intrinsic values to which Williams here appeals are non-impersonal moral values and commitments. They are lower-order moral commitments that can without difficulty be taken into account from the impersonal standpoint in the articulation of higher-order projects.
[45] Ibid., p. 112.

least, good reasons not to kill even to promote overall happiness.[46] I am committed to avoid killing, and you are committed to avoid killing. From the 3rd person observer's evaluative standpoint, however, your avoiding such a rights violation is no better a thing to happen than is my avoiding such a rights violation, and a better outcome is one upon which fewer rather than more such rights not to be killed are violated, all other things being equal, regardless of whether or not I am in certain cases the one doing the violating. If we have good reasons to promote the best overall state of affairs, and among the intrinsically worthwhile projects recognized by rational agents are such projects as respecting the autonomy and rights of others, then pursuit of our higher-order projects will be hopelessly skewed if the impersonal evaluation of states of affairs does not take such intrinsic non-impersonal moral reasons into account. If each person is committed to avoiding telling lies, it will be a better overall outcome, all other things considered, upon which fewer rather than more such lies are told.

Williams' suggestion, then, is that rational agents have a range of commitments, including distinctively non-impersonal moral commitments, that provide them with reasons relevant to the determination of what they have reasons to do. We have seen that it does seem appropriate to adopt the impersonal standpoint towards both non-moral commitments and non-impersonal moral commitments in the determination of better and worse overall states of affairs. Indeed, it is just such a recognition that the impersonal standpoint can and properly should be taken up not just towards pleasure and well-being, but towards these distinctively moral commitments of deliberating agents as well, that is often taken by consequentialists themselves to breathe new life into the theory.[47]

This seemingly innocuous expansion of the values to be taken up impersonally, however, threatens to undermine the third member of our triad, the consequentialist theory of moral standards (CMS). One result of such expansion is that operation of the impersonal standpoint in the determination of the best overall state of affairs presupposes the recognition of certain non-impersonal moral values that either have non-impersonal rationales or do not need such rationales for their legitimacy. Such non-impersonal first-order moral commitments to intrinsic moral values are recognized as playing a role in the determination of what a rational deliberating

---

[46] Kamm (1996, p. 263).   [47] See, e.g., Railton (1988).

agent has reasons to do in the very impersonal determination of better or worse overall states of affairs. But this suggests that impersonally articulated higher-order moral considerations are best understood as at most some among the relevant moral considerations that are appropriately taken into account by agents, and that the impersonal standpoint for evaluating states of affairs as better and worse is not the fundamental standpoint for the moral evaluation of actions. The adoption of the impersonal standpoint towards the lower-order non-impersonal moral commitments of agents presupposes that whatever higher-order impersonal moral commitments agents have are merely some among that agent's moral commitments, including lower-order non-impersonal moral commitments. Such a pluralistic consequentialism not only presupposes that higher-order impersonal reasons are merely some among the rational agent's contending reasons, it presupposes that they are only some among the rational agent's contending moral reasons, including first-order non-impersonal moral reasons. Recognition that the impersonal standpoint is a higher-order standpoint that, qua higher-order, comprehends lower-order non-impersonal moral values is recognition that it is not a comprehensive standpoint of moral evaluation. The higher-order moral commitment comprehends these first-order moral commitments as its content, but precisely for this reason it is no longer plausible to see the impersonal standpoint as a comprehensive moral standpoint. If non-impersonal moral values are among the lower-order projects that are appropriately taken into account in higher-order impersonal evaluation, then the most plausible articulation of the impersonal standpoint and the claims that it makes upon us undermines the claim that this standpoint of impersonal evaluation exhausts the standpoint of morality, in the process undermining CMS. Consequentialism is best understood not only as presupposing that its moral project is merely one project among others, it is best understood as presupposing that its moral project is only one moral project among others, a higher-order moral project that presupposes the relevance of other non-impersonal lower-order moral projects in its evaluation of overall states of affairs. Recognition of lower-order moral commitments suggests that it is a mistake to treat the standpoint from which one particular higher-order moral commitment is articulated as a comprehensive moral standpoint. Rather, such higher-order moral commitments seem most plausibly understood as merely some moral commitments among others, including other non-impersonal moral commitments. Of course a consequentialist can in principle grant the existence of such independent lower-order moral projects, but claim that an agent's higher-order moral commitments are always morally decisive in cases of conflict with such first-order moral commitments. But the argument for such decisiveness has typically appealed to the claim that the ultimate rationale for moral commitments is based in the appeal to impersonal value.[48] Williams' point is that on his diagnosis impersonal evaluation presupposes that there are lower-order non-impersonal moral commitments with non-impersonal rationales. In short, it presumes that the ultimate rationales for such non-impersonal moral commitments are not impersonal. Intuitively, impersonal moral commitments often fail to be decisive in the face of countervailing non-impersonal moral commitments. The traditional consequentialist maintained that such apparently countervailing non-impersonal moral commitments are in fact derived from impersonal commitments. But Williams' diagnosis suggests that impersonal evaluation is more plausibly understood as presupposing that agents have non-derivative lower-order moral and non-moral projects and commitments.

The suggestion is that the impersonal standpoint, plausibly understood, presupposes that certain non-impersonal moral reasons with non-impersonal rationales (or perhaps simply not in need of such rationales) already play a role in practical reason and deliberation, and that such non-impersonal moral considerations are taken up among the lower-order inputs in the very determination of the better and worse things that can happen overall. Any indirect consequentialist rationale for justice, fairness, or rights, on such a view, is oddly beside the point, since independent moral commitments to such lower-order moral values as justice, rights, and fairness are presupposed as among the inputs into the impersonal determination of better and worse states of affairs at the foundational level.[49] Rights, for example, purport to provide non-impersonal and non-partial moral grounds for action. If these are legitimate grounds, it is important to take them into account in any accurate 3rd person determination of better and worse things that can happen: it will be a better state of affairs in which more rights are upheld. But this is to recognize non-impersonal lower-order moral grounds for action at the most fundamental level in the very adoption

---

[48] Such arguments will be considered in more detail in the next chapter.
[49] A point that will be developed in more detail in Chapter 7.

of the higher-order impersonal standpoint, grounds that presuppose a non-impersonal rationale. If Williams and contemporary consequentialists are right that it is appropriate to take up such non-impersonal moral grounds in any impersonal evaluation of states of affairs, then the standpoint of impersonal evaluation is not the moral standpoint; indeed, the impersonal standpoint, properly understood, is taken up towards non-impersonal moral considerations with non-impersonal rationales, considerations which then must be taken into account alongside whatever relevant impersonal moral considerations there might be.

Peter Railton's sophisticated consequentialism is an example of such a recent version of the theory that rejects a monistic account of value, adopting instead "a pluralistic approach in which several goods are viewed as intrinsically, non-morally valuable, such as happiness . . . autonomy, solidarity, respect, and beauty."[50] Railton is committed to seeing the moral standpoint, the standpoint of right action, as the standpoint that takes into account non-moral values, determines "the weighted sum of these values," and establishes the right action as the one that furthers this weighted sum of non-moral values over the long run. Surely Railton is right that such considerations as autonomy, respect, etc. are relevant to the determination of the best overall state of affairs. It seems equally clear, however, that many of these are lower-order moral values. The respect in question, for example, is a moral value, a commitment to recognize each person as having a distinctive moral standing. It seems extremely plausible that such respect functions as an appropriate input into any determination of impersonal value, but it also seems clear that in such contexts it functions as a moral input, and in particular as a lower-order non-impersonal moral input relevant to the evaluation of states of affairs from the higher-order impersonal standpoint. If it is appropriate to take up such non-impersonal moral values from the impersonal standpoint, this is to grant that there are relevant non-impersonal moral values with non-impersonal rationales, hence that the impersonal standpoint appropriate to the evaluation of overall states of affairs cannot itself be the appropriate standpoint for the moral evaluation of actions as right or wrong.

Further sharpening of the challenge to consequentialism along these lines will be undertaken in Chapter 6, focusing in particular upon recent

---

[50] Railton (1988, p. 163).

discussions of the prospects for a consequentialism of rights. I will show that consequentialist presuppositions concerning the relevant values to be viewed impersonally cannot be reconciled to their own claim that the impersonal standpoint is the standpoint of morality. I will demonstrate, moreover, that these consequentialist presuppositions provide the outlines for just the sort of rationale for non-impersonal moral considerations that consequentialists frequently assert is lacking, and that this rationale provides the tools to set aside one traditional rationale for CMS that is not undermined by the arguments offered in Chapter 5. Before moving on to the deployment of the challenge to consequentialism against traditional rationales offered in support of consequentialism, I will first consider certain alleged analogies and disanalogies between the spheres of theoretical and practical reasoning. Certain of these analogies and disanalogies initially obscure the challenge to consequentialism, but when properly framed they allow us to bring both the challenges of and to consequentialism into sharper focus.

4.6 Analogies and Disanalogies Between the Theoretical and Practical Spheres

The traditional act consequentialist's appeal to the impersonal standpoint as the standpoint of morality de jure and reason de facto, an appeal that our Williams-inspired diagnosis has called into question, also might seem to be invited by certain alleged parallels between theoretical reasoning, roughly reasoning about what to believe, and practical reasoning, roughly reasoning about what to do. One such parallel is suggested by the role that reflection plays in our perception of a stick half in/half out of the water. Ordinary perceptual evidence suggests that the stick is bent at the water line. But scientifically informed theoretical reflection leads us to the conclusion that—such visual appearances notwithstanding—it really isn't. Relying on our everyday visual perceptual evidence, we judge that the stick is bent. But it is not. We are led in our theoretical (here as opposed to "practical") reasoning about what to believe to discount our perceptual evidence as illusory, and to continue to do so even if the stick continues doggedly to look bent. Similarly, the morally relevant considerations of rational agents suggest that morality often permits us to pursue our own projects and interests out of proportion to their impersonal value, and sometimes prohibit us, for example, from violating someone's right or betraying a friend even in certain cases when by doing so we can prevent more rights violations overall from happening and promote more friendships overall. But some consequentialists take reflection to demonstrate that such appearances are misleading. Reflection leads us to the impersonal assessment of better and worse states of affairs as the sole consideration relevant to the determination of right and wrong actions, and such an assessment leads us to discount apparent non-impersonal moral and non-moral reasons as only apparently relevant to the determination of what morality requires, permits, and prohibits.[51] Theory, the consequentialist argues, leads us to discount the apparently relevant non-impersonal considerations that appear to be morally relevant, and to continue to do so even if violation of rights in such cases continues to strike us as morally wrong, and preference to our own children does not.

Such an alleged parallel fails to support the case for consequentialism, however. First, only the most extreme views concerning the theoretical sphere hold that the non-perspectival perspective of foundational science, what Williams refers to as the absolute conception,[52] supplants the standpoint of theoretical reasoning and deliberation about what to believe, providing the only ultimate source of epistemic justification. Rather, such reasoning draws upon testimonial, mnemonic, perceptual, and logical reasons—as well as reasons from the most fundamental sciences—for believing that certain propositions are true and correspond to the way things really are.[53] These other reasons play no role from the non-perspectival standpoint of the absolute conception, and cannot be given a scientific rationale from that standpoint. But it is common to resist any conclusion that this somehow undermines their role in the proper theoretical reasoning and deliberation of rational agents. To take the absolute conception of science somehow to supplant or displace the standpoint of theoretical reason, on such an approach, would be to lose access to good reasons for beliefs about everything ranging from colors and minds to chairs and values. It would be

---

[51] Kagan (1989, ch. 1). The bent stick example presented above is taken from Kagan. Although not himself a consequentialist, Thomas Nagel's account also often appears to suggest an argument along similar lines. Consideration of Nagel's argument will be postponed to Chapter 7.

[52] See, e.g., the middle chapters of his *Ethics and the Limits of Philosophy* (1995).

[53] See, e.g., Chisholm (1977, pp. 122ff.) for one standard account of the various sources of knowledge.

to discount good reasons, hence to come to believe falsely, and to do so (ironically) in the name of truth and reality via the absolute conception.

Similarly, the consideration of rights, autonomy, friendship, our own interests and projects, etc. seems to provide us with good morally significant reasons that result in moral permissions to pursue our own interests and moral prohibitions against violating the rights of others. But the impersonal standpoint may be taken to provide us with grounds to discount such reasons; indeed, to hold that there are decisive moral reasons to discount our own interests and projects, violate the agent's rights, etc. However, much as perception, logic, and testimony appear to provide real reasons to believe that are not revealed as illusory by the standpoint of the absolute conception, so too rights, friendship, and an agent's projects and interests appear to provide real non-impersonal moral and non-moral reasons, reasons that are not voided or revealed to be illusory by appeal to the impersonal standpoint. Indeed, as we have seen, the appropriateness of taking up the impersonal standpoint towards such non-impersonal reasons seems most plausibly to be understood as itself presupposing that practical rational agents have good non-impersonal reasons to pursue ends and honor commitments. These non-impersonal reasons appear to be relevant to the determination of what is morally right and wrong, just as perceptual, logical, and testimonial reasons appear to be relevant to the determination of what to believe—to take to be true. The parallel suggests that the impersonal standpoint does not supplant the various moral and non-moral reasons that appear to be relevant to the determination of what it is good or bad, right or wrong to do. To take it somehow to supplant such reasons is to come to take right actions to be wrong in many cases, and to do so, ironically, in the name of rightness and goodness via the impersonal standpoint.

In our everyday practical reasoning we take ourselves to have good distinctively moral non-impersonal reasons to avoid violations of the rights of others, and these reasons are often decisive in establishing the wrongness of such courses of action, just as perceptual reasons are often decisive in establishing the truth of some particular belief. An approach which takes the impersonal standpoint to undermine such non-impersonal reasons parallels an approach in epistemology that appeals to the general intuition that true beliefs correspond to reality, but stipulates that only reasons for believing from the standpoint of the absolute conception are ultimately authoritative in the determination of what is real. The result will be an approach that discounts perception, memory, and testimony, recognizing only science as a source of reasons relevant to the determination of what it is true to believe. The temptation to restrict relevant reasons to such a subset is understandable in the theoretical sphere, and arguments have been offered for doing so. But the argument cannot be that there is no rationale supplied by the absolute conception for perceptual or logical reasons, or, by analogy, no impersonal rationale for prudential or rights-based reasons. Such claims, like their counterparts, would straightforwardly beg the question. What would be needed, rather, is a rationale for restricting relevant reasons for believing something to be true to the apparently relevant subset of reasons supplied from the standpoint of the absolute conception, and for restricting the relevant reasons for the rightness of action to the apparently relevant impersonal subset. This would require an account of why such apparently good reasons are in fact good, while others are not. Barring such a demonstration, it seems most plausible to take the impersonal standpoint to presuppose that the lower-order non-impersonal reasons towards which it is adopted are relevant to the determination of right and wrong action. The impersonal standpoint, in turn, seems best understood as properly invoked to articulate only some of the reasons that are relevant to the determination of right and wrong action.

The consequentialist advocate who attempts to draw support from this parallel may concede, however, that perception, logic, and testimony do provide other legitimate sources of reasons for believing, reasons in addition to whatever reasons are provided through appeal to the absolute conception. But he may nonetheless insist that the non-perspectival perspective, the standpoint of the absolute conception, is authoritative in all cases in which such sources of reasons conflict. The idea would be that although these other sources have seats at the justificatory table in the theoretical sphere, justification from the standpoint of the absolute conception has a privileged seat at the table, such that reasons from such a standpoint are decisive whenever they conflict with those arising from these other sources. If the impersonal standpoint has, by analogy, such an authoritative seat at the table of practical reason and justification, this will provide the consequentialist all that she requires from the parallel with the theoretical sphere. Such a parallel, if it is plausible, will allow her to recognize the agent's interests, special obligations, and perhaps even rights as providing other legitimate sources of reasons that are relevant in the determination of what it is right and wrong to do, but insist that the impersonal standpoint is authoritative in any cases in which such sources of reasons conflict.

The claim that the standpoint of the absolute conception is a source of reasons that is authoritative in this sense, the claim that forms the basis for the alleged parallel, is itself extremely controversial.[54] But the arguments in Chapter 3 and the earlier parts of this chapter have put us in a position to see that whatever the role of the absolute conception as a source of reasons in the theoretical sphere, the alleged parallel with the role of the impersonal standpoint in the practical sphere is not defensible. Whether or not the standpoint of the absolute conception is ultimately authoritative in the theoretical sphere, we have ample evidence to doubt that the impersonal standpoint is in this sense authoritative in the practical sphere. Indeed, it became apparent in Chapter 3 that the fundamental challenge confronting the consequentialist theory of moral standards is to show how the standpoint of impersonal evaluation can have any place at the table of practical reason and deliberation at all. Our preference theoretic consequentialist, for example, takes the satisfaction of the agent's own preferences to be the source of authoritative practical reasons, and takes preference satisfaction viewed impersonally to set the standard for right action. Impersonal evaluation would only appear to be a source of practical reasons at all on such an account if among some agent's preferences is a preference to maximize the satisfaction of the agent's of all agents' preferences overall. At best this will be one among other competing preferences.

In the earlier sections of this chapter Williams' arguments revealed the impersonal standpoint for what it is: a 3rd person observer's standpoint towards what persons have good reasons to value, a standpoint that becomes an evaluative standpoint and a source of reasons at the table of practical reason only to the extent that among the agent's good reasons are certain higher-order reasons to maximize the satisfaction overall of the ends that persons are recognized as having good reasons to value. An agent with such a good higher-order reason has a reason that comprehends the reasons that she and all other agents have in the same sense that a higher-order desire comprehends her other desires. But ex hypothesi it is not a comprehensive reason any more than such a higher-order desire is a comprehensive motive.

---

[54] See, e.g., Putnam (1992) for a sustained argument against this claim.

Nor, as we have seen, is there any reason to take one such good reason among others to be authoritative with respect to these other reasons, as the absolute conception is taken by some to be authoritative with respect to all other theoretical reasons. Rather, this diagnosis leads us to what many consequentialists concede, ordinary experiences suggests, and Williams' own examples help us to confirm: that impersonal evaluation is involved in articulating at most some of a rational agent's good reasons among others, reasons that give way or prove to be decisive in particular circumstances depending upon the centrality of the interests to be sacrificed, the overall disvalue that can be avoided, the nature of the special obligations involved, etc.

4.7 Refining the Challenge of Consequentialism

RAMS claims that we typically have decisive reasons, and in this sense are rationally required, not to do what we know to be wrong, much as its theoretical analogue assures us that we have decisive reasons, and in this sense are rationally required, to believe what we know to be true. If (1) the impersonal standpoint is taken to determine what is better and worse in the relevant sense, and (2) it is always not just right for the agent, but morally required of the agent, to do what's best in this sense (what will bring about the best state of affairs overall), then if (3) we are rationally required, as RAMS suggests, to do what is morally required, it will follow that (4) we are always rationally required to do what's best, understood as what promotes the best overall state of affairs. All reasons for action will be channeled through this non-perspectival standpoint as a result of adopting the distinctive impersonal account of the "best" as determining what it is always morally right to do.

If the conclusion (4) doesn't follow, the most likely culprit is the claim that the impersonal standpoint is in the relevant sense the sole authority for the best that it is always right to do. What does not seem to be the culprit is claim (2), linking rightness (wrongness) and goodness. The general intuition that it *is* always right to do what's best seems as fundamental and noncontroversial as the theoretical claim that true beliefs *do* always correspond to the way things really are.[55] If, however, "it is

---

[55] To endorse such a claim is not, of course, to endorse a correspondence theory of truth. Rather, correspondence theories constitute one set of strategies for interpreting such a general claim. Putnam,

always right to do what's best" is an uncontroversial claim concerning the relationship between rightness and goodness, as "true beliefs correspond to reality" is an uncontroversial general claim concerning the relationship between truth and reality,[56] where does the claim go wrong that, as consequentialists insist, this general intuition, coupled with the rational authority of moral requirements, drives us towards a usurpation of practical reason and deliberation by the impersonal standpoint, that is towards Williams' "agent as utilitarian"? If, as the consequentialist maintains, this powerful intuitive general contour, that it is always right to do what's best, is most plausibly interpreted in a way that results in CMS, then at the very least the consequentialist theory of moral standards appears to hold its own against RAMS and NIR, and is not the obvious claim to be discarded. Indeed, it would appear to be provided with a powerful independent rationale that is grounded in a deep intuition concerning the relationship between rightness and goodness.

But what does the appealing intuitive contour relate? One of the relata is clearly rightness of actions, and the other is goodness. But of what? The consequentialist proposes goodness of states of affairs impersonally considered. One possibility is that the general intuition that it is always right to do what's best is being misinterpreted by the consequentialist, that although rightness in this general intuition is properly understood as rightness of actions, goodness is not properly understood as goodness of states of affairs impersonally considered. To make the case for such a misinterpretation would be to demonstrate that although there is nothing wrong with the general intuition that it is always right to do what is best, the impersonal standpoint is not in the relevant sense authoritative in the determination of the best properly understood. In short, it would be to demonstrate that the "best" that this general intuition

e.g., distinguishes those who endorse such a claim as part of a "nominal definition of the truth" from those who interpret it in terms of the correspondence theory (1981, pp. 63ff.). Strawson as well emphasizes that while of course one must "say that a statement corresponds to . . . the facts," this need only be understood as "a variant on saying it is true" (1971, pp. 194–5). McDowell takes some such claim articulating "the bearing of empirical judgments on reality" to be a central component of any plausible picture (1994, p. 5), but argues against any role for the traditional correspondence theory in such a picture.

[56] Indeed, as the previous footnote concerning the correspondence theory of truth suggests, the issue in each case isn't whether the claim is true, but whether it is a "mere" platitude or instead a substantive general intuition that lends support to some particular theory of true belief, such as the correspondence theory, or some particular theory of right action, such as consequentialism.

relates to right action is not the consequentialist's "best overall state of affairs".

But is there any support for such a diagnosis? The impersonal standpoint does appear to be the appropriate standpoint from which to determine better and worse things that can happen overall. Critics of consequentialism have often taken themselves to be compelled to deny this, but such denials are not plausible. If it is always right to do what's best, and "best" understood as the consequentialist understands it (as a property of overall states of affairs) leads ineluctably to CMS, and CMS itself is both intuitively and theoretically problematic for the reasons suggested earlier, the obvious response is that the consequentialist's proposal for interpreting the "best" that it is always right to do by way of the impersonal standpoint, as a property of states of affairs impersonally considered, must be a misinterpretation. But then what is the right way to understand the appeal to the "best" in this powerfully intuitive claim? If there is no viable alternative to the consequentialist proposal, the challenge of consequentialism reasserts itself. Critics of consequentialism often concede that what's best in the relevant sense is what brings about the best state of affairs impersonally considered. But this leaves them committed to the position that to reject consequentialism is to reject the powerful general intuition that it is always right to do what's best, and to defend the claim that, contrary to intuition, it is sometimes wrong to do what we know to be best. This seems as bizarre and paradoxical as claiming that true beliefs sometimes do not correspond to the way that we know things really are.[57] If consequentialism offers the only plausible way to unpack the general intuition that it is always right to do what's best, or even the most plausible way, then there will be a rationale for CMS at least as compelling as those for RAMS and NIR, its initial intuitive implausibility notwithstanding. The challenge will be maintained, and its force will be clarified. A response to this more focused challenge of consequentialism

---

[57] Indeed, Tyler Burge maintains not only that "the representational function of a system of beliefs . . . is to represent veridically" (2003, p. 506), but that it is "apriori that a *representational* function of a psychological system of beliefs is to form true beliefs" (2003, p. 509, his emphasis). True beliefs correspond to the way things really are. It is of course also true that particular justified beliefs that agents take to be true nonetheless fail to be true, that is, fail to correspond to the way things really are. Brute mistakes occur—the world can play tricks on us—leading us to have false beliefs that we are nonetheless justified in holding. For discussions of the apparently paradoxical nature of agent-centered restrictions understood as claims that it is sometimes wrong to do what's best, see Nagel (1986), Scheffler (1982), and my own (1997).

must demonstrate that the consequentialist interpretation of this general intuition invokes the wrong—because impersonal—interpretation of the best that it is always right to do. But if the consequentialist's interpretation of this general intuition is wrong, what is the right interpretation? This is the central challenge that must be answered to deflect the consequentialist challenge.

4.8 Outline of an Alternative Interpretation of the General Intuition

My suggestion will be that the considerations that appear to lead us ineluctably to consequentialism have the apparent force they do because they effectively elide the role of good and bad as properties of actions and reasons for actions. The general intuition fueling consequentialism is that it is always right to do what's best, but the arguments and rationales offered in support of consequentialism turn on what can plausibly be viewed as a systematic misinterpretation of this general intuition, hence upon a systematic misappropriation of its force. The best action for an agent to perform is determined through appeal to practical reasons and deliberation. The goal of theoretical reason is true belief; the goal of practical reason is the best action (when there is such a uniquely best action). The general intuition is most plausibly understood as claiming that it is always morally right to do what it is best to do thus understood. As such, this general intuition complements the general intuition captured in RAMS (the rational authority of moral requirements), that it is, in effect, always bad to do what's morally wrong; indeed, that the agent typically has decisively good reasons not to perform such actions. The rational authority of moral requirements sets out one central contour of the relationship of morality to practical reasons and deliberation, that we never have sufficient reasons to do what's wrong, but the intuition that it is always right to do what's best, properly understood, sets out another, that it's always right to pursue the best course of action, the course of action supported by the best reasons. Each captures a deep general intuition concerning the relationship between reason and morality.

I will argue in the next chapter that the considerations that appear to lead us towards consequentialism swap out goodness as a property of actions and reasons for action with goodness as a property of overall states of affairs, effectively hijacking these general intuitions regarding goodness, rightness, and reasonableness. The theory is able to usurp de facto the standpoint of practical reason and deliberation that it eschews de jure because, in explicating the general intuition that it is always right to do what's best, it swaps out goodness of reasons and actions for impersonal goodness of states of affairs. The claim concerning goodness and rightness of actions does capture a plausible general intuition: that what the agent has the best reasons to do—the best course of action—will not be morally prohibited. The swapping out provides illusory support for the counter-intuitive claim that agents are always morally required to bring about the best overall state of affairs. Such a hijacking precludes an accurate account of the role of impersonal determination of the best state of affairs in relation to rightness and goodness as properties of actions. Moreover, it misrepresents goodness as a property of states of affairs (not actions) as having a relationship to rightness of actions that leads ineluctably to consequentialism, and results in a portrayal of all other alternatives as seemingly flying in the face of our deepest convictions concerning the relationships among rightness, goodness, and practical reason. Once goodness as a property of actions and reasons for action is restored to its proper role in relation to rightness and the impersonal goodness of states of affairs, the traditional considerations that have been taken to lead ineluctably to consequentialism lose much if not all of their force.

5

Deflating the Challenge
of Consequentialism

5.1 The Pull Towards Consequentialism

I have argued that there is a serious tension among the consequentialist theory of moral standards (CMS), the fundamental non-impersonality of many practical reasons (NIR), and the rational authority of moral requirements and prohibitions (RAMS). In the previous chapter I interpreted Williams as arguing that advocates of CMS presuppose NIR in the very articulation of consequentialist moral standards, and that such lower-order reasons appear routinely to provide sufficient or decisive reasons to perform actions identified by consequentialist moral standards as wrong. This tension puts consequentialism under tremendous pressure, pressure augmented by the many particular counter-intuitive implications of the theory. This pressure is only intensified by the 2nd Williams-inspired sharpening of the challenge to consequentialism, which suggests that the very plausibility of the claim that the impersonal standpoint is properly adopted toward a plurality of values, including certain non-impersonal moral values, undermines the consequentialist claim that the impersonal standpoint is the fundamental standpoint of moral evaluation. Not only does the consequentialist presuppose certain lower-order reasons in the very articulation of consequentialist moral standards, the most plausible account of impersonal evaluation presupposes lower-order non-impersonal moral commitments as well. Impersonal evaluation seems best understood as presupposing not only that reasons to adhere to consequentialist moral standards are merely some reasons among others that often appear to be stronger, but in addition that such higher-order consequentialist moral commitments are only some moral commitments among others that often appear to be morally decisive.

Critics and defenders nonetheless typically allow that powerful countervailing considerations draw the reflective inquirer, against her particular moral judgments, ineluctably towards consequentialism. If these countervailing theoretical grounds drive us, even in the face of this multitude of newfound obstacles, towards consequentialism, they must appear powerful indeed, sufficient to support the commitment to CMS in the face of the pressure brought to bear upon it by the appeal of RAMS and NIR. They must, in short, be forceful enough to justify proposals to bite the bullet on either RAMS or NIR rather than to reject CMS, or to accept post hoc proposals for their reconciliation. Both consequentialists and their critics recognize that these traditional considerations purport to provide just such overwhelming countervailing force. T. M. Scanlon characterizes this state of affairs nicely. Consequentialism, he argues,

is not the view which most people hold. . . . But . . . it is the view towards which they find themselves pressed when they try to give a theoretical account of their moral beliefs.[1]

Critics of consequentialism present arguments for resisting the pull of these theoretical considerations, while advocates take them to provide compelling support for CMS and set about mitigating the apparently troubling tensions among it and the other two components of the triad. These theoretical considerations are commonly recognized as sufficient, unless they are countered, to shift the burden of proof on to opponents of consequentialism.

I will argue in this chapter that the pull of many of these countervailing considerations is illusory. They do not provide a path of theoretical reflection that leads to consequentialism. That they appear to, I will argue, results from what can profitably be seen as a misappropriation of general intuitions concerning the relationship between good/bad and right/wrong as properties of action, and their misguided deployment as general intuitions concerning the relationship between good/bad as a property of states of affairs impersonally considered and right/wrong as a property of actions. It is this misappropriation that underwrites the claim that CMS provides the

---

[1] Scanlon (1982, p. 267).

most plausible interpretation of the general intuition that it is always right to do what's best. In what follows I will rehearse what I expect will be a familiar set of considerations that have been thought to tell powerfully in favor of CMS. I will argue that these considerations all depend for their apparent plausibility upon the aforementioned conflation of claims about goodness as a property of actions and goodness as a property of states of affairs considered impersonally. This leads to a conflation of the relationship between good actions and right actions with the relationship between good states of affairs impersonally considered and right actions. With this conflation in view, a return to the considerations that apparently favor consequentialism will show that their apparent support collapses.

In the next section I will lay out five interrelated considerations that have been thought to support consequentialism. In the process I will make clear the central role in these considerations played by a particular interpretation of the intuitive link between rightness and goodness, a link captured by such platitudes as that it is always right to do what's best. In Section 5.3 I will proceed to develop an alternative interpretation of the intuitive link between rightness and goodness. I will argue in Section 5.4 for the superiority of this alternative interpretation. This alternative interpretation, and certain of its implications, will be developed in Section 5.5. In Section 5.6 I will demonstrate that the apparent support for consequentialism provided by the traditional rationales collapses once the more plausible interpretation of the intuitive link between rightness and goodness is accepted. Finally, in Section 5.7 I will demonstrate that one traditional rationale for consequentialism, the impartiality rationale, is not undermined by acceptance of the more plausible interpretation. The apparent force of this remaining rationale will be clarified. This remaining rationale will be the focal point of Chapters 6 and 7.

5.2 The Traditional Considerations and the General Intuition

In this section I will present some of the considerations that appear to lead us ineluctably away from our particular considered moral judgments and towards consequentialism, and demonstrate that they rely upon a particular interpretation of the intuitive connection between rightness and goodness.

There is considerable overlap among the considerations I present; indeed, all draw in different ways upon the same interpretation of the intuitive link between rightness and goodness. Moreover, I do not claim that these considerations exhaust the case for consequentialism. Indeed, certain considerations offered in support of consequentialism, considerations that do not obviously draw upon this interpretation of the link between rightness and goodness, can only come fully into view once these other alleged sources of support are recognized as illusory.[2]

Consideration 1: CMS can seem to be a straightforward and illuminating explication of powerful general intuitions about the relationship between rightness and goodness, intuitions usefully captured by the claim that it is always right to do what's best. The theory can seem to fall out of a more rigorous formulation of this intuitive link between rightness and goodness, upon which an action is right just in case it promotes the best overall state of affairs. Right and wrong are clearly properties of actions; good, better, and best are clearly properties of states of affairs impersonally considered. If it is always right to do what's best, the temptation presents itself to unpack this as the claim that it is always right to do what will promote the best state of affairs overall. This is the first consideration in support of consequentialism, that it provides what might seem to be the obvious, indeed, the only plausible interpretation of the fundamental intuitive link between rightness and goodness.[3]

Consideration 2: It is but one of the many additional sources of the appeal of CMS that it emphasizes two distinct types of considerations that clearly do play a role in most alternative accounts of practical reason and deliberation. First, facts about what will be better or worse for me clearly count as reasons for and against different courses of action. It will be better for me if the typhoon veers South of my boat, if I don't return the lost money to

---

[2] In particular, certain arguments for factoral/normative consequentialism that reject foundational consequentialism can only come into view when the traditional considerations for foundational consequentialism are set aside. Arguments for factoral/normative but not foundational consequentialism by Brad Hooker, David Cummiskey, and Derek Parfit will be taken up in Section 8.5.

[3] I will focus here upon only one side of the consequentialist biconditional, the claim that if an action brings about the best overall state of affairs, then it is the right action to perform. Additional work would have to be done to establish, through appeal to these various considerations, the second component of the biconditional, that if it is the right action, then it brings about the best state of affairs. It is the first of these conditionals that is the target of the criticisms to follow.

the person who will use it for famine relief, if I save a rich and notoriously grateful person from the riptide, etc. Second, facts about what will be better or worse overall clearly count as reasons for and against different courses of action. It will be worse if the typhoon veers toward a populated island rather than continuing out to sea, if the famine reliever does not get her money back, and worse if I fail to pluck three swimmers from the riptide rather than the rich and grateful one (assuming I can save either the three or the one). Facts about what is better or worse for me and better or worse overall clearly provide agents with reasons for action. Moreover, it seems clear that the best thing that can happen to me and the best thing that can happen overall need not coincide. It is better for me if the typhoon veers away from my boat and towards the island, but better overall if it continues out to sea and towards my boat. It is better for me if a lifeguard saves me from the riptide instead of the three, but better overall if she saves the three instead. It may well be better for me if the tax cut package becomes law, but overall people might do far worse. Consideration of what is best for me seems particularly relevant to prudential assessments; consideration of what is best simpliciter seems particularly relevant to moral assessments. The lifeguard who saves the one rather than the three may be doing what is best for the one or best for himself, but he is not doing what is best overall, and it seems right to say that what he is doing is wrong because it fails to prevent a worse overall state of affairs. The consequentialist's claim is that these facts about what state of affairs is best overall, facts that all agree are rationally and morally relevant, exhaust the considerations that are relevant for the determination of what morality requires, at least at the foundational level. An agent is morally required to perform the action that brings about the best overall thing that can happen simpliciter.

Nor does there appear to be any great mystery about what is involved in taking up this impersonal standpoint. As the previous examples suggest, we do it all the time. To occupy such a standpoint is to take into account the relevant ends or goods such that the disvalue of a harm that the agent herself does, for example, is exhausted from such an evaluative standpoint as merely another harm that will happen. What may well be distinctively desirable for her, for example her own happiness, is from such a standpoint viewed as but one among other ends that an agent has reasons to pursue. Many have taken issue with the characterization of this standpoint as impersonal, but such a characterization does capture one of its central features: the standpoint depersonalizes the harm, allowing the agent, to the extent that she occupies this standpoint, to consider even harms to herself from an observer's standpoint—as some among other undesirable harms that will happen to someone. Hence, to have recourse to the earlier example, my death from the typhoon may well appropriately have distinctive relevance for me (not just as my death, but as a death it is particularly desirable for me to prevent), but from the impersonal standpoint such distinctive personal relevance is eliminated, and mine has value as but one among other deaths that may or may not happen. My drowning is bad, but it seems clear (even to me) that more drownings will be a worse thing to happen overall, and that the impersonal standpoint is appropriate for such determinations. The second consideration in support of consequentialism, then, is that it can seem to offer the most plausible interpretation of the important roles of appeals to the best outcome for me and the best overall outcome in the evaluation of action. The former, as we have seen, is closely linked to prudence, the latter to morality. If it is always right to do what's best, and the impersonal determination of what's best simpliciter is clearly relevant to the determination of right action, it is tempting to conclude that the search for the best in light of which we determine what's right has come to an end.

Consideration 3:   These two considerations are sometimes bolstered by a third, that the "rational way to respond to any value is to promote it."[4] To recognize something, for example well-being, as valuable, is to have reason to promote well-being. We have more reason to promote more value, and the most reason to promote the most value, for example to bring about the most well-being. If the appropriate rational response to values is their promotion, then the rational response to overall value will be to perform precisely that action identified by the consequentialist as right, the action that brings about the best overall state of affairs. If it is rational to promote overall value, and it is right to promote overall value, then *pace* NIR consequentialist rightness and reason coincide after all.

Consideration 4:   A fourth consideration is the role of the appeal to facts or states of affairs in the determination of right and wrong actions. As Philippa

---

[4] Tim Mulgan (2001, p. 14); Phillip Pettit (1993*b*, pp. 230–3). See also the discussion by David McNaughton and Piers Rawling (1991) of the consequentialist "vacuum cleaner".

Foot points out, recognition that some course of action "will not *have the best results*"[5] suggests that there is a better course of action available. Results are relevant to the determination of the right action, but the puzzle can seem to be what else besides facts about what will be better or worse overall can be relevant. It is not clear how it could ever be wrong to do what will bring about better results, and consequentialism is the view that establishes standards for the rightness of actions entirely through appeal to the best results, understood as the best overall states of affairs. The burden can seem to reside with any approach that takes something besides the goodness and badness of the consequences of an action impersonally considered to be relevant to the determination of whether or not the action is itself morally justifiable.

Consideration 5:   The final consideration is that appeals to the badness of overall states of affairs clearly provide a rationale for certain of our judgments that actions are right or wrong. The lifeguard in our previous example should save the three rather than the one because three deaths are a worse thing to happen. Moreover, such an impersonal value-based rationale appears to comprehend all other values; indeed, it can seem to take such values more seriously than other alternatives. If rights violations have intrinsic disvalue, shouldn't we minimize the extent to which they occur? Rights, autonomy, happiness, and well-being are all values the violation or diminution of which is bad, and the badness of such violations provides agents with at least some grounds for holding that an action that promotes such badness is wrong. Since this impersonal value-based rationale comprehends all other values, and in a way that can seem to take them more seriously than the alternatives, it can become hard to see what a plausible alternative candidate could look like. The temptation is strong to see the impersonal standpoint as not merely providing a rationale that comprehends all other values, but as providing a comprehensive rationale, a rationale that will serve as the basis for any other legitimate appeal to moral value.[6]

---

[5] Foot (1988, p. 227, her italics). Although there are significant differences between Foot's argument in this essay and my own, I am following her lead here in focusing upon the problematic nature of the consequentialist interpretation of the best that it is always right to do.

[6] We have already seen in Chapter 4 that there are reasons for being suspicious of such an argument.

I have now rehearsed many different considerations that might seem to lead theorizing about morality ineluctably in the direction of a consequentialist theory of moral standards (CMS), but the subsequent considerations each depend crucially upon the first. For example, once what's best in the relevant sense is interpreted as what promotes the best state of affairs impersonally considered, the general intuition that it is always right to do what's best leads ineluctably to the conclusion that morality requires agents to bring about not what is best for me but what is best overall—our second consideration falls out as a consequence. Our fourth consideration is but another consequence—nothing but the consideration of overall consequences will be relevant to the determination of right actions. Finally, our fifth consideration also seems a natural consequence of the first. If overall value is the relevant "best" in light of which right actions are properly determined, it is natural to expect that such appeals to impersonal value will provide the ultimate rationales for all claims that actions are right or wrong.

I will suggest in the next two sections that there is an alternative way of unpacking the general intuition that it is always right to do what's best, and that this interpretation, once clearly in view, is clearly more plausible that the consequentialist alternative. The clarification of this more plausible alternative allows us to see that the considerations offered in the previous section in support of consequentialism rely for their apparent plausibility upon a misinterpretation of this intuition, one which misrepresents the fundamental contours of the relationship between rightness and goodness properly understood.

5.3 Good, Better, and Best Actions

In the preceding section we saw that many of the traditional rationales for CMS draw upon a particular interpretation of the intuitive link between rightness and goodness, an interpretation upon which such intuitions are understood as linking the rightness of actions to the goodness of overall states of affairs. In this section I will articulate an alternative interpretation of the intuitive link between rightness and goodness, and in particular of the "best" that it is always right to do. This alternative candidate for the best that it is always right to do emerges naturally within the context of practical reason and deliberation. Rational agents deliberate to determine what they should believe and what they should do. Such deliberation presupposes the possibility of being mistaken. As Thomas Nagel points out in the case of practical deliberation:

> The ordinary process of deliberation, aimed at finding out what I should do, assumes the existence of an answer to this question. And in difficult cases especially it is often accompanied by the belief that I may not arrive at the correct answer. . . . In deliberation we are trying to arrive at conclusions that are correct in virtue of something independent of our arriving at them.[7]

The rational agent attempts to determine what she should do and what she should believe. Sufficiently good theoretical reasons lead such agents to the conclusion that some particular belief is true; sufficiently good practical reasons lead such agents to the conclusion that some course of action is good, better, or best. Theoretical deliberation aims at true belief, but as Gary Watson points out, one's aim in practical deliberation "is to make a commitment to a course of action by making a judgment about what is best (or good enough) to do."[8] Using David Velleman's useful terminology, Stephen Darwall suggests that just as "the formal aim of belief is to believe whatever there is good reason to believe," so too the "formal aim of action is to do whatever there is (normative) reason to do."[9] Equivalently, Darwall suggests, "we could say that the formal aims of belief and action are, respectively, to believe and act . . . as is best supported by normative reasons (and so, in this sense, as is best)."[10]

Up to this point I have restricted myself to Parfit's characterization of practical reasons as sufficient and decisive. But sufficient reasons are simply reasons that are in Watson's phrase "good enough," and an agent has decisive reasons to do something when it is the best thing to do in the circumstances, the action supported by the best reasons. Virtually every account of practical reason recognizes that practical reasons can conflict; moreover, that these conflicting reasons can differ in their "strength, weight, or force."[11] If an agent has stronger, weightier, or more forceful

---

[7] Nagel (1986, p. 149).

[8] Watson (2004b, p. 127). For an extended discussion of the nature of theoretical deliberation, see the first two chapters of John McDowell's *Mind and World* (1994) and Richard Moran's *Authority and Estrangement* (2001). For discussions of relevant analogies and disanalogies between theoretical and practical deliberation, see Scanlon (1998, ch. 1) and Watson (2004b).

[9] Darwall (2006, p. 279).   [10] Ibid.   [11] Parfit (2008, ch. 1, sec. 1).

reasons to act one way rather than another, the agent has better reasons to act that way than the other, and the first course of action is a better course of action.

Neither course of action, however, might be a good course of action to pursue in the circumstances, a course of action supported by "good enough" reasons. To have good enough reasons to act some way is simply to have what we have been characterizing as sufficient reasons to act that way. An agent might have better reasons to perform an action that harms two people than he does to perform an action that harms three, while not having good enough (sufficient) reasons to perform either action. The person who has sufficient reasons is the person who has reasons that are sufficient for her to perform such an action in the circumstances. Accounts of practical reasons also typically allow that in certain circumstances the reasons an agent has to act some way are not only good enough to act that way, but are stronger than the reasons she has to act any other way. Such an action is the action that an agent has the best reasons to perform in the circumstances, and the course of action supported by such reasons is the best available course of action. Parfit characterizes such cases in which an agent has stronger reasons to act one way than any other as cases in which the agent has decisive reasons to act that way. Thus, an agent has decisive reasons in Parfit's sense to act some way when she has the best reasons to act that way, and the action in question is the best course of action.[12]

The fundamental role of the properties "good" and "bad," "better" and "worse" and "best" within practical reason is as properties of actions and reasons for action. This is not to deny that "right" is a property of actions as well, nor that "good" ("better" and "best") is a property of states of affairs impersonally considered as well as a property of reasons and actions. It is only to point out that reason determines what it makes sense to do and to believe, and that just as good reasons for believing provide evidence for holding beliefs that we take to be true, good reasons for acting provide evidence for taking certain courses of action to be good, the best, or at least

---

[12] If an account of practical reason allows that an agent who has the best reasons to act one way may nonetheless have sufficient—good enough—reasons to act some other way, it may make sense on such an account to restrict the set of decisive reasons to cases in which the agent has the best reasons to act one way and does not have sufficient reasons to act any other way. I will follow Parfit; however, in characterizing an agent as having decisive reasons to act some way when she has the strongest reasons to act that way, i.e. when such a course of action is the best course of action available, the course of action supported by the best reasons.

better than certain others. Practical reason appeals to what we have reasons to do to determine which courses of action are better or worse, and in certain cases which one is uniquely best. We recognize often that we have better reasons for believing p than for believing q. When such evidence for p is decisive, we take ourselves to have compelling reasons to believe that p is true. We recognize that we have better reasons to do p than to do q. When such evidence for p is decisive with respect to any other q, we take p to be the best course of action available.

Consequentialists no less than their critics typically appeal to better and worse as properties of actions and reasons for action. Consider, for example, the weighing model of practical reason and justification utilized by many consequentialists.[13] Good reasons to take into account are reasons that in fact have a place on the scales of reason in the circumstances. A good reason should be given its appropriate weight. The weight appropriately given to good reasons, moreover, is understood to be rational weight, not moral weight. When there is a course of action decisively supported by the weight of relevant reasons, including the relevant non-impersonal reasons, this is the course of action that it makes sense for the agent to pursue, the best course of action available to the agent all things considered. The best course of action, when there is such a uniquely best course, is the course of action decisively supported by good reasons. The action is supported by the strongest reasons, but this is normative strength, such that the action we have the strongest reasons to pursue in the circumstances is the best course of action all things considered. Here, then, is an alternative candidate for interpreting the "best" in the our intuitions that it is always right to do what's best, an alternative upon which the "best" in question is not a property of overall states of affairs, but a property of actions. Agents should perform the action that is best supported by reasons, and to perform such an action is to do what's best.

That good and bad are properties of reasons and the actions they support (or don't) within the framework of practical reason and deliberation may seem an obvious point. But it is a point worth dwelling upon both because there is a tendency to lose sight of it in moral theory and because it plays an important role in the arguments that follow. Outside the confines of moral

---

[13] For the deployment of and discussion of such a weighing model, see Scheffler (1988, pp. 243–60) and the first several chapters of Kagan (1989).

theory, good and bad are widely and uncontroversially recognized as the fundamental evaluative properties of actions and reasons for action. Thus, Davidson characterizes incontinent action as action upon which the agent "does x intentionally" although "the agent judges that, all thing considered, it would be better to do y than to do x."[14] He is clear, moreover, that judgment that some action is better is judgment that the agent "has a better reason" for performing that action. Indeed, his principle of continence, which he holds that any rational agent must accept in applying practical reasoning, requires the agent to "perform the action judged better on the basis of all available reasons."[15] In developing these specific formulations deploying good and bad as properties of reasons and actions, Davidson is merely making explicit what is implicit in the standard characterization of the weak willed agent as knowing the better and doing the worse. Such an agent knows that there are better reasons for doing one thing, hence that it is the better of the two courses of action, but does something worse.

Virtue ethicists routinely appeal to good and bad as properties of actions. Aristotle takes it as obvious that happiness, for example, is "doing well in action," and results from engaging in the "best activities," which are "good and fine as well as pleasant."[16] Philippa Foot is clear that the ultimate goal of a virtue ethics is to yield answers to questions "about good or bad action in particular circumstances."[17] Allen Wood points out that for Kant, "to see an *action* as good is to see it as one that should be performed in consequences of a rational principle of some kind."[18] In each case goodness and badness are recognized in the first instance as properties of actions.

Our ordinary practical evaluative practices certainly suggest just such a fundamental role for evaluation of actions and the reasons for them as better and worse. We attempt to find the best thing to do in the circumstances, and attempt to determine whether there might be a better course of action than the one we are contemplating. What is my best option here? Which course of action do I have better reasons to undertake? As practical reasoners we are in the business of determining what reasons we have to do one thing rather than another. In so doing we determine better and worse courses of action, good enough courses of action, and, when such reasons are decisive, a uniquely best course of action.

---

[14] Donald Davidson (1980, p. 22).   [15] Ibid., pp. 40 and 41 respectively.
[16] Aristotle (1999, pp. 19 and 21 respectively).   [17] Foot (1988, p. 235).
[18] Allen Wood (1999, p. 55).

5.4 Good Actions and Good States of Affairs: An Interpretation of the General Intuition

We now have two alternative interpretations of the intuitive link between rightness and goodness. One links right actions to the best overall states of affairs:

(a) It is always right to do what will bring about the best overall state of affairs impersonally considered.

The other interpretation links right actions not to better and worse overall states of affairs, but to better and worse courses of action:

(b) It is always right to pursue the best course of action available to you, to do what you have the best reasons, all things considered, to do.

With these two distinct types of goodness now in view, goodness of overall states of affairs and goodness of actions, it is appropriate to return to the intuitive linkage between rightness and goodness that is reflected in the claim that it is always right to do what's best. Is this claim better understood, as the consequentialist rationales assume, as an intuition concerning the rightness of actions and the goodness of overall states of affairs, or is it more plausibly understood as an intuition concerning the rightness of actions and the goodness of actions? The stakes for the consequentialist are high. We have already seen that consequentialists, like their critics, allow that non-impersonal reasons are relevant to the determination of the best available course of action. When such non-impersonal reasons are decisive, the best course of action will presumably not be the course of action that will bring about the best overall state of affairs. If the alternative interpretation of the intuitive link between goodness and rightness is the more plausible one, and it is always right to do what it is best to do, then, since it will often not be best to do (taking into account all relevant reasons, non-impersonal and impersonal) what will bring about the best overall state of affairs, it will often be morally right not to do what will bring about the best overall state of affairs, and CMS will be undermined.[19]

---

[19] Even if rational agents merely have sufficient reasons to pursue courses of action that will not bring about the best outcome, reasons which establish not that some course of action is best, but merely that it is in Watson's sense "good enough", this will be sufficient on such an alternative

Nor, as we have seen, does consequentialism fare any better with the appeal to particular considered judgments. Indeed, consequentialism runs afoul of many particular considered judgments concerning agent-centered restrictions and agent-centered permissions. Instead it is consequentialists' appeal to deep intuitions concerning the linkage of rightness and goodness that they take to drive us on reflection away from such judgments and towards their account of moral standards. If these intuitions are better understood as capturing the relationship between rightness and goodness of actions, and the claim thus interpreted undermines rather than supports consequentialism, the traditional rationales will be undermined. I will argue in this section that goodness of actions does in fact do a better job of capturing the intuitive force of claims such as that it is always right to do what's best than does goodness of overall states of affairs.

Thomas Nagel points out that goodness of actions and goodness of overall outcomes often appear to pull apart, that although "*things* will be better, what *happens* will be better . . . I will have done something worse."[20] Critics of consequentialism often focus upon rightness and wrongness as properties of actions and goodness and badness as properties of states of affairs. But the naturalness of Nagel's characterization brings out the contrast that has been highlighted above between assessments of actions as good and assessments of overall states of affairs as good. Nagel's point is that the best course of action, as determined through appeal to reasons, frequently appears to diverge from the action that promotes the best thing that can happen overall. What we take it to be best to do in some situation, all relevant things considered, often differs from the action that brings about the best state of affairs impersonally considered. Indeed, we have seen that consequentialists themselves presuppose that reasons involving appeal to the impersonal standpoint typically figure in our practical reasoning concerning what it is best to do as only some reasons among others. We have reasons

interpretation of the claim that it is always right to do what's best to derail the consequentialist who is committed to the rational authority of his moral standards. Such an agent will often have good enough reasons—sufficiently good reasons—to pursue some course of action other than the course of action that brings about the best overall outcome. But this is just to have good enough reasons in such cases to do what consequentialist moral standards prohibit. The consequentialist claims not just that it is always right to do what's best, but that it is always wrong to do anything else. If the "best" in question is a property of actions rather than overall outcomes, a consequentialaist committed to NIR will grant at least that rational agents often have good enough reasons not to do what they identify as right, and to do what's wrong.

[20] Nagel (1986, p. 180).

that involve minimizing overall pain, for example, but we also each have partial reasons to want not to be in pain, and reasons of both sorts, both partial and impersonal, play a role in the determination of what the agent has the most compelling reasons to do in the circumstances—what it is best to do. Only considerations of the latter sort, by contrast, play a role in the determination of the best thing that can happen. Reasons involving consideration of better and worse things that can happen appear to be only some of the reasons relevant to the determination of what it is better or worse to do.

But our question concerns the relative plausibility of the two very different interpretations of our intuitions concerning rightness and goodness, interpretations in which goodness of actions and goodness of overall states of affairs offer competing alternatives. One factor that appears to support the alternative interpretation is that the consequentialism friendly interpretation clashes with so many of our deeply held particular considered judgments. The intuitive appeal of agent-centered restrictions, for example, suggests that it is sometimes wrong to do what is in the consequentialist's sense the best—what brings about the best overall state of affairs. Such an interpretation also clashes with the deep intuitive appeal of agent-centered permissions: intuitively, agents can frequently act in ways that fail to bring about the best overall outcome without having done anything wrong. The alternative interpretation, by contrast, is compatible with both permissions and restrictions. If among the good reasons are reasons to pursue the agent's own plans, projects, and commitments, then it is to be expected that in certain circumstances it will be best to do something other than what will bring about the best overall outcome. If it is always right to do what's best in this sense, then morality will permit actions that fail to bring about the best overall outcome. If other relevant non-impersonal reasons are provided by considerations of the rights and status of others, such an alternative interpretation can readily also generate agent-centered restrictions upon bringing about the best overall outcome as well. The consequentialist interpretation conflicts with such considered judgments; the alternative interpretation does not.

A consequentialist committed to the rational authority of moral requirements, moreover, would appear to be under considerable pressure to reject the interpretation of the intuitive link between rightness and goodness that supports her traditional rationales for adopting CMS, and to accept the alternative interpretation. The considerations that generate this pressure to support the alternative interpretation have already been put forward. Consequentialists, like their critics, are committed to recognizing that good, better, and best are properties of actions, not just of outcomes. Unless such consequentialists endorse the second interpretation, however, they cannot be committed to the rational authority of moral standards (RAMS). RAMS maintains that rational agents have decisive reasons to do what morality requires, and avoid what it prohibits. But unless it is always right do what it is best to do, what is supported by the best reasons, RAMS will be violated.

The considerations that generate pressure to abandon the consequentialist interpretation of the intuition that it is always right to do what's best follow with the addition of NIR. We have seen that consequentialists typically adopt accounts of practical reasons that support NIR, accounts upon which agents have some fundamentally non-impersonal reasons in light of which courses of action other than that which promotes the best overall outcome are often evaluated as good enough or even the best courses of action. Thus for such a consequentialist the best course of action will sometimes be a course of action that does not bring about the best overall outcome, but the right course of action will always be the course of action that does bring about the best overall outcome. In such cases the best thing to do will not be what the consequentialist identifies as the right course of action; indeed, the best thing to do will be morally prohibited by the consequentialist. But to be committed to RAMS is to deny that there can be such cases. The consequentialist must accept the alternative interpretation of the claim that it is always right to do what's best, but such an interpretation, conjoined with NIR and RAMS, is difficult to reconcile with the consequentialist interpretation, upon which it is always right to bring about the best overall state of affairs and wrong to do otherwise.

In addition the alternative interpretation seems to capture a deep intuitive link between morality and reason, between the course of action supported by reason—the best course of action—and what morality prohibits or permits. If an option is properly determined to be the best of those available, the option supported by the best reasons, then surely such an action will not be morally prohibited. Stephen Darwall and others have approached this deeply held intuition through our concept of blame. They take the intuition to support an even stronger result. It is not necessary to show that one has the best reasons to do what one does to show that one's action is not morally wrong, only that one has sufficient reasons to justify performing the action in question. Darwall argues that it is part of the very concept of moral blame, holding someone accountable for a moral wrong, that it makes "no sense to blame someone for doing something and then add that he had, nonetheless, sufficient reason to do it, all things considered." If an agent "can establish that he had sufficient reason to do what he did, then he will have accounted for himself, and shown thereby that blame is unwarranted."[21] The case is even clearer if the agent had not merely sufficient reasons to do p, but decisive reasons to do p rather than any other q. In such cases, the reasons aren't merely sufficient—in Watson's sense 'good enough'—but decisive, and demonstrate that p is the best available course of action. If an agent pursues such a best course of action, he is not acting wrongly, and blame is not appropriate.[22]

Interpreted in this way, the general intuition that it is always right to do what's best captures a central contour of the relationship between morality and reason. As such, it complements RAMS, which captures another central contour of the relationship between morality and reason. Specifically, whereas RAMS is a commitment concerning the rational authority of moral standards, this interpretation of the claim that it is always right to do what's best is a commitment concerning the moral authority of rational standards (MARS), a claim that what reason establishes as the best course of action will not be morally prohibited, and that acting for such reasons will not be morally blameworthy.

The consequentialist's counter-intuitive interpretation of this general intuition, upon which what's "best" is what promotes the best overall state of affairs, loses its apparent plausibility once this alternative interpretation comes into view. Given the alternatives, it seems plausible that what are best in the relevant sense are not states of affairs impersonally considered, but actions and the reasons we have for performing them. Whether or not it is always right to do what will bring about the best thing that can happen overall, it *is* always right to perform the action that the rational agent has the

---

[21] Darwall (2006, ch. 2, p. 25). See also Gibbard (1990, p. 299) and Williams (1995, p. 42).

[22] This intuitive link is also reflected in our legal practices., in which reasonable conduct is commonly seen as sufficient grounds for avoiding legal responsibility, e.g. in tort law. I might have harmed you, but if I acted reasonably I did not legally wrong you, ceteris paribus. See, for example, Arthur Ripstein (1999, pp. 6–7 and 56–60).

best reasons to perform in the circumstances, to pursue the best available course of action. Moreover, because this alternative interpretation does not lead to a consequentialist theory of moral standards, it avoids the serious theoretical obstacles, articulated in Chapters 1–3, of an interpretation that does. Such an interpretation, in addition, also avoids other counter-intuitive implications of the alternative. We have already seen that on the alternative that takes "best" to be "best overall state of affairs," the claim that it is always right to do what's best is interpreted such that (1) it is always wrong not to do what's best, and such that (2) doing what's best is always morally required. Conformity to moral standards becomes extremely confining.

But neither of these counter-intuitive implications follows from the claim that the best course of action is always right, that is, among the morally permissible courses of action. It follows neither that no other alternatives are morally permissible, nor that the best course of action is morally required. If there is a uniquely best course of action, any other course of action would be supported by less compelling reasons. But only if we were always morally required to do the best thing that we can do would such acts be morally prohibited, and such a requirement does not seem at all plausible. Moreover, if more than one course of action were supported by sufficient reasons, such an alternative interpretation could readily allow that all of these actions would be right—morally permissible acts that the agent has good enough reasons to perform—and none of them would be wrong.[23]

The intuitions linking rightness and goodness maintain their intuitive force when goodness is interpreted as a property of actions, and lose their intuitive force when it is interpreted as a property of overall states of affairs. We appear to have compelling grounds, even on the consequentialist's own terms, to endorse the alternative interpretation. But this suggests that the traditional rationales that the consequentialist relies upon to lead the reflective inquirer to a consequentialist theory of moral standards draw upon an implausible interpretation of the relationship between rightness and goodness. We have now seen that a plausible alternative interpretation is readily available. It will become apparent that the traditional rationales do not fare at all well once this plausible interpretation is brought clearly into view.

The more plausible interpretation of this general intuition, upon which it is a claim regarding the moral authority of rational standards (MARS),

---

[23] Railton discusses such features of rightness (2003, p. 238).

coupled with RAMS, which is a claim concerning the rational authority of moral standards, suggests that the proper business of a moral theory is to provide an account of moral and rational standards that provides plausible rationales for both of these intuitions (or diffuses the intuitive appeal of either or both). But the traditional considerations offered in support of consequentialism, I am suggesting, are best understood as built upon a misinterpretation of one of these commitments (MARS). This misinterpretation redirects this intuitive support towards a moral theory, consequentialism, which in turn precludes a plausible rationale for the second commitment, RAMS, even as it presupposes this very commitment.

Other traditional alternatives to consequentialism present accounts of their moral standards as distinctive good reasons, such that when the standards are morally decisive the reasons are rationally decisive as well (RAMS), and when reasons generally are decisive the moral standards will not proscribe the course of action they identify as best (MARS). They offer rationales for both RAMS and MARS. Consequentialism, by contrast, appeals to RAMS, but does so on the basis of a misinterpretation of an intuition concerning the moral authority of rational requirements (MARS) as establishing instead the moral authority of the overall evaluation of states of affairs. Such a misinterpretation of the claim concerning the moral authority of rational requirements as a claim concerning the moral authority of overall states of affairs supports an account of moral requirement that usurps the place of rational requirement. The result is a theory upon which moral authority is always moral requirement (never merely permission), and moral requirement is always rational requirement.

5.5 Alternative Moral Theories and the Alternative Interpretation

With this alternative interpretation clearly in view, traditional alternative moral theories can be seen not as ignoring or failing to anticipate the force of the consequentialist challenge, but as avoiding the misinterpretation of the intuitions concerning rightness and goodness upon which much of its appeal is based. Traditional alternatives to consequentialism, including Aristotelian, Kantian, and Hobbesian alternatives, all offer accounts of practical reason and deliberation—of the proper determination of what it is better and worse to do. Such accounts are then harnessed to articulate accounts of moral standards, and rationales for both RAMS and MARS.[24] For example, the traditional Hobbesian holds that the best course of action available to an agent is the one that most effectively secures her own preservation, appetites, utility, and/or preference satisfaction. As we saw in Chapter 3, moral standards of right and wrong, for the Hobbesian, are a set of constraints that we have decisive reasons to adopt. Agents typically have decisive reasons to avoid moral wrongdoing on such an account because standards for the determination of moral wrongness are rationally justified constraints upon the reasons we have for acting. Hence the rational authority of the Hobbesian's moral standards (RAMS) is taken to be secured. Moreover, it is always right to do what's best on such an account because the best course of action available to the Hobbesian is one which involves the adoption of moral standards as constraints upon the determination, in particular circumstances, of what it is best to do. Thus, the moral authority of Hobbesian rational standards (MARS) is taken to be secured. The Hobbesian theory, then, is a theory of the relationship of what it is best for an agent to do, properly understood, to standards of moral rightness, a theory which offers accounts of both RAMS and MARS.[25]

Such accounts also often provide a rationale for the relationship between evaluations of actions as right and as good, and the impersonal evaluation of overall states of affairs as better and worse. Kantians and Aristotelians, in particular, often provide accounts of the important but circumscribed role that appeals to impersonal evaluations of states of affairs play in the determination both of what it is best to do and of what it is right to do.[26] Philippa Foot, for example, provides a broadly Aristotelian approach upon which such impersonal evaluations play a role "within morality" in the articulation of merely some among the reasons that are relevant to the determination of better and worse, and morally permissible and impermissible, courses of

---

[24] Indeed, for both Kantians and Aristoteleans the question becomes whether, and if so to what extent, what we have been characterizing as standards for morally right action are already comprehended on such views by standards for goodness as a property of actions and reasons for action properly understood, such that the claim that it is always right to do what's best truly becomes a platitude within the context of such accounts. I have benefited from conversations with Pierre Keller and Michael Nelson on this topic.

[25] See the early chapters of Gauthier (1986).

[26] I will focus in what follows upon Foot's neo-Aristotelean account of the proper role of impersonal-involving reasons. For Tim Scanlon's neo-Kantian account of the proper role of impersonal-involving reasons, see ch. 3 of *What We Owe to Each Other*, especially section 6.

action. Her virtue-based approach recognizes benevolence as one among other virtues, and any benevolent person "must often aim at the good of others and call it 'a good thing' when for instance a far-away disaster turns out to have been less serious than was feared."[27] The benevolent person, then, recognizes some sort of requirement to promote the well-being of others that involves making impersonal assessments of well-being. Such a requirement to promote the happiness or well-being of others is an "essential part of morality," but it makes all the difference, she maintains, that "we have found this end *within* morality, and forming part of it, not standing outside it as the 'good state of affairs' by which moral action in general is to be judged."[28] Some sort of impersonally articulated requirement of beneficence will be recognized by a benevolent person, but benevolence is only one of the virtues along with justice, friendship, and many others. Each of these will involve the recognition of other relevant moral reasons by a person who possesses the relevant virtues, and many of these reasons will generate limitations upon the relevant impersonal considerations of beneficence. Within this virtue ethics framework, Foot concludes, "we have no reasons to think that whatever is done with the aim of improving the lot of other people will be morally required or even morally permissible."[29]

It is useful at this point to locate the results of these arguments within the framework of our triad of claims. We saw in Chapter 2 that the first two members of our triad, RAMS and NIR, are difficult to reconcile with CMS. But countervailing grounds for CMS have been thought to arise from its being the most plausible interpretation of the general intuition that it is always right to do what's best, an intuition that captures one of the fundamental contours of the relationship between rightness and goodness. We have now introduced an alternative interpretation of this general intuition, not as the claim that it is always right to do what will bring about the best overall state of affairs, but as the claim that it is always right to do the best that you can do, to perform the action supported by the best reasons. Unlike the consequentialist interpretation of the general intuition, this interpretation preserves its intuitive force and is not in tension with the other members of the triad. Such an interpretation of this general intuition, moreover, puts us in position to identify the nature of the misappropriation of the intuitive force of this relationship at work

---

[27] Foot (1988, p. 235).   [28] Ibid.   [29] Ibid. See also Foot (2001, pp. 10–13).

in the considerations offered in support of CMS. I will work through these considerations one by one in the next section and demonstrate that, with the alternative interpretation in place, such alleged considerations fail to support consequentialism: the traditional challenge of consequentialism collapses in the face of the challenge to consequentialism.

I have pointed out that just as theoretical deliberation aims at true belief, practical deliberation aims at good action. It is the goodness of intentions and actions that stands to practical reason and deliberation as the truth of belief stands to theoretical reason and deliberation. Reasons appealing to the impersonal good of states of affairs, like reasons appealing to the agent's own well-being, or her special obligations to others, or to consideration of the rights and autonomy of others, appear to be but one subset of the set of reasons relevant to deliberations concerning what it is best to do; indeed, only one subset of the moral subset of the set of such reasons.

If the role of goodness as a property of actions is left offstage, and goodness is treated exclusively as a property of states of affairs impersonally considered while rightness is treated as the relevant evaluative property of actions, then intuitions concerning rightness of actions and goodness of states of affairs impersonally considered will be hopelessly skewed. In particular, our various intuitions concerning the relationship of rightness and goodness as properties of actions will be shifted onto the relationship between rightness as a property of actions and the only goodness recognized—goodness as a property of overall states of affairs. I will argue in the next section that many of the considerations traditionally offered in support of consequentialism depend for their apparent force upon just such a skewing. The intuitive relationship between rightness and goodness as properties of actions is subtly transposed into the consequentialist relationship between rightness of actions and the goodness of states of affairs impersonally considered, and we are driven ineluctably towards the view that it is always right to do what brings about the best available state of affairs impersonally considered. The view, coupled with RAMS, leads to the view that agents are always rationally required to do what brings about the best overall state of affairs.

For contemporary opponents of consequentialism the tendency to accept the restriction of rightness to actions and goodness to states of affairs considered impersonally has equally problematic results. Often such opponents recognize as the only relevant appeal to the "best" that involved in the impersonal evaluation of states of affairs, and fail to countenance a role for "best" in the evaluation of actions and reasons for action. As a result they find themselves flying in the face of general intuitions concerning rightness and goodness, maintaining instead that it is often wrong to do what's best.[30] With the proper role of goodness as a property of actions recognized, the critic of consequentialism has an obvious alternative. Of course it is always right to do what's best, since it is always right to perform the action that is the best of those available. But of course it will often not be the best thing to do to produce the best state of affairs impersonally considered, since only some of the reasons relevant to determining the best available course of action involve such impersonal considerations of better and worse overall states of affairs. When other reasons are sufficient, it will not be better all things considered to act in the way suggested by these impersonal involving considerations taken alone. Full consideration of my own well-being, special obligations of mine, the rights of others, etc. in addition to the relevant impersonal involving considerations will result in its often being worse to do what will promote some better overall state of affairs; indeed, perhaps in its sometimes being morally wrong to perform such an action.

My suggestion, then, is that the considerations that appear to lead us ineluctably to consequentialism have the apparent force that they do precisely through eliding the role of good and bad as properties of actions from the practical landscape, and treating the features of the relationship of rightness of actions and goodness of actions as though they are features of the relationship between rightness as a property of actions and goodness as a property of states of affairs impersonally considered. Such a misappropriation, once it is allowed, leads ineluctably to consequentialism, and renders all alternatives seemingly at odds with our deepest moral intuitions concerning rightness, reasonableness, and goodness. In the next section I will show this misappropriation at work in the other considerations offered in support of consequentialism. Once the more plausible interpretation of our claim as linking rightness and goodness is introduced, the traditional rationales for the move to consequentialism lose their force.

---

[30] Barbara Herman offers a similar diagnosis in "Leaving Deontology Behind," *The Practice of Moral Judgment* (1993).

5.6 Collapse of the Traditional Rationales

I have now laid out many traditional rationales for consequentialism, demonstrated that they depend upon a particular interpretation of the intuitive linkage of rightness and goodness, introduced an alternative to this interpretation, and demonstrated that even by the consequentialist's own lights it is this latter interpretation, upon which it is goodness and rightness of actions that are intuitively linked, that is more plausible. I will demonstrate in this section that once this alternative is accepted, the traditional rationales for consequentialism that were introduced in Section 5.2 lose much if not all of their force.

Consideration 1: We have already seen that the first consideration, that it is always right to do what's best, provides no support for consequentialism. Support is only generated if this general intuition is most plausibly interpreted as the claim that it is always right to do what will promote the best overall state of affairs. But there appears to be a more plausible interpretation of this general intuition as relating the right action to the best course of action available to an agent, the course of action supported by the best reasons all things considered. This latter interpretation will only lead to consequentialism if the best action, the action that an agent has the best reasons to perform, is always the action that will promote the best overall state of affairs. But reasons appealing to the impersonal standpoint for their articulation appear to be at most some of the reasons relevant to the determination of what it is best to do; indeed, consequentialism seems to presuppose that this is the case. This suggests that what it is best to do will often not be the action that promotes the best overall state of affairs. If it is always right to do what it is best to do, then it is right in such cases not to bring about the best overall consequences, and the consequentialist theory of moral requirement must be abandoned.

Consideration 2: The second consideration suggests that much as prudence is related to determinations of the best thing that can happen for me, morality—rightness—is related to determinations of the best thing that can happen simpliciter. Our alternative interpretation of the general intuition suggests what is right about this consideration, that rightness has a distinctive relationship to determinations of the best simpliciter. But it also suggests where this consideration goes wrong. The general intuition does not relate rightness to the best overall state of affairs, but to the best course of action all things considered. We have already seen that consequentialists and others who sympathize with central features of consequentialist moral theory recognize the independent rational significance at the foundational level of non-impersonal reasons, including partial considerations of what is better or worse for the agent in question. Non-impersonal considerations involving evaluation of better and worse things that can happen to me are relevant, in addition to impersonal considerations of better and worse things that can happen overall, in the determination of what it is best for me to do. But if it is the best course of action that it is always right to pursue, then only an illicit swapping out of "best" as a property of actions with "best" as a property of states of affairs impersonally considered creates the misguided impression that it is these evaluations of overall states of affairs which, contrary to intuition and in the face of daunting theoretical obstacles, have the requisite intuitive link to right action.

Consideration 3:   The third consideration offered in support of the consequentialist theory of moral requirement turns on the claim that the rational way to respond to any value is promotion. If we accept the consequentialist interpretation of our general intuition, upon which it claims that it is always right to do what promotes the best overall state of affairs, then values will be relevant to the moral evaluation of actions only insofar as they figure in the determination of the best overall thing that can happen. The appropriate moral response to impersonal values is promotion. But once the more plausible interpretation relating rightness of actions to goodness of actions comes into view, the plausibility of the claim that the rational response to any value is promotion is undermined. Indeed, it is clear that promotion is not the rational response to either of the values in question. It is the best action that is the right action to perform, and the rational response to the determination that some action is the best available to me is not to promote that course of action but to perform it. Goodness of actions is not a value that it is rational to respond to by promotion at all. The same is true for rightness itself: the rational response to the determination that an action available to me is right is not to promote such an action but to perform it.[31] The general intuition, properly understood, relates evaluations of actions as right to evaluations of actions as good, and in neither case is the proper response to such evaluations one of promotion. If the general intuition is misinterpreted as relating right actions to the best overall states of affairs, the result will be a tendency to maintain that, despite appearances, rightness fundamentally concerns states of affairs to be promoted rather than actions to be performed. Such an interpretation, however, is not plausible in light of the alternative, and the alternative relates moral and non-moral evaluations of actions, evaluations for which the rational response is not promotion of a state of affairs, but performance of an action.[32]

Of course it will always be better to do what will prevent the worse outcome impersonally considered from occurring all other things being equal, just as it will be better to do what will prevent the worse outcome *for me* from occurring all other things being equal. But other things would rarely seem to be equal. Such reasons that involve considerations of the best outcome for me and the best outcome overall are themselves often in conflict with each other, and are only some among the reasons that everyday practical reason and deliberation suggests are relevant to the determination of what it is both right and best to do.[33]

---

[31] This argument will be developed considerably in Chapters 7 and 8. In Chapter 7 I will take up Nagel's characterization of practical reasons in terms of states of affairs to be promoted (rather than in terms of actions to be performed), and in Chapter 8 I will take up Parfit's characterization of desires as attitudes towards events/outcomes to be promoted.

[32] For additional arguments against the claim that the rational response to value is promotion see Scanlon (1998, ch. 2), Rahul Kumar, particularly (1999, pp. 278–80), and Gerald Gaus (1990, pp. 136–40).

[33] Keeping in view the fundamental role of rightness and goodness in the evaluation of actions to be performed suggests where Philip Pettit's (2000) recent arguments against non-consequentialist alternatives go awry. Pettit often appeals to this natural characterization of rightness and wrongness as properties of actions: "If we think that it is right for one agent in one circumstance to act in a certain way, but wrong for another, then we commit ourselves to there being some further descriptive difference between the two cases" (2000, p. 179). But he shifts from this talk of rightness as a property of actions to rightness as a property of "certain patterns" that "are to be instantiated in the agent's behaviour" (ibid., p. 175). Although it is extremely plausible, as we have seen, to maintain that acts are right even though the overall realization of certain patterns is not promoted, the claim comes to seem counter-intuitive if it is glossed, following Pettit, as equivalent to a claim that certain patterns are to be instantiated in the agent's behavior even if the overall realization of these very same patterns is not promoted. If rightness is understood as a non-problematically universalizable property of actions to be performed, not of patterns the instantiation of which is to be promoted, the apparent difficulties that Pettit raises for the non-consequentialist do not arise.

Consideration 4:   The fourth consideration is that every view recognizes states of affairs impersonally considered as relevant to the determination of right actions, but it is not clear what else could be relevant. To include something else besides facts relevant to the impersonal determination of the best overall states of affairs, it can seem, is to allow that it is wrong to do what promotes the best overall result, but how can it not be right to do what's best? The response suggested by our alternative interpretation of the general intuition is that appeal to such a consideration involves a slide—from the implausible claim that it is sometimes not right to do what's best, to the quite plausible claim that it is sometimes not right to do what brings about the best overall state of affairs impersonally considered. On the consequentialist interpretation, the best is the best overall state of affairs; on the alternative interpretation, the best is just the best course of action. The result of practical deliberation is action, and the best action is supported by decisive reasons. Such an interpretation of the general intuition can readily allow that it is always right to do what's best, that what's best cannot be morally prohibited. But if what's best in the relevant sense is the action identified by practical reason as best, there is no reason to expect that the best action will always, or even frequently, be the action that promotes the best overall consequences impersonally considered. Indeed, we saw in the previous chapter that traditional consequentialism presupposes that this is not the case. Evidence that an action is the best available to me is that I have decisive reasons to perform it. The best result of practical deliberation is the action supported by such decisive reasons. If this is not the action that promotes the best outcome impersonally considered, promoting the best overall state of affairs impersonally considered in such a case will not be the best course of action available to me, hence will not be in the relevant sense the best result of practical deliberation. The alternative interpretation suggests that the best thing to do, the action identified as best as the result of practical deliberation, will often not be the promotion of the best overall state of affairs.

Such an interpretation also opens the space for a sense in which the action that will promote the best overall state of affairs is rejected through appeal to the relevant facts or states of affairs.[34] Among the facts that often

---

[34] On this point see also Foot (1988). This view is further elaborated in the Chapter 7 discussion of Nagel and the discussion of Parfit's arguments in Chapter 8.

seem relevant in determining the best course of action, for example, are (1) that certain courses of action would result in more pain for me, and (2) that certain courses of action would result in more pain happening overall. Similarly, among the facts that seem relevant are (3) that I would have to harm someone, and (4) that more harms will be done. In each case one of the apparently relevant facts is impersonally relevant and the other is not. To limit the morally relevant facts to (2) and (4), as the consequentialist proposes, is the practical equivalent of limiting the relevant facts that can be appealed to in theoretical deliberation to those accessible from the scientific standpoint/absolute conception. The point isn't that the latter is not a viable view, it is that it is a very controversial view about which facts we are limited to in theoretical deliberation, a view that can plausibly be thought to deprive us of relevant considerations. The same is true of limitation only to the facts that are relevant from the impersonal standpoint. Under the guise of insistence upon taking into account all of the relevant facts, such an approach systematically eliminates from the determination of the right course of action entire classes of the facts that even the consequentialist typically allows are relevant to the determination of the best course of action. But if it is always right to do what it is best to do, such elimination of non-impersonally relevant facts cannot but be mistaken.

When our rational deliberations lead us to reject a course of action because it will unacceptably undermine our well-being, or will involve treating others unfairly, or will require us to lie or do harm, we cite facts—that I will have to lie or do harm, that my well-being will be undermined—that we take to provide us with non-impersonal reasons to avoid the action in question. Citing such relevant facts ("but that would require me to lie"; "but that would cripple me financially") is thus invoking reasons not to do what will promote the best overall state off affairs. To cite a fact as evidence for believing is to cite a state of affairs that counts in favor of the belief in question, and to cite a fact as relevant to acting is to cite a state of affairs that counts in favor of pursuing some course of action. In light of all such relevant facts, it will in certain cases not be best to do what will bring about the best impersonal results.

Every alternative to consequentialism appeals in this sense to facts/states of affairs as reasons, and appropriately so. The Kantian rejects some course of action because it would require him to lie or harm someone, and such a fact, that it would require him to lie or harm someone, counts decisively against the proposed course of action. The consequentialist is not the only moral theorist who appeals to facts as counting for or against courses of action; rather, she is the only moral theorist who counter-intuitively restricts the relevant facts/states of affairs to those that are relevant from an impersonal standpoint. When the Aristotelian refuses to betray a friend, and the Kantian refuses to break a promise, and the Hobbesian refuses to appropriate the resources of another, each can cite the facts that she takes to provide reasons for taking the action in question to be wrong. Limitation to only impersonally relevant facts will result in limitation to actions promoting impersonally relevant outcomes. But other views appeal both to such impersonally relevant facts and to other facts the relevance of which is non-impersonal. That I would have to lie is a fact that counts non-impersonally on such views against the rightness of a proposed course of action, but the consequentialist can only count its relevance as a lying that will happen, hence, from the Kantian's standpoint, cannot appreciate why such facts often provide decisive reasons for the agent not to perform the action in question. My lying is a bad thing to happen, but it is an even worse thing to do, since its badness as a thing for me to do is not fully captured by its impersonal badness as a thing that will happen. That a course of action will involve my lying is a good reason not to pursue it, but this is just to say that the fact that it is *my* lying is relevant in addition to the fact that it is *a* lying. Interpreting our general intuition as the claim that it is always right to do what brings about the best overall consequences effectively limits us to the consideration of impersonally relevant facts (e.g. that something is a lying). But the alternative interpretation suggests that this is a shortcoming of the consequentialist view of the facts/states of affairs that are morally relevant to the determination of right and wrong, good and bad actions.

5.7 The Fifth Consideration: Two Types of Value-based Rationale

This brings us to the fifth consideration that can seem to push moral theory ineluctably towards consequentialism. This consideration, recall, is that a moral theory should provide a rationale for particular judgments that actions are right and wrong, and for the particular reasons offered in support of such judgments. Appeals to the impersonal badness of outcomes clearly do provide rationales for at least certain of our moral judgments. Moreover, such an impersonal rationale appears to comprehend other values, and to do so in a way that might seem to take such other values more seriously than the alternatives. Thus, the impersonal standpoint can comprehend rights as intrinsically valuable, and purports to take such rights more seriously than the alternatives: if rights are intrinsically valuable, shouldn't we minimize the extent to which such rights violations happen overall?

Recourse to an impersonal rationale does seem inevitable once the general intuition that it is always right to do what's best is interpreted as the claim that it is always right to do what promotes the best overall state of affairs. On such an interpretation the rationale for any claim that an action is the right action to perform will be provided, whether directly or indirectly, through the appeal to impersonal value. That an action on my part will violate Smith's rights can establish that it is wrong, but on such an interpretation this is only because such a violation of Smith's rights is a bad thing to happen, and it is only wrong if this bad thing to happen is not a consequence of the action that brings about the best overall consequences (for example, an action that prevents two rights violations by others from happening).

The alternative interpretation of our general intuition, however, provides an alternative appeal to value in which the rationale for the rightness of actions can be based, an appeal not to the best state of affairs impersonally considered, but to good and bad, better and worse understood as properties of reasons and the courses of action they support. Hobbes and Kant offer value-based rationales of just this sort, rationales that are based in appeals to the goodness and badness of actions and reasons for performing them.

Rationales for moral rightness of actions based in the value of actions and reasons for action are dictated if the "best" in the general intuition that it is always right to do what's best is interpreted as appealing to the best course of action, the one supported by the best reasons. Rationales for moral rightness of actions based in the impersonal value of states of affairs are dictated if best is interpreted as what promotes the best overall state of affairs. Each in a sense comprehends the other. The appeal to the rationale based in the goodness of reasons comprehends determinations of impersonal value to the extent that the rational agent has good reasons involving such determinations. The appeal to the rationale based in the goodness of overall states of affairs comprehends all good reasons because it is a higher-order standpoint that is taken up towards what rational agents' good reasons reveal that they value.

With our alternative interpretation in view, however, there appear to be compelling reasons to hold that an adequate value-based rationale for right action will be based in an appeal to goodness as a property of actions and the reasons for them rather than in an appeal to goodness as a property of states of affairs impersonally considered. It has already been shown that the former provides a better interpretation of general intuitions concerning the relationship of rightness to goodness. It is always right to do the best that we can do (what is supported by the best reasons), not to promote the best thing that can happen overall. The impersonal value-based rationale for right actions is based in an implausible interpretation of the general intuitions linking rightness and goodness. Coupled with the rational authority of moral standards, such an interpretation usurps the very rational standpoints of agents that it presupposes. As a result, it is precluded from recognizing the full range of good reasons that are relevant to practical reason and deliberation concerning what it is right and best to do. A plausible strategy for articulating a value-based rationale for the rightness of actions that can account for the rational authority of moral standards would appear to be one that appeals to the distinctive good reasons involved in the determination that actions are not just worse, but morally wrong, and demonstrates the decisiveness of such reasons, qua reasons, whenever they are decisive qua moral standards for right and wrong action.

Even if it is granted, for the sake of argument, that appeal to the best overall state of affairs provides an ultimate rationale for right action, a rationale is still necessary for taking there to be reasons to perform right actions thus understood. In short, a rationale based in the appeal to the goodness of reasons and actions is necessary to account for the rational authority of any rationale for right actions that is based in the appeal to impersonal value of states of affairs. A rationale for rightness through appeal to goodness of overall states of affairs asserts the *moral* authority of goodness as a property of states of affairs impersonally considered in the determination of the moral rightness of actions. But it does nothing to establish the *rational* authority of such appeals to overall states of affairs, or, by extension, of rightness and wrongness. To establish such rational authority, it would be necessary to provide a rationale that bases the appeal to better and worse states of affairs impersonally considered in the appeal to better and worse reasons for acting. Consequentialists who maintain RAMS, then, are not avoiding appeal to a rationale that appeals to better and worse reasons and courses of action, they are merely locating the place for such a rationale at a different point in their theory. Moreover, we have seen in the previous two chapters that the consequentialist appears to be committed to an account of good reasons and actions that is ill suited to the task of providing such a plausible rationale.

The consequentialist appeals to the impersonal, value-based rationale to reject any considerations concerning moral rightness and wrongness that cannot be provided with such a rationale. This leads, via commitment to the rational authority of moral standards, to rejection of any ultimate considerations of apparently good reasons that cannot be provided with an impersonal, value-based rationale. But for the appeal to an impersonal, value-based rationale to have rational authority, it must itself be based in appeal to good, better, and best reasons and actions. Such an impersonal value-based rationale only has rational authority to the extent that a rationale based in the goodness and badness of reasons for action can be provided for taking such impersonal considerations into account. Only to the extent that such an impersonal, value-based rationale is involved in the articulation of certain of the good reasons relevant to the determination of what it is good and right to do will the impersonal value-based rationale have rational authority. To the extent that other good non–impersonal reasons are relevant to the determination of what it is good and right to do, the rational authority of appeals to impersonal value will also be limited. Any claim that it is the appeal to the good states of affairs impersonally considered that delimits acceptable reasons, rather than the appeal to good reasons that delimits the relevance of appeals to the goodness of states of affairs impersonally considered, would appear to be but one more product of the misinterpretation of the general intuition that it is always right to do what's best.

These five traditional considerations all lose their intuitive force in the face of the more plausible interpretation of the general intuition that it is always right to do what's best as a claim about what it is best to *do*, not about the best thing that can happen. But another prominent consideration remains. By virtually all accounts moral evaluation is impartial evaluation,

evaluation that manifests a robust form of equal concern for all persons. The impersonal standpoint would appear to be an impartial standpoint, an evaluative standpoint that manifests a form of equal concern for persons in the ranking of states of affairs as better or worse. Derek Parfit has rightly pointed out that impartiality is a concept that allows for many different conceptions.[35] The impersonal conception of impartiality might thus merely be one among other alternative conceptions of impartiality. But if the impersonal conception that is involved in ranking overall states of affairs from better to worse, a conception clearly relevant to a moral evaluation of actions, is not the central conception involved in the moral evaluation of actions, what is the central conception of impartiality at work in this latter case? And if impersonality is the fundamental conception of impartiality for a moral evaluation of actions, how can consequentialism be avoided? Arguments that there is no rationale for moral judgments other than the impersonal value-based rationale can be understood as arguments that despite the debilitating challenges that have been raised to consequentialism, there is no viable alternative to impersonality as the fundamental conception of impartiality relevant to the moral evaluation of actions. Moral evaluation of actions is impartial, on this view, because it is based in the impartial evaluation of states of affairs as better and worse. It is to such impartiality arguments that I will now turn. In the next chapter I will argue that these very arguments purporting to demonstrate that there can be no such alternative conception of impartiality appropriate to the moral evaluation of actions inadvertently provide the outlines for just such an alternative conception, an interpersonal conception that is central to the impartial evaluation of actions as right and wrong much as the impersonal conception is central to the impartial evaluation of actions as good and bad overall.

[35] See, e.g., Parfit (2004, sec. 8).

6

From Impersonality to Interpersonality: Alternative Conceptions of Impartiality

6.1 Introduction

The arguments in Chapter 4 helped to refine two challenges to consequentialism. Each rational agent has good non-impersonal reasons to maintain her commitments to friends and causes, pursue her own tastes and interests, etc. These and other good non-impersonal reasons that persons have are taken into account in the impersonal determination of the best overall state of affairs, and such impersonal considerations, in turn, appear to be involved in the full articulation of certain good higher-order reasons. The first challenge is that the good non-impersonal reasons each person has, reasons presupposed in the very determination of the best overall state of affairs, are often sufficient—good enough—for agents to pursue courses of action that do not bring about the best overall state of affairs. If the right action is the action that brings about the best overall state of affairs, this suggests that agents often have sufficient reasons not to do what CMS identifies as right, and to do what is wrong. But such a result is difficult to reconcile to the rational authority of moral requirements (RAMS), authority insisted upon even by most consequentialists themselves. Such considerations seem sufficient, absent compelling countervailing reasons, to challenge the plausibility of CMS. Consequentialists take there to be such countervailing considerations in support of their theory of moral standards, but in Chapter 5 it became apparent that many of these traditional considerations are best understood as relying upon a misappropriation of the claim that it is always right to do what's best. Such a claim, properly understood, relates right actions to good actions and reasons for action. The traditional considerations offered in support of consequentialism misappropriate this general intuition relating rightness and goodness of actions, presenting it instead as a claim linking rightness of actions and goodness of overall states of affairs. With such a misappropriation exposed, the force of these traditional rationales for CMS is undermined.

The second challenge, which will be developed more fully in the next section, arises from the recognition that impersonal evaluation adopts a higher-order standpoint towards what rational persons recognize as valuable; not just their own pleasure and well-being, but in addition rights, autonomy, justice, fairness, loyalty, solidarity/friendship, and/or respect for persons as ends in themselves. It is a better overall state of affairs in which well-being is enhanced, but it is also better overall if rights violations are minimized, treatment of people as ends in themselves is maximized, and friendship and autonomy are promoted. But lower-order reasons are non-impersonal reasons; moreover, some of them appear to be non-impersonal moral reasons, and to have such non-impersonal moral reasons is to recognize non-impersonal moral values. To recognize such non-impersonal moral values as among the appropriate values to incorporate into impersonal evaluations of outcomes is to presuppose non-impersonal rationales for such fundamental non-impersonal reasons and values, or at least that there are non-impersonal moral values that require no such rationales. This is to presuppose that the impersonal standpoint is not the moral standpoint, but at most what ordinary morality takes it to be—a standpoint that is involved in articulating some relevant moral reasons among others. Moreover, this suggests that a moral rationale based in the appeal to impersonal value is a rationale that captures only some relevant moral reasons among others, others that may conflict with relevant impersonal moral considerations. Impersonal evaluation articulates a higher-order moral reason that comprehends other lower-order moral reasons in its object, but for this very reason seems to be an implausible candidate for providing comprehensive moral reasons. To recognize the relevance of such non-impersonal moral values in the evaluation of overall states of affairs is to recognize just the sorts of non-impersonal moral reasons that ordinary morality suggests are often sufficient to establish the wrongness of acting to bring about the best overall state of affairs.[1]

After sharpening this challenge in the next section, I will take up arguments by Samuel Scheffler that unlike impersonal moral values, non-impersonal moral values cannot be provided with a plausible rationale. I will demonstrate both that a consequentialism of rights must presuppose that they can be provided with such a rationale, and in addition that Scheffler's argument against any such rationale for non-impersonal moral values inadvertently provides the outlines of just such a rationale. I will demonstrate that this rationale, in turn, provides a response to the final consideration that has been taken to support foundational consequentialism—the appeal to the impartiality of morality. Morality demands impartial concern for others. The impersonal standpoint can be understood as involving a form of impartial concern in the ranking of states of affairs. If this impartial standpoint appropriate for ranking states of affairs does not capture the impartiality appropriate for evaluating actions as right or wrong, there must be a distinctive conception of impartiality appropriate to the evaluation of actions. Unless such an alternative conception of impartiality can be articulated, and the outlines of a rationale for non-impersonal values provided, no response will have been provided to consequentialist claims that the impartiality central to the evaluation of actions as right and wrong *is* the impartiality of impersonal rankings of overall states of affairs (and that there is no rationale for any alternative conception of impartiality). By the end of this chapter; however, the outlines of just such an alternative conception of impartiality will emerge together with the outlines of a rationale for its adoption. This interpersonal conception of impartiality, in contrast with the impersonal conception, is in the first instance appropriate for the evaluation of actions (rather than overall states of affairs). I will argue in Chapter 7, moreover, that it avoids the structural obstacles to accounting for the rational authority of moral requirements that confront accounts based in the impersonal conception.

[1] The phrase "moral reasons" is being used here and in the discussions to follow in the sense identified by Kagan, a sense that does not presuppose the rational authority simpliciter of reasons that are introduced as relative to some particular (in this case the moral) standpoint or point of view. See the discussion in Section 3.4.

6.2 Consequentialism of Rights

It will help sharpen this second challenge to focus upon one particular class of lower-order intrinsic values—rights.[2] Until recently consequentialists have defended the value of rights, when they defended it at all, only instrumentally. Defenders of the intrinsic value of rights were opponents of consequentialism. Robert Nozick's off-hand sketch of a "utilitarianism of rights"[3] ushered in a dramatic transformation of this landscape. Much of the debate between consequentialist sympathizers and their critics has shifted from the question of whether or not to recognize rights as intrinsically valuable to a debate concerning how the intrinsic value of rights is appropriately recognized. In particular, sympathizers with various aspects of consequentialism have maintained that even if rights are intrinsically valuable, morality will require (or at least permit) agents to bring about the state of affairs that minimizes the violation of rights overall, even if this involves the violation of particular rights of particular agents. Rights can seem to be but one more value to be thrown into the consequentialists' impersonal calculus.[4] Such a stance towards rights purports to take them more seriously than more traditional accounts. Indeed, an air of paradox can seem to attach to any view which claims that rights are intrinsically valuable, yet takes agents to be morally constrained from acting in ways that can prevent more rights from being violated.[5] Defenders of more traditional, common sense approaches to rights, upon which rights also constrain what can be done in pursuit of the goal of minimizing rights violations, have struggled to provide a rationale for their view. Such a rationale must, it seems, be more plausible than that offered by the consequentialist of rights, and must be able to dispel the air of paradox surrounding any view that does not aim to minimize their violation. This argument in the case of rights is merely one instance of a pervasive general strategy harnessed by recent

---

[2] The arguments in this section develop work that has already appeared in Section 5 of my essay "Does Consequentialism Make Too Many Demands, or None at All?" (Hurley 2006).

[3] Nozick (1974, pp. 28–33).

[4] For representative treatments of this debate concerning consequentialism of rights see Samuel Scheffler (1982, ch. 4), Shelly Kagan (1989, pp. 24–32), Derek Parfit (1984, ch. 4), David Cummiskey (1996, chs 5 and 8), Jeffrey Brand-Ballard (2004), Frances Kamm (1996, chs 9 and 10), Stephen Darwall (1986), and Thomas Nagel (2002, pp. 31–52).

[5] Scheffler (1982, ch. 4) and Nagel (2002, pp. 34–7) characterize this air of paradox.

consequentialists for shifting the burden of proof on to their opponents, a strategy which concedes that rights, autonomy, fairness, and/or respect for persons as ends in themselves may well be intrinsically valuable, but contends that impersonal consideration of these very values provides decisive moral reasons whenever they conflict with other moral considerations. On such views proper reflection on moral values such as rights, fairness, and respect for persons as ends is taken to result in a moral requirement to bring about the state of affairs that promotes such values overall.

It is certainly important for any advocate of the intrinsic value of rights to provide such values with a plausible rationale. But it is not necessary to produce such a rationale in order to dispel the apparent air of paradox surrounding non-consequentialist accounts of rights. The reason is that the consequentialist of rights must also presuppose that there is some such non-impersonal rationale in order for rights to be available for impersonal consideration (or, alternatively, must allow that no such rationale is necessary in order to appeal to such values). The demonstration that the consequentialist of rights must presuppose a non-impersonal rationale for rights dissipates the apparent air of paradox surrounding non-consequentialist accounts of rights. Moreover, it provides grounds for concluding that the air of paradox at work in this debate, properly understood, clings instead to the consequentialist of rights.

That the consequentialist of rights must presuppose a non-impersonal rationale for rights can be seen by developing the contrast between consequentialism of rights and classical utilitarian consequentialism. For classical utilitarian consequentialists such as Bentham and Mill, moral standards result from adopting the impersonal standpoint towards whatever rational agents are properly recognized as having lower-order reasons to value. Such consequentialists are monists rather than pluralists, maintaining that there is only one ultimate non-moral, non-impersonal value that each agent has decisive reasons to pursue, for example that agent's own pleasure, happiness, or well-being. The impersonal standpoint from which right actions are determined thus takes into account only this one non-moral end from an impersonal standpoint. The rational action aims at an agent's own pleasure or happiness; the right action promotes overall pleasure or happiness.[6] Her own happiness is a partial end that each rational agent has, an end that can be taken up along with the partial ends of all other rational agents from the impersonal standpoint. The view generates moral standards by adopting an impersonal standpoint towards what agents have partial reasons to value. Thus, for Mill it is the agent's own happiness that she has reasons to value, and moral standards result from adopting the impersonal standpoint towards what reason reveals as valuable.[7] The right action maximizes overall happiness. Such a classical utilitarian approach, despite its many drawbacks, does at least supply a rationale for the counter-intuitive claim that impersonal considerations are morally decisive: Impersonal considerations are morally decisive because the impersonal standpoint *is* the moral standpoint. Moral standards result from adopting the impersonal standpoint towards what is intrinsically valuable, hence impersonal consideration of values is morally decisive consideration of values. The agents have partial reasons to value their own happiness or well-being, for example, or the satisfaction of their own preference, and the impersonal standpoint is adopted towards what agents have such decisive partial reasons to value.

Such monistic accounts that recognize practical reason as aiming to realize one ultimate non-moral value have been rejected as impoverished by most contemporary consequentialists. They reject monism,[8] and they typically recognize a plurality of intrinsic values towards which it is appropriate to adopt the impersonal standpoint. Some of these values appear to be distinctively moral.[9] This is to adopt an impartial standpoint, the impersonal standpoint, towards values that, qua moral, are taken to be impartial. The consequentialist of rights, in particular, adopts the impersonal standpoint towards intrinsic values that are themselves distinctively *moral* values. To

---

[6] Recall, however, Williams' argument that non-impersonal moral values can be smuggled in even on accounts with this structure in the form of certain of the projects that flow from the agent's commitments.

[7] J. S. Mill (2001, chs 2 and 4). For an insightful discussion of these aspects of Mill's account see Geoffrey Sayre-McCord (2001).

[8] See, e.g., Railton (1988, pp. 108–10, 2003, pp. 264–7), Scheffler's elaboration of "pluralistic lexical consequentialism" (1982, ch. 2), and Kagan (1989, pp. 6–7).

[9] Scheffler's characterization of his pluralistic lexical consequentialism (1982, ch. 2) in terms of Rawls' list of primary good, a list that includes among such goods rights and liberties, suggests a commitment to such distinctly moral values among those to be promoted overall. See also Railton's list of goods (1988, pp. 109–10), and the arguments in Chapter 3 that certain of these goods are best understood as distinctly moral goods. See also Cummiskey (1996), which includes distinctly Kantian moral values among those to be viewed by the consequentialist from the impersonal standpoint.

recognize the intrinsic value of rights is to recognize the fundamental lower-order moral reasons that agents have not to interfere (at least) with others, reasons that support moral claims by each agent not to be interfered with. To recognize the moral reasons one has to promote the recognition of such lower-order moral claims, and to promote the conditions for acting on such lower-order moral reasons, is to recognize the non-impersonal moral value of such lower-order moral claims. It is overall recognition of these lower-order moral claims, and actions in accordance with such lower-order moral reasons, that is to be promoted. But this is to recognize the legitimacy of non-impersonal moral claims that would appear routinely to conflict with the higher-order moral reasons agents might have to promote their overall recognition. Because they are not impersonal values, but are (qua moral) impartial values, such impersonal recognition of rights appears to presuppose an alternative conception of impartiality that is involved in moral valuation. On such an account morality cannot be the output of the adoption of the impersonal standpoint towards what is valuable, because lower-order moral (hence impartial) reasons and claims, reasons that can conflict with whatever higher-order moral reasons there are to promote the recognition of such claims overall, are already present among the inputs to the impersonal standpoint.

What can the source of a rationale for these intrinsic moral values be? It cannot be found through recourse to the impersonal standpoint—rights are lower-order moral inputs into this higher-order standpoint towards what persons value, not higher-order reasons that are articulated through appeal to this standpoint. Nor will such a rationale for the intrinsic value of rights emerge from the relevant non-moral partial considerations of individual rational agents. Values such as rights and respect for persons as ends are manifested as moral constraints upon acting on such partial reasons, and it seems unlikely, pace Hobbes, that a rationale for rights as intrinsically valuable can arise from such considerations upon which they function as independent constraints. To appeal to such intrinsic moral values is to presuppose a rationale for such impartial values from a source other than the impersonal or partial standpoint. Of course the impersonal standpoint can then be taken up towards such non-impersonal moral values. But the impersonal standpoint can no longer exhaust the standpoint of morality for the consequentialist of rights, since appeal to non-impersonal moral values such as rights presupposes a non-impersonal rationale for non-impersonal but impartial values. Without such a non-impersonal rationale, these non-impersonal lower-order intrinsic values, values that provide agents with lower-order moral reasons, cannot even be available for consideration from the impersonal standpoint.

Another way to put this point is that the appeal to rights as intrinsically valuable, hence as among the values to be taken into account in the evaluation of states of affairs, presupposes aspects of a "buck passing" account of what is good and valuable of the sort articulated by Scanlon and adopted (with qualifications) by Parfit.[10] Buck passing accounts of value are typically introduced by way of contrast with the teleological accounts of goodness and value typically adopted by consequentialists. On a teleological account, "the primary bearers of value are states of affairs," and "what we have reason to do . . . is to act so as to realize those states of affairs that are best."[11] It seems clear that an account recognizing the intrinsic value of rights cannot adopt a purely teleological account of value. Rights function as moral constraints on acting to bring about both states of affairs that are best and states of affairs that are best for me. The rationale for such intrinsically valuable constraints on the promotion of valuable states of affairs cannot be found in the appeal to the value of the states of affairs whose promotion they constrain.

An account that takes rights to be intrinsically valuable, then, must recognize, in keeping with Scanlon's buck passing account, that "value is not a purely teleological notion," and that "judgments about what is good or valuable generally imply practical conclusions about what would . . . be reasons for acting or responding in a certain way."[12] To recognize rights as intrinsically valuable is to recognize that rational agents have good moral reasons not to interfere with other agents, reasons that often conflict with whatever moral reasons they have to promote better states of affairs. Such reasons ground moral claims not to be interfered with, claims that can be morally decisive even in cases in which such interference promotes the overall value of resulting states of affairs.[13]

---

[10] Scanlon (1998, pp. 95–100); Parfit (2008, ch. 1).
[11] Scanlon (1998, pp. 79–80).   [12] Ibid., p. 96.
[13] Such an appeal to rights as intrinsically valuable, however, can remain agnostic on the second aspect of Scanlon's buck-passing account, his claim that "being valuable is not a property that provides us with reasons" (ibid., p. 96).

On the classical utilitarian approach impersonal reasons are morally decisive because the impersonal standpoint is the standpoint of morality, a standpoint that is adopted towards lower-order non-moral partial values. The identification of the impersonal standpoint as the standpoint of morality provides a rationale for the claim that impersonal considerations are morally decisive. But no such rationale for the decisiveness of the impersonal standpoint is available to the consequentialist of rights. He must countenance a non-impersonal but impartial moral rationale for the non-impersonal moral values towards which he takes up the impersonal standpoint. The standard debate between, for example, advocates of a consequentialism of rights and advocates of a non-impersonal rationale for rights[14] is mis-posed, since an impersonal stance towards rights must presuppose the acceptability of some such non-impersonal but impartial rationale for the rights towards which the impersonal stance is adopted. To accept some such non-impersonal rationale for certain moral values is to reject the classical consequentialists' grounds for taking the impersonal standpoint to be morally decisive, and to do so without offering any other grounds to take their place. It is, in addition, to recognize grounds—the presence of countervailing non-impersonal moral values—for rejecting the moral decisiveness of impersonal considerations in the moral evaluation of actions.

If we see rights, as Frances Kamm has suggested, as having two components, one which generates constraints upon, for example, killing to save other lives, and one which generates constraints upon killing to "prevent violations of the same or a less significant right," then a consequentialism of rights must accept the first component, but reject the second.[15] Yet to accept the first component is already to accept that there are non-impersonal moral constraints upon the legitimate pursuit of

[14] Versions of such an account are developed by Warren Quinn (1993), Nagel (2002, pp. 34–42), and most thoroughly by Kamm (1996, ch. 10). Nagel characterizes their common element as a focus "on the status conferred on all human beings by the design of a morality which includes . . . constraints of this kind. The status is that of a certain kind of inviolability." (2002, pp. 36–7).

[15] Kamm (1996, p. 263). My only disagreement with Kamm here is with her characterization of rights that manifest only the first component as ordinary rights, and rights that manifest both components as "super rights." It is ordinary rights, I suggest, that manifest both components. Ordinary rights constrain the pursuit of impersonal ends, including the impersonal end of minimizing rights violations. Attempts to justify violation of rights in the legal system through appeal to the minimization of rights violations overall (See, e.g., Nagel 2002, p. 38) strike us as violations of those rights, just as attempts appealing to other impersonal ends, e.g. maximization of utility, strike us as violations of such rights.

impersonal goals, for example minimizing the number of lives lost. The consequentialist of rights must maintain both that there is a non-impersonal rationale for such impartial moral constraints upon impersonal ends, and that, contrary to intuition, whatever rationale this is does not extend to constraints upon minimizing rights violations.

Certain rationales that have been offered for the intrinsic value of rights do extend to constraints of this sort.[16] But it is not enough for the consequentialist of rights simply to reject some particular rationale—or even all particular rationales—for the intrinsic value of rights. Rather, the burden is upon her to provide an alternative non-impersonal rationale for rights upon which they morally constrain the agent from pursuing some impersonal ends, but not the particular impersonal end of minimizing rights violations overall. Absent such a rationale, the air of paradox in this debate surrounds the consequentialist of rights herself, who, while insisting upon the decisiveness of the impersonal consideration of rights, must allow that to recognize the intrinsic value of rights is to accept that there is a non-impersonal rationale for moral constraints upon impersonal considerations.

The consequentialist of rights proposes to view non-impersonal moral values impersonally—from the outside in, so to speak. But to recognize such intrinsic moral values is to presuppose a non-impersonal rationale within which rights, for example, come into view as moral constraints upon acting for both partial and impersonal reasons. To borrow Stephen Darwall's metaphor, it is to presuppose a view from the inside out.[17] On such a view, however, whatever paradox is in the air again would appear to cling to a consequentialism of rights itself. Such consequentialism recognizes rights as moral constraints upon impersonal considerations, but takes impersonal consideration of such constraints themselves somehow to be exempt from the very constraints it recognizes. To recognize the intrinsic value of rights is to embrace an inside-out approach that generates non-impersonal moral constraints upon the pursuit of impersonal ends. But to adopt a consequentialism of rights is to persist, in the face of such a presupposed rationale for such constraints, in taking an outside-in approach towards such rights themselves. The consequentialist of rights presupposes a rationale for such non-impersonal values

---

[16] See Nagel's argument to this effect (2002, pp. 36–40).   [17] Darwall (1986).

that constrain impersonal ends—the burden is not on her opponent to provide one. The burden, rather, is on the consequentialist of rights herself to provide a rationale for her assumption that the impersonal end of minimizing the violations of rights is somehow exempt from this presupposed rationale and the constraints it generates.[18] Without such a rationale the view appears to provide a rationale for rejecting the moral decisiveness of reasons based in the impersonal evaluations of states of affairs.

I have argued that consequentialism cannot consistently recognize the intrinsic value of rights while maintaining that the impersonal standpoint is the moral standpoint. But a similar argument can be made regarding a consequentialism that attempts to take into account the intrinsic value of fairness, or justice, or respect for persons as ends in themselves, or robust autonomy. The consequentialist of fairness, or autonomy, or respect for persons as ends in themselves is certainly right that such values ought to be taken into account from the impersonal standpoint. All other things being equal, we ought to maximize the extent to which people are treated fairly and respected as ends in themselves. But to recognize such non-impersonal moral values as proper inputs into impersonal assessments is at the same time to presuppose the relevance of certain impartial but not impersonal moral values, and to presuppose the incompleteness of any consequentialist theory of moral standards.

Either a consequentialism that recognizes intrinsic moral values such as rights presupposes a non-impersonal rationale, or it presupposes that such a rationale is not necessary in order to recognize such non-impersonal moral values. Either way pressure is brought to bear upon the consequentialist's claim that the impersonal standpoint is the moral standpoint. It is of course open to the consequentialist to respond that because there is no such rationale, it is the appeal to the intrinsic value of rights and any other non-impersonal moral values that should be rejected. One problem with this strategy has already become apparent: consequentialists themselves have argued that any moral theory that cannot recognize some such intrinsic values (whether or not the list includes rights) is impoverished. Another problem is that it does seem appropriate, as such consequentialists point

---

[18] See Cummiskey (1996) for one attempt to provide such a rationale.

out, to recognize intrinsic moral values from the impersonal standpoint. We should promote autonomy, rights, respects for persons as ends, etc. But this is to recognize that it is appropriate to take into account from the impersonal standpoint certain non-impersonal moral values, impartial values that presuppose non-impersonal rationales. This, in turn, is to presuppose that the impersonal standpoint is not the fundamental standpoint for the moral evaluation of actions.

6.3 Scheffler—The Rationale

Arguments have nonetheless been made by sympathizers with central features of the consequentialist program that there simply is no rationale for such non-impersonal intrinsic moral values. Scheffler has argued that there is no rationale for agent-centered restrictions—decisive moral reasons not to act in ways that bring about the best state of affairs. Agents have good non-impersonal reasons, he argues, reasons that are often sufficient to free agents from any rational requirement to bring about the best overall state of affairs. If CMS is accepted, such agents will often have sufficient reasons to do what such moral standards prohibit. The rational authority of morality will be undermined unless the consequentialist account of moral standards is rejected, and the independent rational significance of non-impersonal reasons is reflected by their independent moral significance as well. Scheffler has suggested that there is a rationale for recognizing the independent moral significance of such non-impersonal reasons (not simply their independent rational significance) such that when they have sufficient weight or force, agents do not have decisive moral reasons to bring about the best state of affairs. But he also maintains the independence thesis, arguing that the obvious rationale for the claim that agents sometimes do not have decisive moral reasons to bring about the best overall states of affairs (that there are agent-centered permissions) is independent of any rationale for the claim that agents sometimes have decisive moral reasons not to bring about the best state of affairs (that there are agent-centered restrictions). Kagan takes the independence thesis in the opposite direction. It is at least clear to him what agent-centered restrictions are, hence what a successful rationale for them would have to look like. But it is not even clear on his view what agent-centered permissions are, or what form a successful rationale could take. Moreover, he suggests that a successful rationale for restrictions would not supply a plausible rationale for permissions.[19]

In this section and the two that follow I will demonstrate that Scheffler's rationale for recognizing the independent moral significance of the personal point of view is most plausibly understood as undermining the independence thesis; that is, as providing a rationale both for my sometimes not having decisive moral reasons to bring about the best consequences (permissions) and for my sometimes having decisive moral reasons not to bring about the best overall state of affairs (restrictions). It does seem plausible, as Scheffler claims, that recognition of the independent moral significance of my own non-impersonal reasons for acting results in my not having decisive moral reasons to bring about the best state of affairs, that is, it results in agent-centered permissions. But it is also plausible that recognition of the independent moral significance of the personal points of view of each other person, and of the non-impersonal reasons that each other person has for acting, results in my having decisive moral reasons not to bring about the best state of affairs. Scheffler's rationale for agent-centered permissions, I will argue, readily extends to a rationale for restrictions as well. Indeed, I only truly am morally permitted to act in certain ways—the independent moral significance of my personal point of view is only truly recognized—if other agents have decisive moral reasons that require them not to prevent me from doing so. The independent thesis fails.

It will become apparent, moreover, that such a rationale deploys a non-impersonal conception of impartiality in the moral evaluation of actions as right and wrong, an interpersonal rather than an impersonal conception of impartiality.[20] Impartial (impersonal) rankings of overall states of affairs may well play a role in such impartial (interpersonal) evaluation

---

[19] It is clear what agent-centered restrictions are. They occur in cases in which moral considerations generate moral requirements upon some agent not to bring about the best overall consequences. But it is not entirely clear how to characterize their complement, agent-centered options or permissions (which result from accepting, in Scheffler's terminology, an agent-centered prerogative). This is in part because the latter are often bound up with particular claims concerning issues such as supererogation. I will stick with a minimal formulation that avoids these auxiliary commitments, one upon which an agent has an option in cases in which she is not morally required to bring about the best outcome, nor is she morally required not to do so.

[20] Parfit suggests that impartiality requires "that everyone matters equally, and has equal moral claims" (2008, p. 274). He then considers several different ways of understanding impartiality. Impersonality is plausibly understood as offering one such conception of impartiality; the interpersonality that will be articulated through the course of this chapter and the next is another.

of actions, but the impartiality suggested by this rationale as appropriate for evaluation of actions as right and wrong, interpersonal impartiality, is not the impartiality appropriate for evaluating overall states of affairs as better or worse. Impersonality is the conception of impartiality suitable for evaluating overall states of affairs as better or worse, but it is not the conception of impartiality suitable for evaluating actions as right or wrong. The impartial evaluation of states of affairs from the impersonal standpoint may play a role in the impartial evaluation of actions from the interpersonal standpoint, and values that emerge from the impartial evaluation of actions as right or wrong, values such as autonomy, rights, and respect for persons as ends in themselves, may well be appropriately taken into account in the impersonal evaluation of states of affairs. But the interaction between the impartial evaluation of actions and the impartial evaluation of states of affairs presupposes the distinctness of the conceptions of impartiality at work. This result undermines the remaining rationale for consequentialism, the rationale that appeals to the impartiality of morality to establish that the impersonal standpoint is the fundamental moral standpoint. The arguments for these conclusions, however, proceed through a closer examination of Scheffler's own arguments. It is to such an examination that I turn in the remainder of this section.[21]

We have seen that intuitively agents are sometimes morally permitted not to bring about the best overall states of affairs—they do not have decisive moral reasons to perform such an action. Moreover, ordinary morality suggests that agents are sometimes morally prohibited from bringing about the best overall states of affairs—they have decisive moral reasons not to act in particular ways. CMS leaves room for neither such permissions nor such restrictions. Scheffler purports to have discovered a rationale for rejecting the act consequentialist's case against permissions. Moreover, he argues that it is not a rationale for rejecting their case against restrictions. Indeed, he argues that there are no prospects even in view for providing a rationale for such restrictions. He introduces his rationale as a response to the Bernard Williams argument we considered in Chapter 4, an argument that consequentialism profoundly undermines the integrity of individuals by alienating them from their interests and ground projects. He contends that only rejection of the first implication of consequentialism, that agents

---

[21] This and the next two sections develop certain arguments originally put forward in Hurley (1993).

always have decisive moral reasons to bring about the best consequences, is necessary to provide a response to such an objection.

A rationale for rejecting such an implication, one which supports the claim that agents sometimes do not have decisive moral reasons to bring about the best state of affairs, is provided, on Scheffler's view, by the fact that commitments are naturally generated from a person's point of view. Each person has a point of view, "a perspective from which projects are undertaken, plans are developed, events are observed, and life is lived."[22] Such a viewpoint constitutes "a locus relative to which harms and benefits can be assessed, and are typically assessed by the person who has the point of view."[23] A person's point of view has independent rational significance—agents properly take their own plans, projects, interests, and commitments to provide them with fundamentally non-impersonal reasons that have weight independent from whatever weight they have from the impersonal point of view.

Scheffler outlines two strategies for recognizing the moral significance of this natural independence of the point of view of each person. The first strategy, the maximization strategy, is the strategy adopted by consequentialism. On such a strategy the *moral* significance of an agent's personal point of view is entirely exhausted for that agent "by the weight that point of view carries in the impersonal calculus."[24] The personal point of view, and in particular the fundamentally non-impersonal reasons that each person has, has *rational* significance independent of the impersonal standpoint, but no independent *moral* significance. Such an account will be difficult to reconcile with the rational authority of moral requirements (RAMS). The second strategy, the liberation strategy, by contrast,

takes account of the natural independence of the personal point of view precisely by granting it moral independence: by permitting agents to devote energy and attention to their projects and commitments out of proportion to the value from an impersonal standpoint of their doing so.[25]

---

[22] Scheffler (1982, p. 56).   [23] Ibid., p. 56.   [24] Ibid., p. 61.

[25] Ibid., p. 62. Notice that the although the personal point of view, as Scheffler characterizes it, clearly will take into account considerations of what is better or worse for the agent, considerations that are relevant from the agent's own partial point of view, it need not be limited to such considerations. For example, among the commitments that an agent can maintain from her personal point of view might well be commitments to fairness and respect for the autonomy of others, commitments that may well often be in conflict with commitments to the agent's own well-being.

Notice that it in no way follows from Scheffler's claim that such natural independence is recognized on such an account as independent moral significance that all of the reasons generated from the personal point of view are moral reasons, only that the good non-impersonal reasons that it generates all have independent moral significance. My own plans and projects do not provide countervailing moral reasons which, when of sufficient weight, provide me with decisive moral reasons not to bring about the best overall state of affairs. Such an account would result in agent-centered moral restrictions, not in agent-centered permissions. Rather, these non-impersonal reasons are reflected in a moral significance for an agent's plans, projects, and commitments that is independent of their impersonal significance, moral significance that is manifested as a moral claim that the agent has to act on such non-impersonal reasons. This moral claim, when it has sufficient moral strength or weight, is sufficient to free the agent from what would otherwise be a decisive moral reason to bring about the best state of affairs. In such cases, recognition of the independent moral significance of my personal point of view results in a moral permission, a moral entitlement to act in a way that does not bring about the best overall outcome. Such a rationale avoids obvious obstacles that undermine consequentialist attempts to accommodate RAMS. It liberates people by freeing them "from the demand that their actions and motives always be optimal from the impersonal perspective."[26] Recognition of such independently rationally significant reasons as reflected in their independent moral significance will plausibly result in cases in which, taking their significance into account, the agent does not have decisive moral reasons, all things considered, to bring about the best state of affairs. In such cases the agent will be morally permitted to act in ways that the consequentialist account identifies as wrong. On Scheffler's liberation strategy an agent may well nonetheless have sufficient reasons to perform the action that consequentialist moral standards would require, but she will not have decisive moral reasons to do so. Scheffler's argument is that a liberation strategy for responding to the natural independence of the personal point of view, which is manifested as its independent rational significance, provides a plausible rationale for recognizing the independent moral significance of the personal point of view. Recognition of such

---

[26] Scheffler (1982, p. 62).

independent moral significance, in turn, allows that in certain cases the agent is not morally required to bring about the best overall state of affairs. She is morally permitted to pursue her interests out of proportion to their weight in the impersonal calculus.

However, Scheffler argues that such a rationale for the claim that agents are not always morally required to bring about the best overall state of affairs is not a rationale for the claim that agents are sometimes morally required not to bring about the best overall outcome, that is that there are agent-centered restrictions. The rationale for cases in which agents do not have morally decisive reasons to act is not a rationale for cases in which agents have morally decisive reasons not to act. Indeed, he contends that his liberation strategy is clearly inappropriate for generating such restrictions, since restrictions do not "liberate," they confine:

The *permission* not to produce the best state of affairs suffices to free individual agents from the demands of impersonal optimality, and thus to prevent them from becoming slaves to the impersonal standpoint. . . . What must be provided is a rationale for going beyond such permissions and *prohibiting* the production of the best state of affairs.[27]

Scheffler thus takes it to be clear that restrictions requiring agents not to bring about the best consequences "go beyond" permissions, such that they must be supported by a rationale independent of and additional to the liberation rationale for such permissions.

6.4 A Subversive Reinterpretation of Scheffler's Rationale

Various objections have been presented against aspects of Scheffler's argument.[28] Before introducing my own, I first want to highlight an aspect of his account the significance of which has not been sufficiently appreciated: that the rationale is the basis for rejecting the impersonal standpoint as the fundamental standpoint for the moral evaluation of actions. It is worth pausing to see both why this is the case, and what aspects of Scheffler's account tend to obscure this point from view.

---

[27] Ibid., pp. 94–5.   [28] See, e.g., Kagan (1989, ch. 1), Kamm (1996, ch. 8), and Hurley (1995).

The liberation strategy recognizes the independent moral significance of the personal point of view: the personal point of view has moral significance independent of its impersonal moral significance. On such an account moral right and wrong, moral permission and prohibition, is determined not from the impersonal standpoint, but from a standpoint that takes into account in addition the independent moral significance of the non-impersonal reasons each agent has in the proper determination of what an agent is morally required or permitted to do. The standpoint from which relevant impersonal and non-impersonal reasons are accorded their appropriate and potentially conflicting moral significance is neither the partial standpoint of what is best for the agent nor the impersonal standpoint of what is best overall, nor can it simply be reduced to the two. Rather, it is the standpoint from which the considerations articulated through such standpoints are themselves accorded their appropriate moral significance in the determination of which actions morality requires, prohibits, and permits. The result, then, is a theory of moral evaluation that rejects the assumption that moral relevance is always determined through appeal to the impersonal value of what happens—a rejection of an impersonal theory of the moral evaluation of actions as right and wrong.

One feature of Scheffler's account tends to obscure from view that his account is not merely rejecting consequentialism, but advocating a standpoint for the moral evaluation of actions within which impersonal considerations play only a circumscribed role. The obscuring feature is that from the impersonal standpoint the independent moral significance of the point of view of the person will manifest itself as disproportionate impersonal moral significance. From the impersonal standpoint it will look as though your happiness, for example, has impersonal value of X for me, while my own has a disproportionate impersonal value of 10X.[29] The relevant weighing, it can seem, is all done from the impersonal standpoint after all suitable multipliers are provided. But of course this cannot but be a misrepresentation. My happiness has the same impersonal value as yours, but its value is not exhausted from the impersonal standpoint. Impersonal moral considerations weigh against the independent moral significance of non-impersonal reasons from a standpoint for the determination of right

---

[29] See, e.g., Scheffler's claim that on such an account each agent is "allowed to give M times more weight to his own interests than to the interests of anyone else" (1992b, p. 378).

and wrong actions that comprehends both. The non-impersonal moral significance of the agent's own personal point of view will *appear* from such an impersonal standpoint to be disproportionate impersonal significance only because the non-impersonal moral significance of the personal point of view can only be misrepresented as disproportionate impersonal moral significance from the impersonal standpoint.

From this standpoint for the moral evaluation of actions, the relevant non-impersonal and impersonal factors are assigned their appropriate moral significance, significance which will then manifest itself from the impersonal standpoint, in the case of certain non-impersonal considerations, as disproportionate impersonal moral significance. The impersonal standpoint cannot be the standpoint from which these initial moral weights for non-impersonal as well as impersonal considerations are assigned; it can only misrepresent (albeit perhaps benignly) the relevant weight of non-impersonal considerations in the moral evaluation of actions as greater impersonal weight.

We have seen that Scheffler recognizes the natural independence of the personal points of view of agents. Such agents have non-impersonal reasons, and the rational significance of such reasons is independent of whatever impersonal rational significance they might have. The independent rational significance of the points of view of persons, he argues, is manifested in independent moral significance, moral significance for such non-impersonal reasons that is independent of their impersonal moral significance. But these independent non-impersonal reasons, although they have independent moral significance, are not on Scheffler's view all independent moral reasons, reasons which, when of sufficient weight, provide agents with decisive moral reasons to do what they have non-impersonal reasons to do. Rather, the independent moral significance of such non-impersonal reasons, and the natural independence of the standpoint of persons that they reflect, takes the form of a moral claim that the agent has to do what he has sufficient reasons to do. Such a moral claim, when it has sufficient weight relative to conflicting impersonal moral reasons, provides decisive moral reasons for the agent to do what he has sufficient reasons to do. Among the actions such an agent has good enough reasons to do may well be the action that brings about the best state of affairs. But if the agent in question performs such an action it will not be because he has morally decisive reasons to bring about the best state of affairs (he does not), but because he has sufficient—good enough—reasons to act this way. Morality does not require such an agent to bring about the best state of affairs, but it does permit him to do so.

Such a proposed modification of standard act consequentialism, however, appears to face a serious obstacle. Morality is impartial, and the impersonal standpoint for the evaluation of actions is an impartial standpoint of equal concern. Scheffler expands the agent's standpoint of moral evaluation, however, to comprehend as well the independent moral significance of her own personal point of view, and of the non-impersonal reasons that she has from her own personal point of view. But the resulting standpoint for moral evaluation is no longer impartial. Rather, it augments an impersonal standpoint of equal concern with recognition of disproportionate moral weight for the agent's own concerns. It is of course possible at this point to jettison the claim that morality is impartial, but this is to jettison the very feature of morality that has been taken by consequentialists to mandate a prominent role for impersonal evaluation. The obvious question is whether there is a rationale for recognizing the natural independence of the points of view of persons as reflected in independent moral significance such that such recognition can be reconciled to the fundamental impartiality of moral evaluation.

There is such a rationale; moreover, Scheffler's own liberation strategy is most plausibly understood as supporting just such a rationale. This rationale for recognizing the independent moral significance of the points of view of persons generates both agent-centered restrictions and agent-centered permissions; indeed, it suggests that agent-centered permissions arise in the special case in which the agent recognizing some person's independent moral significance and the person whose independent moral significance she is recognizing are not two distinct people, but one and the same person. Recognition of the independent moral significance only of my own point of view in moral evaluation leads to a standpoint of moral evaluation that is not impartial. Recognition of the independent moral significance of the personal points of view of each person, of the equal moral claim of each person to act for the good non-impersonal reasons that he or she has, would result in a standpoint of moral evaluation that is impartial, and that recognizes the independent moral significance of the points of view of all persons. Indeed, such impartial recognition of the independent moral significance of each person by each person seems to provide the most plausible interpretation of Scheffler's liberation rationale. If the natural independence of my personal point of view is plausibly reflected in moral significance for me, independent of whatever significance it has from the impersonal standpoint, should we not expect the natural independence of your personal point of view also to be reflected in significance for me independent of the significance it has from the impersonal standpoint? Surely this is a far more consistent application, one upon which each person's natural independence is recognized in the evaluation of actions by each person as independent moral significance.

Agents, after all, can become "slaves of the impersonal standpoint" in two distinct ways. First, a moral theory can provide me with decisive moral reasons to alienate myself—directly so to speak—from my good non-impersonal reasons to act. Scheffler identifies these as cases in which a theory "violates the integrity of agents by virtue of what it directly requires them to do."[30] Second, it can provide you with decisive (or sufficient) moral reasons to alienate me—indirectly so to speak—from my good non-impersonal reasons to act. These are cases in which the theory provides decisive or sufficient moral reasons "to force particular people to do things that will undermine their integrity."[31] My taking into account the independent moral significance of my own personal point of view, my moral claim, so to speak, not to be alienated from my good non-impersonal reasons by impersonal moral reasons, safeguards me from direct enslavement to the impersonal point of view. It frees me from what would otherwise be decisive moral reasons to alienate me from doing what I have good non-impersonal reasons to do. But only if others take into account the independent moral significance of my personal point of view for them will my indirect enslavement to the impersonal standpoint be prevented. It is this recognition by them of my moral claim not to be alienated from my good non-impersonal reasons to act that liberates me from what would otherwise be decisive moral reasons for them to alienate me from acting on such reasons. Without this latter component you are always morally permitted (and sometimes required) to kill me for my inheritance or forcibly remove my organs for transplant, and in general to prevent me from acting for good reasons, whenever such an action on your part will bring about the best state of affairs.

---

[30] Scheffler (1982, p. 38).   [31] Ibid., p. 38.

Recognition by each person only of the independent moral significance of her own personal point of view will result in what we can label "license permissions"—permissions that prevent direct enslavement but permit indirect enslavement. By contrast, recognition by each person of the independent moral significance of each other person's point of view is necessary to account for true "liberation permissions"—permissions that prevent both direct enslavement to the impersonal point of view at the agent's own hands and indirect enslavement at the hands of others. Only such liberation permissions free me from alienation not only by me, but by each of you as well. The issue, then, is whether recognition of the independent moral significance of the personal point of view is most plausibly reflected in a true liberation strategy, one that generates liberation permissions that avoid indirect as well as direct enslavement to the impersonal standpoint, or in Scheffler's liberation as license strategy, which generates a license permission that avoids only direct enslavement.

To see how recognition of the independent moral significance of each person by each person will generate the sort of robust moral permissions required by the liberation strategy, and provide a rationale for restrictions as well as options, consider what is involved in the recognition of both the impersonal moral significance and the independent moral significance of each person by each person. Person A, the agent, recognizes the impersonal moral significance of each person's point of view, and such recognition provides her with an agent-neutral moral reason to interfere with the plans, projects, and commitments of any person P, the patient, whenever doing so will bring about the best overall state of affairs. Recognition by person A in addition of the independent moral significance of each person is recognition of a moral claim that each person P has to act without interference for good non-impersonal reasons. We have already seen that when A and P are the same person, Ps independent moral significance, and his resulting moral claim to act without interference, provide A with a moral reason not to interfere with P's acting on such reasons—to allow P, in this case himself, to do what he has good (including good non-impersonal) reasons to do. A is morally required to permit P to act for such reasons. Because A is P in such cases, A is morally permitted to act for such reasons. If A has sufficient reasons to bring about the best overall state of affairs, A has sufficient reasons to do what would be morally required by consequentialist moral standards, but is not morally required to perform such an action.

Indeed, she may have sufficient reasons to pursue other courses of action as well.

When A and P are different people, P's independent moral significance, and her resulting moral claim to act without interference, provide A with a moral reason not to interfere with P's acting on such non-impersonal reasons—to allow P, in this case some other person, to do what she has good (including good non-impersonal) reasons to do. When the claim has decisive strength, A has morally decisive reasons to permit P to act for such non-impersonal reasons. Because A is not P in such cases, the morally decisive reasons to permit P to act are moral restrictions upon A, moral prohibitions upon interfering with P's actions even to promote the best state of affairs. When A and P are different people, recognition of P's independent moral significance results in a moral restriction on A; when A and P are the same person, recognition by A of his own (P's) independent moral significance results in a moral permission for A. In each case P's claim, when it is decisive, permits P by providing A with morally decisive reasons not to interfere to bring about the best state of affairs. When A and P are the same person, the morally decisive reasons that she has result in a moral permission to do what she has good reasons to do; when A and P are different people, the morally decisive reasons that A has result in a moral permission for P to do what she has good reasons to do by way of a moral restriction upon interference by A.

P's recognition of her own moral claim in virtue of her independent moral significance generates an agent-centered moral permission for her; the recognition by others of her moral claim in virtue of her independent moral significance generates an agent-centered restriction upon them. Her recognition of her own claim, sans recognition of this claim by others, would generate the sort of pyrrhic permission that results from the license strategy, a permission to act that is consistent with a permission (or even moral requirement) by others to prevent her from doing so. But recognition by each person of her claim generates the sort of robust, true permission required by a true liberation strategy. Agent-centered restrictions and agent-centered permissions are both generated by recognition of the independent moral significance of the points of view of persons; indeed, agent-centered permissions are simply the special case in which the agent A in question, and the person P whose claim provides A with moral reasons not to interfere, are the same person.

On a true liberation strategy you will not have decisive reasons to promote the best state of affairs when the moral claim reflecting the moral independence of your personal point of view is of sufficient significance. But I will have decisive moral reasons not to interfere with your acting for non-impersonal reasons when the moral claim reflecting the moral independence of your personal point of view is of sufficient significance. Morality permits you to do X only if (1) you do not have decisive moral reasons to do some other Y, and (2) I and others do not have morally decisive reasons to interfere with your doing X. I have argued that only in a pyrrhic sense are you morally permitted to do something that I am morally required and able to prevent you from doing. Yet it is only this pyrrhic sense of permission that Scheffler's liberation-as-license strategy would secure. Such an alternative would seem to be improperly characterized as a liberation strategy at all, because it secures only license, and liberty is not license. True permission for me requires restriction upon you—I am not morally permitted to do something that you are morally required to prevent me from doing. Morality only truly permits me to act if it doesn't provide any of you with morally decisive reasons to prevent me from acting. The very same feature, my independent moral significance, that frees me from enslavement at my own hands by impersonal moral requirements will on a true liberation account free me from enslavement at the hands of others by impersonal moral requirements.

There is a misreading of Scheffler's view which can seem to suggest that recognition of the independent moral significance of each person's point of view is not possible.[32] If my independent moral significance appears as disproportionate weight from the impersonal point of view, then it might seem that recognition of everyone's independent moral significance must appear as disproportionate weight for each person's plans and interests from the impersonal standpoint. But everyone's weight cannot be disproportionate—add the same multiplier to everyone's plans and projects, and we have not given universal disproportionality, we have merely restored the original proportionality.

Here, however, our earlier insight, that disproportionate weight from the impersonal point of view is a misrepresentation even of my own independent moral significance, proves helpful. That the independent

---

[32] I have benefited on this point from an exchange years ago with Michael Otsuka.

moral significance of others cannot be similarly misrepresented from the impersonal standpoint as disproportionate impersonal significance is hardly an objection to recognizing it. Indeed, once we free ourselves of this impersonal misrepresentation it seems clear how we would recognize the independent moral significance of others consistently from the distinctive standpoint presupposed by Scheffler for the evaluation of actions as right and wrong. Morality permits me to pursue my personal plans and projects in a way that cannot be represented—only misrepresented—from the impersonal standpoint. Morality also permits each and every other person to pursue her plans and projects—that is what it is to recognize their independent moral significance. But they are only permitted if I am morally prohibited from interfering with other agents' pursuit of their plans and honoring of their commitments in the pursuit of impersonal goals. Scheffler's appeal to liberation rather than license is thus exactly on point. Liberation is freedom with respect to the rights—or in this case the independent moral significance—of others; license is "freedom" that undermines the freedom of others and one's own freedom at the hands of others. License is not true freedom, in short, precisely because it fails to recognize the independent moral significance of others as well as oneself. Recognition of the independent moral significance of others will naturally manifest itself from the impersonal standpoint not as disproportionate impersonal weight, but as constraints upon acting from that standpoint when doing so interferes with an agent's pursuit of her plans, projects, and interests. This is the natural and full articulation of a liberation rather than a mere license strategy.

I have suggested that such recognition of the independent moral significance of each person's point of view by each person suggests a distinctive standpoint for the articulation of moral claims and reasons, an impartial standpoint of equal concern by each person for each person. For Scheffler each person's point of view has the same moral significance, reflected in the equal disproportionate weight of each from the impersonal standpoint. But it has this independent moral significance only for the person herself. The resulting standpoint for the moral evaluation of actions is not an impartial standpoint. On a true liberation strategy, by contrast, each person's point of view has the same independent moral significance for each person, herself included. The result is that such recognition of the independent moral significance of each person by each person provides a form of equal concern for each person by each person. This resulting standpoint for the evaluation of actions would appear to give rise both to moral permissions not to bring about the best overall state of affairs in cases in which their own independent significance is relevant, and to restrictions upon bringing about the best overall state of affairs when the independent moral significance of others is relevant.

The nature of this alternative standpoint of equal concern can be clarified by the following example. Bob and Carol will be killed unless I (Ted) kill either myself or Alice. Scheffler's view suggests that the moral independence of my own personal point of view is such that if my claim against interference is of sufficient weight, it frees me from any impersonal moral requirement to kill myself. Recognition of my own independent moral significance protects me from my own impersonal moral reasons to kill myself to bring about the best overall state of affairs, and morally permits me to do what I have sufficient or decisive reasons, including non-impersonal reasons, to do. This result is suggested by Scheffler's liberation-as-license strategy. But on a true liberation strategy, a strategy that morally evaluates actions from a standpoint of equal concern, I must also recognize each of the others involved, Bob, Carol, and Alice, as having moral significance independent of their impersonal moral significance. They are each freed from enslavement to the impersonal standpoint only if I and others are each prohibited from treating each of them as having merely impersonal moral significance. Such a prohibition will result if each person's natural independence as a person is reflected in her equal independent moral significance. If the moral independence of each is of sufficient moral significance, the moral claim that each has to act for good reasons provides me with decisive moral reasons not to kill any one of them on impersonal grounds, including the impersonal grounds that doing so will prevent the deaths of the other two from happening.[33] Each, then, has a moral claim equal to my own, and equal to each other, which provides each other person with a moral reason

---

[33] Of course such a general framework allows for the possibility that impersonal grounds of sufficient significance will also require the agent to do harm in order to prevent very significant harm from happening. The crucial point is that recognition of the independent moral significance of the personal point of view can give rise on such an account to morally relevant non-impersonal considerations that must be taken into account in addition to whatever impersonal-involving moral considerations are relevant. What the agent is morally required to do will then be a function of the relative significance of these potentially countervailing considerations.

that weighs against any impersonal moral reason to kill them. In light of the recognition of the equal independent moral significance that each of them has, and assuming in this case that this independent significance is sufficient, I (Ted) have decisive moral reasons not to kill either Bob or Carol or Alice in the pursuit of impersonal goals. Each has an equal moral claim upon me, a reflection of his or her equal independent moral significance, that is independent of whatever impersonal claims they make upon me; indeed, each person has such claims upon each other person. When this independent moral significance is sufficiently compelling relative to the relevant impersonal considerations, I am morally required not to kill each of them on impersonal grounds. Although in the circumstances I can prevent Bob and Carol from being killed by killing Alice, I am morally prohibited from doing so. I am not permitted to kill Alice to prevent the deaths of Bob and Carol from happening, just as I would not be permitted to kill Carol, for example, to prevent the deaths of Bob and Alice.

Recognition of my own independent moral significance, as Scheffler emphasizes, generates a moral permission not to kill myself. But recognition of the independent moral significance of other persons generates agent-centered moral restrictions against, for example, killing Alice even to prevent the killings of Bob and Carol from happening. Recognition of my own independent moral significance results in a moral permission not to kill myself even to prevent twice the killing from happening overall; recognition of Alice's independent moral significance results in a moral prohibition against killing Alice even to prevent twice the killing from happening. In each case, the case in which killing myself will prevent the deaths of Bob and Carol, and the case in which my killing Alice will prevents the deaths of Bob and Carol, Bob's and Carol's deaths figure only impersonally. But in the former case my independent moral significance frees me from the moral requirement of impersonal sacrifice, and in the latter case Alice's independent moral significance requires me not to sacrifice her on impersonal grounds.

I have suggested that to recognize this equal independent moral significance of each and every person (myself included) from the impersonal standpoint in determining what it is right for me to do is to deploy an impartial conception of equal concern. Here I am following Parfit's suggestion that the appeal to impartiality, properly understood, is an appeal to a standpoint or fundamental principle according to which "everyone matters equally, and has equal moral claims." To invoke the concept of impartiality, he suggests, is to invoke the intuitive idea that "we should not single ourselves out for special consideration or treatment."[34] The requirement that morality is impartial, a requirement that is taken to support one of the central arguments for consequentialism, is a requirement that moral standards be articulated from such a standpoint upon which the agent herself is not singled out for special treatment; moreover, upon which everyone matters equally and has equal moral standing. Parfit also emphasizes that such a general conception of impartiality allows for alternative conceptions of impartiality that flesh out these general notions of mattering equally and equal moral claims in different ways. It seems clear that impersonality itself can be articulated as such a distinct conception of impartiality, of what it is for each to count as one, and no one to count as more than one. It provides one way of articulating the general concept that no one can be singled out for special consideration. It is a conception of how it is that everyone matters equally that is widely recognized, even by critics of consequentialism, as relevant to the overall evaluation of states of affairs.

What has emerged as a natural articulation of the liberation strategy, however, is an alternative conception of impartiality that appears to have particular relevance to the moral evaluation of actions. Recognition of the natural independence of persons as reflected not only in the independent rational significance of the standpoints of persons, but in the independent moral significance of each person by each person, provides a second conception of the "equal moral claims" that impartiality requires each person to recognize, a conception upon which any person is precluded from singling herself out for special moral consideration or treatment. On such a conception the natural independence of Alice's personal point of view is reflected in the moral significance of Alice's personal point of view, a moral significance that is independent of its impersonal moral significance and of whatever significance it has from the partial standpoint of any other person. Alice's recognition of her own independent moral significance frees her from moral enslavement to the impersonal standpoint at her own hands. Each other person's recognition of her independent moral significance frees

---

[34] The first quotation is from Parfit (2008, p. 274). He takes the second quotation from O'Neill (1989, p. 94).

her from moral enslavement to the impersonal standpoint at their hands. Alice's recognition of the equal moral significance of each other person independent from his or her impersonal moral significance frees each of them from moral enslavement to the impersonal standpoint at her hands. From this alternative impartial standpoint, an interpersonal or intersubjective rather than an impersonal impartial standpoint,[35] each person's equal independent moral significance, a moral significance Scheffler's account suggests that they each have in virtue of the natural independence of their respective points of view, is a source of equal moral claims that each person has upon each other person not to be interfered with for impersonal reasons.

Although the moral reasons generated from this standpoint are, like the reasons generated from the impersonal standpoint, impartial reasons generated from a standpoint of equal moral claims, the reasons generated from the impersonal conception are agent-neutral reasons, reasons for anyone to promote some state of affairs impersonally evaluated as best, while reasons generated from the alternative conception are agent-relative reasons, reasons for some particular person or persons not to act in some way. Ted's recognition of his own independent moral significance provides him with moral reasons that are decisive with respect to the impersonal moral reasons that he has to enslave himself to the impersonal standpoint. Ted's recognition of Alice's independent moral significance provides him with moral reasons that are decisive against the impersonal moral reasons that he has to enslave Alice to the impersonal standpoint. They are moral reasons for Ted not to interfere with Alice, reasons that are indexed specifically to Ted, just as Bob and Carol have reasons not to interfere with Alice that are indexed specifically to Bob and Carol respectively. These are non-impersonal but impartial reasons, agent-relative moral reasons for Ted, and Bob, and Carol not to interfere with Alice.

Crucially, not only are such reasons indexed to some particular agent, some particular "I," they are also indexed to some particular patient, some "you." Ted's recognition of Alice's independent moral significance provides him with an agent-relative moral reason not to interfere with Alice, and Alice's recognition of her independent moral significance provides

---

[35] See Scanlon (1982, sec. III) for a characterization of a conception of impartiality of this sort as interpersonal, and Korsgaard (1996) for a characterization of a conception of impartiality of this sort as intersubjective.

her with an agent-relative moral claim against Ted not to interfere, a claim against each particular person not to act in a way that will result in her enslavement to the impersonal standpoint. Such impartial agent-relative moral reasons not to interfere generated through appeal to such an alternative conception of impartiality are thus reflected in corresponding agent-relative claims not to be interfered with.

Such impartial but non-impersonal reasons and claims, agent-relative reasons and claims that would be generated from such an alternative conception of impartiality, are reasons in the first instance to perform or not to perform certain actions, not agent-neutral reasons to prevent or promote certain overall states of affairs. To summarize, recognition of the independent moral significance of each person by each person (1) invokes an alternative to the impersonal conception of impartiality, an interpersonal conception. Such an alternative conception (2) generates non-impersonal (agent-relative) impartial moral reasons, that reflect (3) corresponding non-impersonal (agent-relative) impartial moral claims. Finally, (4) these are not in the first instance reasons to promote overall outcomes, but impartial moral reasons for distinct and assignable people not to do things to distinct and assignable others, reasons reflecting claims that distinct and assignable others have against actions being done by other persons.

6.5 Consequences of the Reinterpretation

Scheffler suggests that the strategy he supplies in support of the claim that agents are not always required to bring about the best overall consequences allows room for what he takes to be the plausible sounding feature at the core of consequentialism, that "one may always do what will lead to the best available outcome overall."[36] I demonstrated in Chapter 5 that the plausible sound of this feature trades upon an ambiguity. We have now seen that the strategy deployed by Scheffler, a liberation strategy that draws upon appeal to the natural independence of the points of view of persons to provide a rationale for the independent moral significance of the personal point of view, undermines rather than supports the problematic consequentialist interpretation of this plausible sounding feature. The very independent

[36] Scheffler (1982, p. 4).

moral significance of the personal point of view that provides a rationale for agent-centered permissions also provides a rationale for agent-centered restrictions: recognition by the agent of her own independent moral significance generates permissions, and recognition by the agent of the independent moral significance of each other person generates restrictions upon impersonal interference with them. Scheffler's independence thesis is thus called into question by an interpretation of his own rationale, an interpretation that is better grounded in the core notion of liberty to which it appeals—a true liberation rather than a liberation as license strategy.

We have already seen that even Scheffler's own treatment of this rationale presupposes a standpoint for the moral evaluation of actions from which partial and impersonal claims are appropriately weighed against each other. It is neither the partial nor the impersonal standpoint, but the standpoint from which a person appropriately takes impersonal moral reasons and the independent moral significance of non-impersonal reasons into account to the appropriate extent in the determination of what it is right or wrong for them to do. With the natural extension of this rationale, however, it has also become clear that this standpoint from which right and wrong actions are determined involves impartial but not impersonal evaluation of actions, an impartiality as interpersonality that is grounded in recognition of the equal moral significance that each person has independent of whatever moral significance she has from the impersonal standpoint.

There is a strong tendency in the literature to identify impartiality with impersonality. If non-impersonal considerations are as a consequence identified with partiality, they are expunged from morality, which is impartial. Thus, if the impartial is identified with the impersonal, agent-centered restrictions, impartial but not impersonal restrictions, are excluded by fiat, at least at the foundational level. What has emerged in the course of this chapter, however, is a rationale for holding that the evaluation of actions as right or wrong involves a distinct conception of impartiality, an interpersonal conception that demonstrates equal concern for each person through recognizing each person's independent moral significance. This conception requires me to take into account each person's point of view independently of any weight that it will have from the impersonal standpoint. If actions in the pursuit of my plans or impersonal goals will fail to recognize the independent moral significance of another person's point of view, I am morally prohibited from performing those actions whenever such independent considerations are sufficiently compelling. The result is an account of agent-centered restrictions that is grounded in the impartial evaluation of the actions available to me. The impartial evaluation of states of affairs as better or worse is impersonal, but the impartial evaluation of actions through recognition of the equal and independent moral significance of each person for each person invokes an alternative interpersonal conception of impartiality that provides a rationale for both agent-centered restrictions and agent-centered permissions.

6.6 Doing and Allowing

This alternative conception of impartiality supports the moral relevance of certain distinctions between doing bad things and merely allowing them to happen. It may be thought that in so doing it begs the question against the consequentialist, whose foundational appeal to the impersonal standpoint precludes the fundamental relevance of any such distinction.[37] This is because traditional act consequentialism, in requiring agents to morally evaluate actions entirely from the impersonal standpoint, requires each agent to adopt what Scheffler has characterized in more recent work as "a purely instrumental view of his own actions and theirs . . . because they assert that each action is to be assessed solely in terms of its optimality relative to the other causal opportunities available to the agent."[38] As a result, Scheffler continues, "the fact that a given action might help realize some value (other than causal or instrumental optimality) about which the agent cares . . . or to contribute to the flourishing of one of his projects or relationships has no direct significance."[39] To take the impersonal conception of impartiality as the foundational conception for the moral assessment of actions is to adopt such a purely instrumental view of one's own actions, hence to reject any foundational moral relevance of the doing/allowing distinction.

Scheffler's characterization allows us to see that exclusive appeal to the impersonal conception in the moral evaluation of actions grounds the rejection of any morally relevant distinction between doing and allowing. From the impersonal standpoint bad things that I do and bad things that I

---

[37] I am indebted to an anonymous referee for pointing out the importance of bringing to bear some of the implications of the arguments presented so far upon the distinction between doing and allowing.
[38] Scheffler (2004, p. 231).   [39] Ibid.

allow others to do are not morally distinguishable. They are all relevant as bad things that will be done, and from the impersonal standpoint the goal is to minimize the badness that will happen, irrespective of whether it is done by me. So too Scheffler's characterization makes it clear that rejection of such an exclusive foundational role for the impersonal standpoint in the moral evaluation of actions will lead to a rationale for accepting a morally relevant distinction between doing and allowing, at least in Scheffler's minimal sense that if non-impersonal reasons are among the morally relevant reasons, agents will sometimes be morally permitted or required to *do* one thing even though in so acting they will be *allowing* something worse to happen. To accept that impersonal-involving reasons are only some of the moral reasons relevant to the moral evaluation of actions will be to recognize that when the moral significance of other relevant non-impersonal reasons is sufficient the agent will be morally permitted and perhaps even required to do certain things even though so acting will allow things that are worse overall to happen.

Notice that the claim here is not that the recognition of such non-impersonal moral reasons will immediately resolve paradigmatic hard doing/allowing cases such as the infamous trolley problem.[40] The point is rather that if an account provides a rationale for taking into account relevant non-impersonal moral reasons, it will be an account upon which determination of the goodness or badness, rightness or wrongness of actions is not exhausted by appeal to the overall goodness or badness of what the agent allows to happen. The appeal to the badness of what will be allowed or prevented will on such an account be only one factor in determining what it is right or wrong, good or bad, to do, and when the other factors are of sufficient strength the agent will be rationally or morally permitted or required to do one thing even though this will allow a worse overall state of affairs to happen. To recognize the relevance of non-impersonal

---

[40] Recognition of the relevance of fundamentally interpersonal reasons provides a general rationale for a morally relevant distinction between doing and allowing, but the articulation and refinement of such reasons is necessary to account for many of the traditional "hard" cases. See Fischer and Ravizza (1992) for a collection of early essays by Philippa Foot, Judith Jarvis Thompson, and others on the trolley problem and other such hard doing/allowing cases. See, in addition, Thompson's recent essay (2008) for a discussion of the current state of the problem in which she maintains that no "convincing account" of the "source" of the relevant distinctions has yet been provided. Scanlon (2008, ch. 1) attempts to provide such an account that aims to resolve many such hard cases through the articulation and refinement of what he takes to be the relevant interpersonal principles.

reasons in the evaluation of courses of action as better or worse, and to recognize the relevance of non-impersonal moral reasons in the evaluation of courses of action as right or wrong, is to recognize that sometimes it will be better or right for agents to do certain things even though worse states of affairs will be allowed to happen as a result.

We have seen in earlier chapters that even most consequentialists allow that non-impersonal reasons as well as impersonal reasons are relevant to the rational evaluation of actions at even the most fundamental level of justification. Hence they are typically committed to accepting that agents will sometimes have sufficient reasons to do, and perhaps even decisive reasons to do, what will allow worse things to happen overall. We might have sufficient reasons not to do harm to our friends or children, for example, even though greater harm to the friends and children of others will be done as a result. In short, such consequentialist sympathizers themselves accept the rational relevance of the doing/allowing distinction in Scheffler's sense, even if they reject the moral relevance of such a distinction. Moreover, even such consequentialists often readily concede the intuitive moral relevance of the doing/allowing distinction. If there is a rationally relevant distinction between doing and allowing in this sense, and a morally relevant distinction is intuitively plausible as well, it can come to seem puzzling why the burden of proof is not upon those who wish to reject the moral relevance of such a distinction.

What is taken to shift the burden on to defenders of the distinction, even in Scheffler's broad sense, is precisely the rationales that have been offered for accepting a consequentialist account of moral standards. If such rationales are compelling, then the moral relevance of the broad doing/allowing distinction is undermined at the most fundamental level. If some such rationale is taken to support the consequentialist theory of moral standards, and this third member of our triad (CMS) is coupled with a commitment to the first member of our triad (RAMS), the result is a rationale for rejecting any rational relevance for such a distinction as well. But because consequentialists recognize a foundational role for non-impersonal reasons in the evaluations of actions and reasons for action as good or bad (NIR), they are under pressure to abandon either a commitment to the rational authority of moral standards (RAMS) or a commitment to the consequentialist theory of moral standards (CMS). The former choice concedes the *rational* relevance of the doing/allowing distinction as the price of rejecting the moral relevance of the distinction. Additional pressure upon the consequentialist to recognize the *moral* relevance of the distinction is generated, as we have seen earlier in this chapter, by the realization that non-impersonal moral values such as robust autonomy, rights, respect, justice, and fairness are appropriately taken into account in the moral evaluation of overall states of affairs. Such recognition of a foundational role played by non-impersonal moral values with non-impersonal rationales in the moral evaluation of actions leads to recognition of the moral as well as the rational relevance of the distinction between doing and allowing.

The acceptance of the second member of the triad (NIR) leads even the consequentialist to recognize that agents will routinely have good reasons to *do* certain things even though this will *allow* worse things to happen. Moreover, if it is always right to do the best that we can do, and the best that we can do may well result in something worse happening overall, then it is sometimes right not to do what brings about the best consequences overall. The force of this general intuition, explored in Chapter 5, augments the pressure upon the consequentialist to recognize not just the rational relevance of distinctions between doing harms and allowing them, but the moral relevance of such distinctions as well.

The rationale for rejecting the moral relevance of the broad distinction between doing and allowing is the rationale for accepting the consequentialist theory of moral standards. But it has been demonstrated in Chapter 5 that many of the rationales offered in support of CMS turn upon a misappropriation, and cease to be plausible once that misappropriation is exposed. Indeed, properly understood, RAMS provides strong support for the moral relevance of the broad distinction between doing and allowing. The rationale for the consequentialist theory of moral standards that survived the arguments in Chapter 5 turns upon the appeal to impartiality. If impersonality is the only (or even the most plausible) fundamental conception of impartiality for morality, and morality is fundamentally impartial, then the moral relevance of any distinction between doing and allowing is again called into question. But the point of the previous sections has been to demonstrate both that it is implausible to take impersonality to be the fundamental conception of impartiality for morality, and that an alternative conception of impartiality is readily available; indeed, that such a conception is developed naturally as a response to certain difficulties that arise from taking the impersonal conception to be fundamental to morality.

This alternative interpersonal conception dovetails with the common sense moral relevance of the doing/allowing distinction, allowing for both moral restrictions and moral permissions. Moreover, because it can recognize non-impersonal moral considerations at the foundational level, it avoids the central difficulty that confronts efforts by consequentialists to establish the rational authority of their impersonal moral requirements.

This alternative conception of impartiality as interpersonality not only allows for the relevance of the broad doing and allowing distinction, the distinction between what it is good or right to do and the badness of what is allowed to happen, but in addition provides support at least for certain paradigmatic doing/allowing cases. Indeed, it provides a rationale for our intuition that it is often wrong to do certain things even though this will allow more such equally bad wrongs to be done. Our previous example involving Bob and Carol and Ted and Alice provides just such a case. Ted can prevent harms from being done to Bob and Carol, but only by inflicting such harms on Alice. But recourse to the interpersonal standpoint accounts for why Ted cannot do certain things to Alice in such circumstances that he will allow to be done by others to Bob and Carol. The impartial recognition of the independent moral significance of each is recognition of the fundamental claim that each has upon Ted not to be interfered with. Their respective claims preclude him from interfering with any of them on impersonal grounds, and may do so even in cases in which this will allow multiple equally damaging interferences with their claims by others. Far from begging the question against the consequentialist's rejection of the doing/allowing distinction, the arguments presented so far have systematically challenged the grounds offered by consequentialists for rejecting the moral relevance of distinctions between doing and allowing. It is their rationales for CMS that provide their argument against the moral relevance of the distinction, and it is precisely these rationales that have been undermined.[41]

---

[41] Scheffler reaches a similar conclusion, arguing that if "we are to hold ourselves and others to norms of individual responsibility at all" (2004, p. 236), norms of the sort that are invoked in the evaluation of actions as good and bad, right and wrong, then "the norms in question will . . . have to provide a standard of assessment that is not purely instrumental" (ibid., p. 236), i.e. that treats "the distinction between doing and allowing as normatively relevant" (ibid., p. 236). Such standards, he argues, tell us that "there is a distinctive kind of normative significance that attaches to what we do—to the primary manifestation of our agency" (ibid., p. 236). He provides a focused argument for the incoherence of attempts to reconcile the consequentialist's instrumentalist standard to a plausible account of individual responsibility.

We began the chapter with two remaining challenges. The first was posed by a set of influential arguments against any rationale for agent-centered restrictions. The second was grounded in the impartiality of morality: if the moral evaluation of actions as right and wrong is impartial evaluation, and impersonality is the only viable conception of impartiality, then only consequentialism can allow for the intuition that the evaluation of actions as right or wrong deploys such a conception of impartiality—of robust equal concern. In response to the first challenge I have argued that a standard strategy for providing a rationale for agent-centered permissions provides a rationale for agent-centered restrictions as well—for moral requirements not to bring about the best overall consequences. Even as Scheffler deploys it, such a rationale presupposes a standpoint from which the rightness and wrongness of actions can be determined through assigning morally relevant reasons, including both partial and impersonal reasons, appropriate weight. When his liberation strategy is articulated in the form of a true liberation rather than a mere liberation as license strategy, the result is the outlines of a rationale for agent-centered restrictions as well as agent-centered permissions. This rationale also provides a response to the second of our challenges by providing the outlines of an alternative conception of impartiality that is relevant to the evaluation of actions as right and wrong, much as the impersonal conception of impartiality is appropriate for the evaluation of overall states of affairs as better or worse. It is not the case that the impartiality appropriate for the determination of right and wrong actions can only be supplied by the impersonal standpoint. Rather, recognition of the independent moral significance of the points of view of persons provides a framework for the impartial evaluation of actions as right or wrong.

The challenge to consequentialism was developed in the first three chapters, and refined into two distinct challenges in Chapter 4. The first of these distinct challenges provided the tools for arguments in Chapter 5 that undermine many of the traditional considerations offered in support of consequentialism. The second of these distinct challenges has been refined in this chapter, and this refinement has provided the tools for setting aside one of the remaining considerations traditionally offered in support of consequentialism—that it alone can account for the impartiality of the moral evaluation of actions. It has become apparent that certain natural responses to the inadequacies of act consequentialism suggest the outlines of an alternative conception of impartiality that points the way beyond consequentialism to a very different account of the moral evaluation of actions as right or wrong, one which reinforces rather than undermines our considered judgments that morality sometimes permits us not to do, and at other times prohibits us from doing, what will bring about the best overall state of affairs. In the next chapter we will see how this alternative conception of impartiality and the account of right action that it suggests fares within the framework of the first two members of our original triad.

7

Impartial Evaluation and Rational Authority

7.1 Introduction

We saw in Chapter 2 that the consequentialist theory of moral standards is one leg of a triad of normative claims that are in considerable tension with each other, and that this tension raises significant obstacles to providing a plausible account of the rational authority of consequentialist moral standards. In Chapters 3 and 4 it became clear that the central problems with consequentialism are not (as is commonly thought) that it is too demanding and too alienating, but that it does not appear to make any demands upon rational agents at all, and that integrated rational agents are not alienated by consequentialist morality but from it. Certain insights of Bernard Williams were developed which suggest that a systematic mistake underlies the standard conviction that consequentialism is instead too demanding and too alienating. Williams' diagnosis suggests that the impersonal standpoint is best understood as a higher-order standpoint that can be taken up towards what rational agents are recognized as having good lower-order reasons to value, non-impersonal reasons including distinctively moral reasons. As a higher-order standpoint towards these lower-order reasons of persons it in one sense comprehends all such reasons and values. But as with the temptation to see higher-order desires as comprehensive desires, there is a temptation to see such a higher-order standpoint towards the reasons of persons as providing comprehensive reasons. Higher-order desires, however, are not only not comprehensive desires, they presuppose, in their very articulation and operation, that they are at most some desires among others. Similarly, whatever reasons might arise from appeal to the higher-order impersonal standpoint are not only not comprehensive reasons, they presuppose, in their very articulation, that they are at most some reasons among others. Moreover, because many of the lower-order reasons towards which this higher-order standpoint is appropriately adopted appear to be moral reasons, such a diagnosis calls into question not just the rational authority of impersonal evaluation but its moral authority as well. The impersonal standpoint may well play a crucial role in the articulation of certain moral reasons, but it appears to do so in a way that presupposes other non-impersonal moral reasons and a non-impersonal conception of impartiality.

It became clear in Chapter 5 that many of the consequentialist's rationales for treating the impersonal standpoint as the fundamental moral standpoint turn on an implausible interpretation of the intuition that it is always right to do what's best upon which it relates rightness of actions to goodness of overall outcomes rather than to goodness of actions. The remaining rationale for a consequentialist theory of moral standards turns on the claims that morality is impartial, and that the only viable candidate for the conception of impartiality fundamental to morality is impersonality. In the previous chapter, however, it was demonstrated that an alternative interpersonal conception of impartiality emerges naturally as a result of efforts to address the deep tensions within a consequentialist approach. This alternative interpersonal conception of impartiality came into view following the collapse of Scheffler's independence thesis, a collapse that is precipitated by consistent application of the very rationales that he cites in his arguments for that thesis. Reason liberates us from moral require-ments (thereby violating RAMS) unless we recognize the independent moral significance of the person's own point of view. Morality enslaves us to the impersonal standpoint unless we recognize the independent moral significance of persons. Recognition of the moral significance that per-sons have independent of their impersonal moral significance is necessary both to secure the rational authority of moral requirements and to fend off enslavement of the agent to the impersonal standpoint by morality. Moreover, whereas recognition of one's own independent moral signifi-cance is necessary to fend off direct enslavement at one's own hands, it is recognition of one's independent moral significance by others that is necessary to fend off indirect enslavement to the impersonal standpoint at their hands.

This liberation rationale suggests the outlines of a robust interpersonal conception of impartiality that is distinct from the impersonal conception of impartiality. Moreover, whereas the impersonal conception captures a form of equal concern for persons that is appropriate, in the first instance, for the evaluation of overall states of affairs as better or worse, this interpersonal conception of impartiality is relevant, in the first instance, to the evaluation of potential courses of action as right or wrong. We saw in the previous chapter that Scheffler's own account presupposes a standpoint for the evaluation of actions as right and wrong—the standpoint from which morally significant impersonal and non-impersonal reasons are accorded their appropriate moral weight. A consistent application of his liberation strategy suggests that interpersonal impartiality plays a fundamental role in this standpoint for the moral evaluation of actions, just as impersonal impartiality plays a fundamental role in the evaluation of states of affairs. Moreover, such a fundamental role for interpersonal impartiality in the moral evaluation of actions provides a rationale for the agent-centered restrictions and permissions that are central to ordinary morality.[1]

What has emerged here is but the barest outline of an alternative to the impersonal conception of impartiality. Like the impersonal conception of impartiality itself, this interpersonal conception has been fleshed out in significantly different ways and supported through appeal to a range of different rationales and theories of practical reason. Kant famously calls upon such an interpersonal conception of impartiality to play a foundational role in both reason and morality.[2] Many contractarian approaches also provide moral theories upon which the interpersonal conception is the fundamental conception for the moral evaluation of actions and institutions, theories grounded in the mutual recognition of and respect for each person by each person.[3] Hobbes and Hobbesians argue that such rationally authoritative

---

[1] Shelly Kagan (1989, pp. 19–32) points out in his critique of views such as Scheffler's that a plausible account of agent-centered permissions must be supplemented with an account of agent-centered restrictions. He then argues that there is no independent rationale for such restrictions. But it has become apparent that no independent rationall is necessary—the very rationale that results in permissions is the rationale that results in restrictions. The constraints that are required to render permissions plausible are provided by the rationale for such permissions.

[2] Kant (1997). For contemporary Kantian accounts, see Barbara Herman (1993), Onora O'Neill (1989), and Christine Korsgaard (1996a, 1996b).

[3] This point is made explicitly by Kumar (1999, pp. 284–7), and it seems clear that Scanlon's account of respecting the value of human life as requiring "us to treat rational creatures only in ways that would be allowed by principles that they could not reasonably reject" (1998, p. 106),

interpersonal moral evaluation of actions can be based in the appeal to practical reason understood as fundamentally partial.[4] My arguments in earlier chapters have demonstrated that the appeal of moral theories that take the impersonal conception of impartiality to be fundamental is largely illusory; my suggestion in the previous chapter is that Scheffler's liberation rationale, a rationale that results from full recognition of the independent moral significance of the personal point of view, provides additional support for an approach that takes the interpersonal conception to play a fundamental role in the moral evaluation of actions.

Even philosophers such as Thomas Nagel, who have questioned whether such an alternative conception of impartiality can play a foundational role in moral evaluation, nonetheless offer articulations of the interpersonal conception of impartiality and identify certain roles that they take such a conception to play in moral evaluation. Many consequentialists themselves do not deny that such an alternative conception has a role to play in moral evaluation. Their claim is rather that this role is derived from impersonal moral foundations. Thus, Mill's account of justice deploys such an interpersonal conception of impartiality,[5] but he grounds such a role for the interpersonal conception in the appeal to impersonal value.

If such an interpersonal conception of impartiality is recognized as playing a fundamental role in the moral evaluation of actions, any moral theory incorporating such recognition will take us beyond consequentialism. But certain influential arguments developed by Nagel challenge the claim that such an alternative interpersonal conception can play such a fundamental role in either morality or practical reason. Nagel's arguments will be taken up in Sections 7.3–7.5. Moreover, it remains to be shown that a theory of moral standards which recognizes a fundamental role for this alternative interpersonal conception of impartiality has prospects for succeeding where standard consequentialism seems so dramatically to fail, by providing at least the outlines of a theory of moral reasons (not just moral standards)

---

especially when interpreted as restricting the justification of principles only to "various individuals' reasons for objecting" (ibid., p. 239), invokes an interpersonal as opposed to an impersonal conception of impartiality in the articulation of the principles governing right action. I will demonstrate in the next section that Stephen Darwall invokes the interpersonal conception of impartiality as fundamental. Darwall takes his own articulation of the interpersonal standpoint to be in various respects Fichtean, Kantian, and contractarian.

[4] For such arguments see Thomas Hobbes (1994) and David Gauthier (1986).
[5] Mill (2001, ch. 5).

upon which agents have decisive reasons to do what such moral standards require and avoid what they prohibit. Such a theory of moral reasons would appear to require recognition of the independent moral significance of each person as reflected, at least de facto, in the recognition of the independent rational significance of each person for each person. If the case for such de facto recognition of the independent rational significance of each person for each person can be established, replacement of the consequentialist's impersonal theory of moral standards (CMS) in our original triad with such an alternative interpersonal theory of moral standards would avoid the tensions that beset the original triad. This challenge for a fundamentally interpersonal theory of moral standards can also be framed in the terms introduced in the fifth chapter. Is there the requisite linkage on such a theory between what it is right or wrong to do and what it is better and worse to do (what the agent has the best reasons to do) such that the agent typically has decisive reasons not to do what such interpersonal moral standards prohibit, and is typically morally permitted (at least) to do what she has decisive reasons to do?

In what follows I will offer a series of considerations in support of the case for the rational authority of the sorts of moral requirements that will be generated by an account that is based upon an interpersonal conception of impartiality. In the next section I will demonstrate that accounts of moral standards that call upon this alternative conception to play a fundamental role can draw for support upon our ordinary moral intuitions concerning the rational authority of moderate moral requirements. We have seen in Chapter 3 that such ordinary moral intuitions work against rather than in favor of the consequentialist alternative. I will also argue that what Stephen Darwall characterizes as impartial second-personal reasons—reasons that he and others have argued are presupposed by the reactive attitudes that fundamentally structure our rational agency—presuppose the rational authority of interpersonal moral reasons.[6]

In Sections 7.3 and 7.4 I will argue that the recognition of a foundational role for the interpersonal conception of impartiality in the moral evaluation of actions is supported by deep structural features of practical as opposed to theoretical reason. This argument will proceed first by arguing against the

---

[6] See also Kumar (1999, pp. 284–7) for such an account of reactive attitudes as presupposing such an alternative interpersonal conception of impartiality.

aspects of Thomas Nagel's account of practical reason which appear to suggest that the deep structural features of objective practical reason preclude a fundamental role for such an interpersonal conception of impartiality in the evaluation of action. These aspects of Nagel's account appear to suggest that objective practical reasons must be grounded at the most fundamental level in the impersonal evaluation of states of affairs, hence that whatever role is played by the interpersonal conception of impartiality must be derivative. I will demonstrate that such aspects of his account draw heavily upon certain alleged analogies between the theoretical and practical spheres, and in particular between the fundamental conceptions of impartiality in these spheres. I will show that these points of alleged analogy are instead properly understood as points at which the spheres are crucially, fundamentally disanalogous, and that the resulting disanalogies suggest that if any conception of impartiality structures objective practical reason, it will have to be a conception that, like the interpersonal conception, can countenance a role for non-impersonal reasons at the most fundamental level.

I will close in Section 7.5 by considering another tantalizing aspect of Nagel's analogy between the theoretical and practical spheres. We have seen that impartial evaluation of actions is not impersonal evaluation of actions. But Nagel's analogy suggests that just as evaluation of beliefs as true is impartial evaluation, and agents have compelling reasons, ceteris paribus, to believe what they impartially evaluate as true, so too evaluation of actions as good, better, and best is impartial evaluation, and agents have decisive reasons, ceteris paribus, to perform the action impartially evaluated as best. If the interpersonal standpoint is the appropriate standpoint for the impartial evaluation of actions as good, better, and best, such an analogy suggests that it is not just the appropriate standpoint for the moral evaluation of actions as right and wrong, but the appropriate standpoint for the rational evaluation of actions and reasons for action as good, bad, and best.

7.2 Ordinary Morality and Second-Personal Reasons

In this section I will provide two grounds for optimism that recognition of a fundamental role for the interpersonal conception of impartiality will result in a moral theory that can satisfy RAMS. The first is that in contrast with consequentialist moral requirements, our ordinary moral intuitions do appear to support, at least in broad outline, the rational authority of the sorts of moral requirements that emerge from the interpersonal evaluation of actions. The second draws upon recent work by Stephen Darwall demonstrating that reactive attitudes such as guilt, resentment, and moral indignation, attitudes that fundamentally structure our interactions with each other as responsible agents, presuppose the distinctive rational authority of interpersonal moral requirements.

As we saw in earlier chapters, even many consequentialists draw regularly upon the intuition that ordinary moral requirements have rational authority. Intuitively, we typically have decisive reasons to do what morality requires and avoid what it prohibits. But our ordinary moral conviction is bound up with our ordinary moral standards. Because these standards hold that we are often not morally required to bring about the best overall states of affairs, and are sometimes morally required not to bring about the best overall states of affairs, this ordinary moral conviction suggests that we are often not rationally required to bring about the best overall state of affairs, and often rationally required not to bring about the best overall state of affairs.

Because the consequentialist's moral standards always yield a moral requirement, and it is always a moral requirement to bring about the best overall state of affairs, these same ordinary moral intuitions would appear to suggest that such moral standards would not have the rational authority that ordinary morality intuitively does. Intuitively, we are often not rationally required to bring about the best overall consequences and often rationally required not to bring about the best overall consequences, hence in all such cases consequentialist moral requirements would appear, intuitively, to lack rational authority. The consequentialist account jettisons ordinary morality but leaves ordinary reason in place. The result is a striking collapse of any intuitive support for the rational authority of its moral requirements.

The case is quite different if we recognize a fundamental role for the interpersonal conception of impartiality in the moral evaluation of actions. This conception, we have seen, would seem naturally to produce agent-centered permissions, allowing that agents are not morally required to bring about the best overall state of affairs in cases in which such actions would fail to take into account the independent moral significance of the person's own point of view. It would also naturally seem to produce agent-centered restrictions, moral requirements not to bring about the best overall state of affairs, in cases in which such an action would fail to take into account the independent moral significance of another person. Taking into account his own independent moral significance may well free Ted from a moral requirement to sacrifice himself in our previous example, and taking into account Alice's independent moral significance can morally restrict Ted from sacrificing Alice (even to save Bob and Carol), thereby freeing her from enslavement to the impersonal standpoint at his hands.

Because such a conception of impartiality lines up, at least structurally, with ordinary moral standards, it can plausibly draw for support upon the intuitive conviction that such ordinary moral standards have rational authority. The interpersonal conception can plausibly be seen as generating the structural features of the ordinary moral standards that, intuitively, do have rational authority, while the consequentialist's impersonal conception offers an alternative to such ordinary moral standards, an alternative upon which, intuitively, moral standards appear to lack rational authority.

A second source of optimism concerning the rational authority of interpersonal moral requirements is suggested by Darwall's recent work on what he characterizes as the second-personal standpoint and second-person reasons.[7] Darwall argues that the reactive attitudes that play a deep and pervasive role in our everyday reasoning and justification, attitudes such as guilt, resentment, and indignation, presuppose the distinctive rational authority of agent-relative reasons generated through recourse to a second-personal standpoint. This second-person standpoint from which such agent-relative reasons are generated is structured by an interpersonal rather than an impersonal conception of impartiality. Darwall's account thus suggests that reactive attitudes presuppose not just the moral authority of interpersonal moral requirements, but their distinctive rational authority as well.

Recall that the interpersonal standpoint which emerged in the previous chapter is (1) an impartial standpoint which generates (2) agent-relative impartial reasons, and (3) corresponding agent-relative impartial claims. Moreover, (4) these are impartial reasons in the first instance for people not to do things to particular people, and claims that people have against

---

[7] This second point, articulated through appeal to Darwall's account of reactive attitudes as presupposing second-personal reasons, is itself a development of one aspect of the first point, that interpersonally structured approaches to morality can draw upon the intuitive rational authority of ordinary morality. I am grateful to Noel Birondo for helping me to see this connection.

particular other people that things not be done to them. All four of these markers are present in Darwall's account of the standpoint that is presupposed by reactive attitudes. Darwall is clear, for example, that the standpoint presupposed by our reactive attitudes is an impartial standpoint, and in particular an "impartially disciplined version of the second-personal standpoint."[8] Moreover, he is clear that the reasons that are articulated through appeal to this impartial standpoint "would be agent-relative rather than agent-neutral,"[9] and that these are reasons to do and not to do, not agent-neutral reasons to promote outcomes:

The reason would not be addressed to him as someone who is simply in a position to alter the regrettable state of someone's causing another pain. . . . It would be addressed to him, rather, as the person causing gratuitous pain to another person, something we normally assume we have the authority to demand that persons not do to one another.[10]

Reactive attitudes thus presuppose, Darwall argues, an impartial standpoint of equal concern from which you and I make and acknowledge claims on one another's conduct and will.[11] This impartial standpoint is the source of agent-relative reasons not to do things to other people, rather than reasons merely to prevent things from happening to other people; moreover, such a standpoint is a source not only of impartial agent-relative reasons not to do things, but also of agent-relative claims and of the authority to demand that persons not do what will violate such claims. In short, the impartial standpoint that Darwall argues is presupposed by reactive attitudes has all of the distinctive markers of the interpersonal alternative to the impersonal conception of impartiality, markers that highlight the contrast with the impersonal conception. This second-personal impartial standpoint generates agent-relative reasons and agent-relative claims that support the authority to make agent-relative demands upon others to act or not act in certain ways.

The authority to which Darwall appeals appears to be precisely the authority that Alice has in our previous example to demand that Ted not kill her even to prevent more killing from happening. The adoption of such an interpersonal conception via recognition of the independent moral significance of each person's point of view will manifest itself, in cases in

---

[8] Darwall (2006, p. 102).   [9] Ibid., p. 7.   [10] Ibid., p. 7.
[11] This is a paraphrase from Darwall (2004).

which it is my own recognition of my independent significance that is at issue, as a moral entitlement to act in ways that do not bring about the best overall consequences, and, in cases in which it is your recognition of my independent moral significance that is at issue, as a moral commitment by you not to interfere with my acting in the ways to which I am entitled. My independent moral significance is the ground both for my own moral entitlement to act and for your moral requirement not to interfere with my action. If I am morally entitled, you are morally committed (albeit perhaps only defeasibly), and vice versa. To have such interpersonal moral entitlements is thus to have impartial but agent-relative claims upon each other person to uphold their corresponding commitments, and to have the authority to make demands upon them when they fail to do so.

The interpersonal conception of impartiality, we have seen, suggests that both Alice and Darwall's pain sufferer have moral significance independent of their impersonal moral significance. This independent moral significance is manifested as a claim against being treated as having merely impersonal moral significance, a claim that can, when sufficient, generate moral prohibitions upon treating them this way. It is Alice's moral claim upon Ted not to treat her this way that constrains him. The point is not that treating her this way would be a bad thing to happen that Ted can prevent from happening: this is merely recognition of impersonal moral significance, not recognition of her moral significance independent of the impersonal point of view. It is instead a claim that anyone, but in this case Alice, has upon anyone, but in these circumstances Ted, that is independent of the badness of such a harming happening—of the act's impersonal moral significance.[12] Alice has an independent claim on Ted, in such a case, not to be harmed by him, a claim that is independent of the third person, impersonal badness of that harm resulting. It is a claim that Alice has on any other "you," any "second person," not to be harmed by that person.

If the only claim were a claim to prevent a worse state of affairs from happening as determined from an impersonal standpoint, there would be no moral prohibition against killing Alice, and no moral significance for such a killing independent of the impersonal standpoint. Alice's is instead a claim upon each other person not to interfere (at least) with her in

---

[12] Such claims, then, are general (see Nagel's characterization of generality (1970, pp. 47ff.)) and impartial, but they are not impersonal, hence are not "agent-neutral" reasons in the sense in which we are using this term, that is, not reasons based in the appeal to the impersonal value of states of affairs.

certain specifiable ways that gives rise to a moral requirement for Ted not to kill her even to prevent a worse overall state of affairs from resulting. Her impersonal moral significance may well be involved in the articulation of a claim upon others to prevent something bad happening to her. Her moral significance independent of the impersonal standpoint, by contrast, gives rise to a claim against anyone, any "you"—in these circumstances Ted—harming her. Darwall emphasizes that such a claim authorizes her to demand that Ted not act against her, and that such a demand "would not be addressed to him as someone who is simply in a position to alter the regrettable state of someone's pain . . . it would be addressed to him, rather, as the person causing gratuitous pain to another person."[13] The moral reason that Ted has in our example not to kill Alice is thus in Darwall's sense a second-personal reason, and the interpersonal conception of impartiality provides the structure within which such impartial but non-impersonal reasons and claims come into view.[14, 15]

Darwall provides a broadly Kantian and Fichtean rationale for recognition of the independent moral significance of the standpoint of each individual person, a rationale that takes the resulting moral requirements to be rooted in our common natures as free and equal.[16] Moreover, he emphasizes one central implication of such recognition, that agents have equal authority to require or demand that we comply with these requirements.[17] To be entitled in virtue of my independent moral significance is to have a claim on you not to interfere, hence to have the moral authority to demand that you recognize my entitlement, a demand that you have a moral obligation to acknowledge.

This recognition that impartial agent-relative reasons presuppose the interpersonal conception of impartiality provides a second ground for

[13] Darwall (2006, p. 7).

[14] See Darwall's characterization of such claims as arising within a "fundamentally intersubjective" and "impartially disciplined" version of the second-person standpoint (ibid., p. 102).

[15] These claims can be viewed impersonally, and we can set out to maximize, from an impersonal standpoint, the extent to which they are recognized; the point here is that they are not impersonal claims. See Darwall (2006, p. 78) for his argument that such second-person reasons are irreducible to impersonal reasons.

[16] One can, of course, adopt a different rationale for the independent moral significance of the standpoints of each individual person, and even a different (less Fichtean) version of a Kantian rationale for such a standpoint.

[17] Darwall emphasizes this point at the outset of "Respect and the Second-Person Standpoint" (2004).

optimism that the moral authority of interpersonal moral commitments is reflected in the rational authority of such commitments as well. This ground emerges from Darwall's analysis of what Strawson famously characterized as reactive attitudes, attitudes such as indignation, guilt, forgiveness, blame, and resentment that fundamentally structure our interactions with each other.[18] For me to experience a reactive attitude such as resentment, Darwall suggests, is to take myself to have claims upon you and your conduct. Such claims presuppose that certain authority relations hold between you and me, relations that presuppose an impartial but not impersonal standpoint of robust equal concern from which the addressee can "take up the very same point of view that an addresser takes up in holding them responsible."[19] Guilt is a reactive attitude, for example, and shame is not, precisely because guilt "feels like the appropriate (second-personal) response to blame," whereas in the case of shame "the relevant regard is not second-personal,"[20] but third-personal. Such reactive attitudes, then, presuppose the authority to make claims from a second-personal standpoint of impartial concern, deploying precisely the interpersonal conception of impartiality that results from recognition of the independent moral significance of the standpoint of each person by each other person. More importantly for present purposes, reactive attitudes presuppose not merely the moral authority of such agent-relative claims generated from an interpersonal standpoint, but "the capacity to hold oneself responsible and . . . determine oneself by a second-personal reason, that is, an agent-relative reason whose validity is grounded in presupposed normative relations between persons and that is therefore independent of the value of any outcome or state."[21] In short, the reactive attitudes that pervasively structure our engagement with others as responsible agents, attitudes without which we are unrecognizable as responsible agents,[22] presuppose not merely the moral authority of fundamentally interpersonal claims, but their rational authority as well. Such attitudes presuppose not just the moral significance of each person for each person independent of her impersonal moral significance, but that this independent moral significance is reflected in independent

---

[18] Although it is Strawson who emphasizes the fundamental and irreducible role of such reactive attitudes, it is Darwall who argues that such attitudes presuppose reasons and claims articulated through appeal to an impartially disciplined second personal standpoint, a standpoint that shares all of the features of the interpersonal alternative to the impersonal conception of impartiality.

[19] Darwall (2006, p. 79).   [20] Ibid., p. 71.   [21] Ibid., p. 78.

[22] See Scheffler's (2004) defense of this claim.

rational significance as well. To make sense of the reactive attitudes that structure our interactions with others, Darwall argues, is to presuppose second-person moral claims with second-person rational authority. To have such attitudes is thus to presuppose "the acceptance of (agent-relative) norms of action," norms that are grounded in an impartial standpoint other than the impersonal standpoint and that presuppose the capacity to take such "moral demands as conclusive reasons for acting."[23] Darwall's analysis of reactive attitudes thus suggests that they presuppose the rational authority of an interpersonally structured impartial standpoint, a standpoint of authority relations that are taken to hold between an addresser and an addressee. Second-personal reasons mirroring claims generated from an interpersonal standpoint appear to be a central component of practical reason and deliberation.[24]

In Chapter 6 we were led to an interpersonal impartial standpoint for moral evaluation by the inability of the impersonal conception to account for the rational authority of moral requirements. Darwall's arguments lead us to the same alternative standpoint for moral evaluation in part by demonstrating the inability of the impersonal conception to account for the authority, both rational and moral, of the claims and reasons implicit in our reactive attitudes. In light of such considerations, it becomes difficult to see how foundational consequentialism can plausibly be maintained. If the interpersonal conception of impartiality plays a fundamental role in practical rational evaluation, this raises considerable obstacles to any consequentialist account of moral standards upon which they purport to have rational authority. That such obstacles to consequentialism have not played a more prominent role in evaluations of the theory is due in part, ironically, to the influence of one of the most persistent and insightful critics of consequentialism, Thomas Nagel. It is to Nagel's arguments that I will now turn.

---

[23] Darwall (2006, p. 78).

[24] Rebecca Kukla and Mark Lance (2008) isolate two distinct elements in Darwall's account of second-personal reasons. One, the component upon which I have focused, is the grounding of certain impartial reasons "in specific, agent-relative relations between persons" (ibid., ch. 5, sec. 4), i.e. in the interpersonal (his second-personal) standpoint. The second concerns the relationship between such agent-relative, impartial reasons and second-personal address. I do not take up this second element here, nor do I take up Darwall's account of the relationship between these two elements. In their own work Kukla and Lance present certain challenges to Darwall's account of the relationship between these two elements (ibid., ch. 5, sec. 4).

7.3 Tensions within Nagel's Ethics

Thomas Nagel is one of the few philosophers who clearly invokes and carefully distinguishes roles for both the interpersonal and impersonal conceptions of impartiality in practical reason and deliberation. He not only (1) clearly distinguishes roles for the two conceptions in ethics, but (2) clarifies the nature of the constraints that interpersonally articulated reasons appear to generate upon action in accordance with impersonally articulated reasons, and (3) emphasizes the agent-neutrality of the reasons generated from one of these impartial standpoints and the agent-relativity of the reasons generated by the other.

Nagel's appeal to the two conceptions is of particular significance because he also provides a series of subtle and extremely influential arguments that appear to undermine any non-derivative role for the interpersonal conception. One such line of argument suggests that objective practical reason is conditioned by an impartial standpoint that is fundamentally agent-neutral. This line of argument appears to imply that any interpersonal, agent-relative claims that agents have upon each other, and with them the purported objectivity of interpersonal reasons, are at best derivative from impersonal, agent-neutral foundations.[25] Another line of argument in Nagel's work suggests that reasons are appropriately articulated within a framework for the evaluation of states of affairs. Although such an account may seem innocuous, because actions are included as constituents of the events/states of affairs that we have reasons to promote, its implications are profound. If the fundamental role of actions in practical reasons is that of constituents of states of affairs that are to be promoted, the fundamental standpoints for rational evaluation become the standpoints for the evaluation of the states of affairs of which such actions are constituents. The obvious standpoints for evaluating such states of affairs determine whether they are the best state of affairs for an agent ("best for me") and the best overall state of affairs. Such standpoints, however, allow no place for impartial but agent-relative considerations: the former is agent-relative but partial, the

---

[25] A similar diagnosis can be found in Korsgaard's (1996b, pp. 275–310) discussion of Nagel. Korsgaard argues that on one understanding of agent-neutrality often suggested by Nagel, an objective realist understanding, his distinction between agent-relative, subjective reasons and values and agent-neutral, objective reasons and values would "leave out an important option," intersubjective values that fit into neither category (ibid., p. 281).

latter is impartial but agent-neutral. If my actions are evaluated entirely as means to or components of states of affairs that are the best for me or the best overall, there will be no fundamental role for interpersonal reasons. Although Nagel is himself an advocate of agent-centered restrictions, even he allows that these aspects of his account render such restrictions, and the interpersonal reasons that give rise to them, "paradoxical."

In the remainder of this section I will demonstrate the role that appeals to both conceptions of impartiality play in Nagel's account. In the next section I will take up one of Nagel's arguments that appears to undermine any fundamental role for the interpersonal conception and interpersonal reasons. I will show that Nagel cannot accept this argument. In Section 7.4 I will show that it is his characterization of practical reasons that renders the appeal to interpersonal reasons paradoxical, and demonstrate that the tools have already been provided in our earlier arguments for rejecting this characterization. It will become apparent that his arguments inadvertently threaten to generate a version of our problematic normative triad that is even more fundamental than the one that plagues the consequentialist. An advocate of such arguments would be committed not just to the position that rational agents often have sufficient reasons to do what is wrong, but to the claim that such agents often have sufficient reasons to do what they have decisive reasons not to do. My suggestion will be that Nagel's commitment to the impartiality of practical reason, coupled with his recognition that there are good agent-relative reasons operating at even the most fundamental level of justification, commits him to a fundamental conception of impartiality in the practical sphere that is not agent-neutral; indeed, to the fundamental status of his own interpersonal conception.

Nagel's View

Nagel clearly appeals to an agent-neutral impersonal conception of impartiality as playing a central role in both the moral and rational evaluation of actions. Less clearly, but importantly, he also consistently appeals to an agent-relative interpersonal conception of impartiality as playing a central role in both the moral and rational evaluation of actions. This alternative standpoint, he claims, involves

a different kind of impersonal judgment from the one which enables us to recognize that what happens to anyone is just as important as what happens to anyone else. In addition, we have to enter into the motivational point of view of each individual and recognize that there are also conditions on what it is reasonable to demand of him, because his personal standpoint imposes certain claims.[26]

Recall that the interpersonal conception of impartiality generates agent-centered reasons and claims, reasons and claims to do and not to do, not to prevent or promote overall outcomes. Although Nagel characterizes his alternative conception as giving rise to "a different kind of impersonal judgment," it is clear that in our terms this is a different kind of impartial judgment from the impersonal, agent-neutral kind. This different kind of impartial judgment is like the impersonal kind in that it arises from a standpoint of equal concern which recognizes that "one is only one among others equally real." Unlike impersonal impartiality, however, it does not proceed via impersonal transcendence of perspectives but through equal "identification with each perspective." Again unlike the impersonal standpoint, this alternative impartial standpoint gives rise not to agent-neutral principles but to "general agent-relative principles."[27] Recognition of the moral significance of the impersonal conception of impartiality accounts for why "murder is an evil that everyone has reason to prevent," but it is the moral significance of the interpersonal conception which accounts for why murder is in addition "an act that everyone has reason to *avoid*"(his emphasis).[28] This standpoint of equal concern recognizes a moral significance of the standpoints of persons that is independent of their impersonal moral significance. It recognizes that each "personal standpoint imposes certain claims" that cannot be captured by the impersonal standpoint. Such impartial but agent-relative reasons and claims, "considerations of what I may do, and the correlative claims of my victim against me" can "outweigh the substantial impersonal value of what will happen." In such cases although "things will be better, what happens will be better" if I act on impersonal moral reasons nonetheless, taking into account the relevant interpersonal reasons, "I will have done something worse."[29] As in Darwall's case, Nagel's alternative conception of impartiality has all of the markers of the interpersonal conception, and recognition of a central role for such a conception as a source of non-impersonal moral reasons

---

[26] Nagel (1991, p. 40). See also Nagel (1986, pp. 178 and 184) for additional characterizations of this distinct conception of impartiality as generating agent-relative claims by agents upon other agents.

[27] Nagel (1991, p. 40).   [28] Nagel (1986, p. 178).

[29] This and the preceding quotation are taken from Nagel (1986, p. 180).

generates agent-centered restrictions on the pursuit of the best overall state of affairs. Nagel often refers to the impersonal standpoint as a view from nowhere—from no particular point of view. This alternative, by contrast, is in effect an interpersonal view from each particular point of view, a standpoint that recognizes independent moral claims that each person has on each other person.

The impersonal standpoint gives rise to agent-neutral reasons for acting to bring about the best overall states of affairs. The interpersonal standpoint gives rise to reasons that, like impersonal requirements, are general and impartial, but unlike impersonal requirements, are non-impersonal. In much of Nagel's work "agent-neutrality," which is identified with the impersonal conception, is the marker of impartiality and objectivity, and "agent-relativity" (non-impersonality) is the marker of partiality and subjectivity. His own interpersonal requirements and reasons, which are general and impartial but not impersonal,[30] do not fit at all comfortably into this framework. To recognize the independent moral significance of each person's point of view is to recognize that each person has a claim on each other person that she not be treated only as a means either to that person's own personal ends or to impersonal ends. Nagel emphasizes rightly that such requirements and reasons are impartial, reasons each person has to, for example, avoid doing harm. In this respect they are like impersonal reasons. There is an interpersonal requirement upon each person not to assault any person, and an impersonal requirement upon each person to prevent such assaults from happening. But although such explicitly interpersonal moral reasons are general and impartial reasons, they cannot, in contrast with their impersonal counterparts, "be explained simply in terms of neutral values."[31] Agent-"neutral" values are here understood by Nagel (as we have been understanding them) as "impersonal" values. The fact that lies will be told to people gives rise, Nagel maintains, to an impersonal and impartial reason for me to prevent them. But the fact that *I* would have to lie to Smith gives rise to an impartial reason that is not based in the impersonal badness of a lie being told. It is a reason for me not to act in this way

---

[30] See Nagel's claim that if the restrictions generated by such reasons exist, they "apply to everyone: they are mandatory and may not be given up like personal ambitions or commitments" (ibid., p. 178). An act prohibited by such mandatory reasons is an act that "everyone has reason to avoid" (ibid., p. 178).

[31] Ibid., p. 176.

above and beyond the fact that it would prevent a state of affairs in which someone lies. Each person has a claim upon me that *I* not lie to her, a claim distinct from any claim she might have that I prevent all such lies from being told.

The nature of such interpersonal impartial requirements and reasons can be clarified through comparison with the operation of partial reasons. Consider a variation upon Scheffler's standard schema: unless I suffer harm to one of my projects five others will suffer equally serious harm to central projects of theirs. In my own practical reasoning my own project, precisely because it is mine, has independent rational significance for me, hence has weight as more than just another project that will suffer harm in the determination of what it is better or worse for me to do. Such partial reasons have rational significance independent of whatever impersonal moral or rational significance they might have.[32] Consider now the parallel interpersonal case: unless I betray a trust, five others will have their trust betrayed.[33] In my own moral evaluation of my actions my betrayal of someone's trust has moral weight as more than just a betrayal of trust that will result. Each of you may well have a claim upon me that I prevent your trust from being betrayed, but each of you also has an interpersonal claim upon me not to betray your trust. Hence the trust that I would have to betray has a moral significance that is independent of its significance merely as a trust that would be betrayed.

7.4 Nagel's Analogy Between the Theoretical and Practical Spheres

Now that the involvement of the two conceptions of impartiality in Nagel's account has been highlighted, we are in a position to consider which, if either, he takes to be the more fundamental conception for practical evaluation and why. If each of these conceptions plays a fundamental role in the evaluation of actions, the result is not consequentialism (at least not at the foundational level). Non-impersonal moral reasons will be arrayed against impersonally articulated reasons upon such an account, resulting in

[32] Nagel considers these under the heading of reasons of autonomy. See Nagel (1986, pp. 166ff.).
[33] Nagel labels such paradigmatically second personal reasons deontological reasons (ibid., pp. 175).

a structure amenable to agent-centered restrictions. If it is the interpersonal conception of impartiality, the view from each point of view, that is fundamental, the prospects for consequentialism, at least at the foundational level, are nonexistent: our fundamental impartial moral commitments will be non-impersonal (interpersonal) impartial commitments. Only if the impersonal conception, the view from nowhere, is fundamental does foundational consequentialism find support. We have already seen that such foundational consequentialist views confront serious obstacles to establishing the rational authority of the resulting moral requirements. In Section 7.2 it became apparent that the prospects are far brighter for accounts that allow a fundamental role for interpersonal impartial evaluation.

Ironically, it is Nagel himself, a staunch advocate of the legitimacy of the interpersonal point of view as a source of moral and rational constraints upon impersonal moral requirements, whose work is a source of some of the most influential arguments that it is instead the impersonal conception that must be fundamental.[34] In what follows I will first articulate this case for the fundamental role of the impersonal conception that can be found in Nagel's writings, an argument that turns crucially upon the interpretation of the relevant disanalogies and analogies between the theoretical and practical spheres. I will suggest that Nagel's interpretation threatens his account of the practical sphere with serious internal inconsistencies, and that a more plausible understanding of the relevant analogies and disanalogies suggests that whether or not objective rational evaluation of beliefs in the theoretical sphere is fundamentally agent-neutral and impersonal, objective rational evaluation of actions in the practical sphere cannot be. Indeed, only an alternative like the interpersonal conception of impartiality holds out the prospect of being able to play such a role.

Practical reason, Nagel argues, has objective purport: "the only acceptable reasons are objective ones."[35] This commitment is carried forward as well into his later work:

The initial data are reasons that appear from one's own point of view in acting. They usually present themselves with some pretensions to objectivity to begin with . . . the ordinary process of deliberation, aimed at finding out what I should do, assumes the existence of an answer to this question."[36]

---

[34] Scanlon (1998, ch. 2, esp. pp. 82ff.) highlights and criticizes this aspect of Nagel's account.

[35] Nagel (1970, p. 96).   [36] Nagel (1986, p. 149).

Good practical reason aims at objective correctness, and such practical objectivity, he argues, requires recourse to an impartial standpoint that involves "a conception of oneself as simply a person among others all of whom are included in a single world."[37] This requirement of practical reason, that one must be able to apply the fundamental principles of practical reason "to the person one is, in abstraction from the fact that it is oneself,"[38] is a feature of Nagel's account that is maintained as well in the *View from Nowhere*:

In the sphere of values or practical reasoning ... we must take up a new, comprehensive viewpoint after stepping back and including our former perspective in what is to be understood.[39]

Practical rational evaluation of actions, like theoretical rational evaluation of beliefs, purports to be objective, and objectivity presupposes an impartial standpoint from which one views oneself as one person among others. Indeed, in the practical sphere Nagel identifies impartiality as the fundamental condition of objectivity:

The condition of *objectivity* ... is the practical expression of ... oneself as merely one person among others, and of others as persons in just as full a sense. (his emphasis)[40]

Nagel, then, is committed to the objectivity of practical reason, and the impartiality of practical objectivity. But such a result, we have seen, underdetermines our choice of the impartiality in question. The impersonal view from no particular point of view and the interpersonal view from each particular point of view are both conceptions of impartiality recognized by Nagel, conceptions that involve recognition of oneself as simply one person among others equally real, and which are sources of universal principles. Moreover, in light of Nagel's commitment to the existence of good non-impersonal reasons of various sorts (including non-impersonal impartial reasons), reasons that can weigh against and in many cases outweigh relevant impersonal reasons, it seems unlikely that the impartiality that is on Nagel's view presupposed by the objectivity of practical reason will be impartiality conceived impersonally. The impartial (impersonal) view from no particular point of view cannot accommodate non-impersonal

---

[37] Nagel (1970, p. 100).   [38] Ibid., p. 108.   [39] Nagel (1986, p. 138).
[40] Nagel (1970, p. 88).

reasons at the foundational level; the impartial (interpersonal) view from each particular point of view can. Given Nagel's conviction that non-impersonal reasons play such a foundational role,[41] the commitment to a foundational role for interpersonal impartiality would appear to be straightforward. His arguments concerning practical impartiality also seem to dictate such an interpersonal conception. The arguments appeal to the reactive attitude of resentment,[42] and, as Darwall has argued, such attitudes appear to presuppose an interpersonal rather than an impersonal conception of impartiality. Practical objectivity, Nagel suggests, requires me to exchange perspectives with you, not to transcend our perspectives, and its fundamental "argument"—"Would you like it if someone did that to you?"[43]—seems more naturally suited to an interpersonal view from each particular point of view (putting me in your particular pair of shoes) than to an impersonal view from no particular point of view.

But certain of Nagel's commitments support just the opposite conclusion—that the fundamental conception of impartiality presupposed by practical reason is impersonality, not interpersonality.[44] These commitments suggest that the impartiality that he takes to be fundamental to both theoretical and the practical reason is impersonality. It is achieved by impersonal detachment, a stepping outside of the self.[45] If the impartial standpoint that is a condition of practical objectivity at the foundational level is impersonal and non-perspectival, non-impersonal reasons that are essentially agent-relative are in Nagel's sense partial, and cannot play anything but a derivative role in good practical reasoning.

Nagel's appeal to impersonality rather than interpersonality as the conception of impartiality that is fundamental to objective practical reason is motivated in large part through appeal to certain parallels that he draws between the theoretical sphere and the practical sphere. In *The Possibility of Altruism* he emphasizes a parallel between the threat of solipsism in the theoretical sphere and the threat of egoism in the practical sphere. Central to his argument in response to the first threat is his claim that the rejection of solipsism invokes our capacity to view ourselves and our circumstances through an impersonal, believer-neutral conception of

---

[41] A conviction the he expresses in his writings after *The Possibility of Altruism*. See below.
[42] See Nagel (1970, pp. 83–5).   [43] Ibid., p. 82.
[44] See Korsgaard's (1996b, pp. 275–310) analysis of Nagel's arguments.
[45] See, e.g., Nagel (1986, p. 181) and Nagel (1991, ch. 2).

impartiality. All of our theoretical judgments "commit us to corresponding impersonal judgments about the same circumstances."[46] Good reasons for me to believe, Nagel argues, purport to be, or to correspond to, good reasons for anyone to believe the same thing. In the theoretical sphere, Nagel argues, agent-relative factors make "no difference in what is to be believed to be the case, but only in *how* it is believed"(his emphasis).[47] My reasons for believing that Paris is the capital of France are good reasons for anyone to believe that this is true. We can put this point, following Darwall, by saying that on Nagel's account all good theoretical reasons are or correlate with good believer-neutral reasons,[48] reasons that purport to justify the belief in question impersonally. Such theoretical reasons presume to have a grounding in the world that is not specific to the particular believer in question, an impersonal grounding that provides believer-neutral reasons.[49]

The claim that all theoretical reasons purport to be impersonal, believer-neutral reasons is widely defended. Darwall has recently argued for such a position:

By its very nature, belief is responsible to an independent order of fact, which it aims to represent in a believer-neutral way. . . . Of course, what reasons people have to believe things about the world depend in many ways on where they stand in relation to it. But ultimately their reasons must be grounded in something that is independent of their stance, namely, what is the case believer-neutrally.[50]

Rebecca Kukla and Mark Lance make a similar point, suggesting that entitlement in such theoretical cases is "agent-neutral, because it purports to express entitlement to facts that are public and in no way agent specific, even if the epistemic conditions that allow these facts to be used . . . are themselves agent specific."[51] It is the transparency of belief to truth, to what is in fact that case, that is taken to account for the believer-neutral structure of theoretical reason. As Richard Moran has argued, "if a person asks himself the question 'Do I believe that P?,' he will treat this much as he would a corresponding question that does not refer to him at all,

---

[46] Nagel (1970, p. 106).   [47] Ibid., p. 112.

[48] Kukla and Lance (2008, ch. 1) characterize a reason as agent or believer-neutral in this sense if "its force is not targeted at anyone in particular," but is instead "inherently available to whomever is perceptive or lucky or interested enough" to avail themselves of them.

[49] This formulation adapts language from Kukla and Lance (2008, ch. 1, sec. 2).

[50] Darwall (2006, pp. 56–7).   [51] Kukla and Lance (2008, ch. 1, sec 4).

namely, the question 'Is P true?' "[52] Evidence for my believing that p will be evidence for the truth of p—evidence for anyone to believe that p.

The key to a successful response to the solipsist, Nagel maintains, lies in the recognition of the impartiality of good reasons for believing, and the recognition that the appropriate conception of impartiality is the impersonal conception: all good reasons for believing are fundamentally believer-neutral, and the standpoint of objective theoretical justification is fundamentally an impersonal, believer-neutral standpoint. Similarly, Nagel argues, the key to mounting a successful response to the egoist is an appeal to the impartiality of good reasons for acting. But he asserts, in addition, that the conception of impartiality that he takes to fundamentally condition theoretical objectivity, the impersonal conception, fundamentally conditions practical objectivity as well. All reasons for acting, this parallel suggests, purport to be agent-neutral reasons articulated at the most fundamental level from an agent-neutral standpoint. The parallel suggests that the standpoint of objective practical reason is fundamentally an impersonal, agent-neutral standpoint. Thus, Nagel is committed not just to the fundamental impartiality of practical reasons, but to the fundamental impersonality of the relevant conception of impartiality. The result would appear to be a commitment to the fundamental impersonality of all practical reasons.

Whether or not the standpoint of theoretical objectivity is fundamentally impersonal and believer-neutral, and whether such believer-neutrality allows for a response to solipsism, are interesting questions in their own right. But the relevant question here is whether there is a persuasive case for Nagel's analogous claim that all good practical reasons, reasons that purport to determine what the agent in fact should do, are fundamentally agent-neutral, impersonal reasons. The advocate of such a position would appear to be driven to adopt not merely a consequentialist theory of moral requirement, but a consequentialist theory of rational requirement. She would reject the second member of our triad, NIR, because all good reasons on such an account are, or correlate with, agent-neutral reasons to bring about the best overall state of affairs.

We have already seen that this is a consequence that even most consequentialists themselves are unwilling to accept. In later works Nagel

---

[52] Moran (2001, p. 60). For additional defenses of what I have characterized as the believer-neutrality of theoretical entitlements see Robert Brandom (1994, ch. 3) and Lance and Kukla's discussion of the agent-neutrality of entitlements to declaratives (2008, ch. 1).

acknowledges both that his earlier arguments commit him to this consequence, to the fundamental impersonality of practical reason, and that such
a consequence is unacceptable:

> I once claimed that there could be no reasons that were *just* agent-relative . . . I
> even suggested that all apparently relative reasons were really subsumable under
> neutral ones. . . . I no longer think the argument works . . . some values are
> agent-relative.[53]

Nagel recognizes by this point that agents have good non-impersonal
reasons for acting at even the most fundamental level. He rejects the
claim that all good reasons are fundamentally impersonal. But he continues
to maintain the fundamental impartiality of practical reason, and the
fundamental impersonality of practical impartiality—the very commitments
that led him initially to conclude that all good reasons are fundamentally
impersonal.[54] How can he recognize practical reasons that are fundamentally
non-impersonal while taking practical objectivity to be not just impartial
but impersonal? Again a parallel between the theoretical and practical
spheres looms large. In the relevant passages of *The View From Nowhere*
the most pressing threat in the theoretical sphere is not solipsism, but the
reductive physicalism that threatens to result from the complete detachment
that objectivity may seem to require. Nagel appears to suggest that a parallel
threat looms in the practical sphere; complete impersonal detachment
threatens to leave no room for good agent-relative reasons. His suggestion
in response, very roughly, is that although objectivity requires impersonal
detachment in both spheres, different degrees of detachment are appropriate
in the theoretical sphere.[55] So too, his account suggests, different degrees
of detachment are appropriate in the practical sphere. Objectivity in each
sphere is still identified with impersonal detachment, but the suggestion is
that just as less detached theoretical reasons can be recognized as among
our good reasons for believing, so too less detached practical reasons can
be recognized as among our good reasons for acting.

---

[53] Nagel (1986, p. 159).

[54] Scanlon notes the persistence of Nagel's (1986) commitment to the fundamental impersonality of
value as well, emphasizing not only that Nagel maintains in particular cases "that value and disvalue
are a matter of being 'to be promoted'," but that "Nagel seems to feel a strong pull toward the view
that this is true of value more generally" (Scanlon 1998, p. 82). My suggestion is that the parallel
that Nagel attempts to draw between the believer-neutrality of theoretical objectivity and the alleged
agent-neutrality of practical objectivity helps to explain this continued pull.

[55] At least for us as we currently are with our cognitive apparatus and present conceptual resources.

But the appeal to detachment here is a red herring. We have already seen that for Nagel all good reasons for believing, formulated from whatever degree of detachment, are believer-neutral. Beliefs about the mental are still supported by believer-neutral evidence, whatever the degree of detachment might be from which they are appropriately formed. Theoretical objectivity is impersonal throughout for Nagel because he endorses the widely held view that good theoretical reasons, at whatever degree of detachment, are believer-neutral reasons grounded in believer-neutral states of affairs. In the practical sphere, by contrast, only fully 'detached' practical reasons are impersonal, agent-neutral reasons; less detached good reasons are non-impersonal, agent-relative reasons. Less detachment in the theoretical sphere is not departure from the impersonal, believer-neutral standpoint, but in the practical case less detachment is precisely more distance from the impersonal, agent-neutral standpoint. Less detached theoretical reasons are not thereby excluded from what he identifies as the impersonal standpoint of theoretical reason, but less detached practical reasons are thereby excluded from what he identifies as the impersonal standpoint of practical reason. The parallel with the theoretical sphere undermines rather than supports an account of objective agent-relative reasons: believer-relative reasons, at whatever level of detachment from the personal perspective, are not for Nagel objective theoretical reasons. The parallel suggests precisely the view to which Nagel recognizes that his arguments commit him in *The Possibility of Altruism*—that agent-relative reasons, at whatever level of detachment, are not objective practical reasons. But Nagel himself recognizes that they are, hence that such a result has the form of a modus tollens argument against his account of practical reason as not just fundamentally impartial but fundamentally impersonal as well.

Nagel can maintain the identification of objectivity with believer-neutral impersonality in the theoretical sphere because he maintains that all good theoretical reasons, at whatever level of detachment, are believer-neutral. But he cannot consistently maintain the identification of objectivity with agent-neutral impersonality in the practical sphere, because he rejects the claim that all good reasons, at whatever level of detachment, are agent-neutral reasons. Rather, only the fully "detached" subset of the set of good practical reasons is agent-neutral. If there are objectively good agent-relative reasons that are in no sense agent-neutral, and Nagel is clear by *The View From Nowhere* that there are, then there are good practical reasons that are not grounded in the impersonal value of states of affairs, reasons that are often sufficient to justify acting contrary to such good agent-neutral reasons.

In *The Possibility of Altruism* Nagel avoids the deeper version of the inconsistent triad, upon which agents have sufficient reasons to do what they have decisive reasons not to do, by biting the bullet and maintaining that there are no good reasons that are "just agent-relative." By *The View From Nowhere* he recognizes that this is too high a price, allowing that there are such good agent-relative practical reasons. But he continues to maintain that practical reason aims at objectivity, that objectivity requires impartiality, and that the conception of impartiality fundamental to both the theoretical and the practical spheres is the impersonal conception of impartiality. This set of commitments does threaten his view with a fundamental inconsistency: practical reasons are fundamentally agent-neutral, but there are fundamentally agent-relative, non-impersonal practical reasons. Agents' agent-relative reasons often provide sufficient reasons for acting contrary to their agent-neutral reasons, but all good practical reasons are fundamentally agent-neutral.[56] Such a position seems to suggest not just that agents have sufficient reasons to do what is wrong, but that they have sufficient reasons to do what they have decisively good reasons not to do.

In the theoretical case the relative positions of believers are taken into account in determining good reasons, all of which are based in the believer-neutral evaluation of states of affairs as true or false. In the practical case, by contrast, it is precisely the good non-impersonal reasons of agents—not just relative *positions* but relative *reasons*—that are taken into account in the agent-neutral evaluation of states of affairs as good or bad. Whatever good reasons agents have that involve such impersonal evaluation of states of affairs are, ex hypothesi, only some among other good reasons that are relevant in the determination of what it is better or worse to do. The "reasons of autonomy" to which Nagel appeals function just this

---

[56] Nagel recognizes that "a certain amount of dissociation is inevitable" on his account (Nagel 1986, p. 170), but he takes it only to be the dissociation of not being motivated by agent-relative reasons "qua objective self" (ibid., p. 170). My point is that because for Nagel justifications must be "objectively correct" (ibid., p. 150), and because he takes the standpoint of practical objectivity to be the agent-neutral, impersonal standpoint, the account implies that any agent-relative reasons, reasons that fail to motivate him "qua objective self," are not good reasons. Because Nagel recognizes that many such reasons are good reasons, the result is not merely dissociation, but a profound and unresolved tension at the core of his account.

way—as fundamental non-impersonal partial reasons that are relevant in the determination of what it is good or bad and right or wrong to do. Nagel is clear that reasons of autonomy often provide agents with sufficient reasons not to bring about the best overall state of affairs. In addition, among practical reasons that are not based in an agent-neutral evaluation of states of affairs (indeed, upon which the latter evaluations, properly understood, are themselves based) Nagel recognizes good interpersonal reasons (his deontological reasons), impartial moral reasons that are capable of providing decisive reasons not to act in ways that will bring about the best overall state of affairs.

The allure of the parallel with the theoretical sphere obscures precisely the sort of double role for non-impersonal reasons in Nagel's account that Williams allows us to identify in traditional consequentialism (see Section 5.3). Nagel's approach suggests that in the theoretical case we take into account the relative positions of believers in the world in the process of generating good theoretical reasons, all of which are good believer-neutral reasons to take something in fact to be the case. In the practical case we take into account not just the relative positions of agents, but the good relative reasons of agents, in the process of generating impersonal evaluations of states of affairs and articulating whatever reasons we might have to promote such states of affairs. But any such higher-order reasons that are articulated through recourse to such impersonal practical evaluations are, ex hypothesi, only some among the reasons relevant to the rational and moral evaluation of actions. For example, if we recognize good interpersonal reasons not to interfere with others, such reasons will be taken into account in the determination of better and worse things that can happen. Such interferences will be bad things to happen, and an agent may well have a good agent-neutral reason to prevent such bad things from being done. But such a higher-order reason to prevent interferences from happening not only does not displace the lower-order interpersonal reason not to interfere, it presupposes such a reason with which it might come into conflict.

Nagel's general strategy is to maintain (1) that reason, whether theoretical or practical, is objective, (2) that good objective reasons are impartial, (3) that the fundamental conception of impartiality suitable to the theoretical sphere is believer-neutral impersonality, and (4) that the fundamental conception of impartiality suited to the practical sphere, by analogy, is agent-neutral impersonality. I have not considered the merits of the first three claims.[57] I have emphasized instead that whatever the merits of the first three claims, the fourth, when coupled with his recognition of good non-impersonal, agent-relative reasons, leads to a profound tension at the core of the account. If practical reason must be fundamentally impartial, but the conception of impartiality in question cannot be fundamentally impersonal, it is necessary to identify the alternative conception of impartiality that is appropriate to the practical sphere, as impersonality is to the theoretical sphere. Nagel himself has already demonstrated that the interpersonal conception of impartiality appears to be relevant to the practical sphere, and we have already seen that such a conception avoids Nagel's threatened contradiction, because it allows for impartial agent-relative reasons; indeed, we have seen that it allows for both permissions not to bring about and restrictions upon bringing about the best overall state of affairs.[58]

There is a second line of thought in Nagel's work, one also initiated in *The Possibility of Altruism*, that also appears to preclude a fundamental role for the interpersonal conception of impartiality in the practical sphere. Indeed, this line of thought results in the apparent paradoxicality of the interpersonal reasons that are distinguished through appeal to such an interpersonal conception. This line of thought develops naturally out of his characterization of practical reasons. Nagel suggests that "every reason can be expressed by a predicate R, such that for all persons p and events A, if R is true of A, then p has a prima facie reason to promote A."[59] A "subjective" or agent-relative reason is then "one whose defining predicate R contains a free occurrence of the variable p," and an "objective" or agent-neutral reason is one that does not contain such a free occurrence, such that "anyone has a reason to promote" the event A in question.[60] The point of particular interest is Nagel's characterization of practical reasons as in every case reasons to promote some event/outcome A: a practical

---

[57] In particular, I have not argued in support of Nagel's commitment to (2), that good objective reasons, in both the theoretical and the practical sphere, are impartial reasons. It is one thing to maintain that moral reasons are impartial. But it is far more controversial to claim, as Nagel does, that all good practical reasons are impartial, developed from a robust standpoint of equal concern. I will briefly consider the prospects for defending such an account of the fundamental impartiality of the practical sphere later in this chapter.

[58] The difference in Nagel's case is that these moral restrictions and permissions would have rational authority as well.

[59] Nagel (1970, p. 90). See also his earlier formulation at p. 47.   [60] Ibid., p. 90.

reason, for Nagel, is a reason to promote the occurrence of an event—to bring about some outcome or state of affairs.[61]

Why characterize practical reasons in terms of outcomes to be promoted rather than in terms of actions to be performed? Given that, for Nagel, "a practical reason is a reason to do or want something, as a theoretical reason is a reason to conclude or believe something,"[62] the natural characterization of practical reasons is as counting for or against actions to be done rather than as counting for or against outcomes to be promoted. Specifically, in place of Nagel's formulation:

For all persons p and events A, if R is true of A, the p has a pf reason to promote A

It seems preferable to adopt the following formulation, a formulation suggested by his emphasis upon practical reasons as reason for doing:

For all persons p and actions A, if R is true of A, then p has a pf reason to perform A

Such a formulation takes seriously Nagel's insistence that practical reasons are reasons for action, and has the advantage of simplicity over his formulation in terms of promoting events/outcomes. Why interpose events/outcomes into an account of all reasons for action unless such an interposition is for some reason necessary? Our ordinary practices of practical reason giving also suggest that the "A" in question is naturally taken to be the action itself rather than an outcome to be promoted through action. That it will harm p's child is a partial, agent-relative reason for p not to perform some action; that it will harm someone is an impartial (impersonal), agent-neutral reason for p not to perform some action; that p will have to harm someone is an impartial (interpersonal), agent-relative reason for p not to perform some action A. Each is a reason of a different sort, but each is also naturally characterized as a reason for performing some particular action. Reasons of the first two sorts can readily be adapted to Nagel's event formulation of practical reasons; reasons of the third sort, however, can only be adapted with a certain amount of awkwardness. This is because Nagel's formulation, upon which A is an event/outcome to be promoted or prevented through action rather than the action to be

---

[61] See Michael Ridge (2006) and Mark Schroeder (2007) for perceptive discussions of this aspect of Nagel's account of reason.

[62] Nagel (1970, p. 64).

performed, invites an interpretation upon which reasons of the third sort, impartial, agent-relative reasons, come to seem paradoxical.

The air of paradox surrounding interpersonal reasons threatens on Nagel's formulation because it suggests that reasons in the first instance count in favor of or against events or outcomes. Such reasons lead us to evaluate some event/outcome positively or negatively, and to take ourselves to have reasons to perform the actions that promote or prevent these outcomes. I have a pf reason to perform an action if there are Rs that are true of the outcome that such an action will promote. The standpoints for distinguishing good reasons (Rs), such a formulation suggests, are the appropriate standpoints for evaluating outcomes and the Rs that count in favor of or against them. The partial standpoint of the person and the impartial, impersonal standpoint are relevant standpoints for evaluating outcomes. But reasons of our third sort, impartial agent-relative reasons, come to seem paradoxical from such standpoints for the evaluation of outcomes.[63] They are not reasons for evaluating an outcome as better for me or better overall, but reasons that often constrain or defeat whatever reasons I have to promote or prevent outcomes thus evaluated.[64] Nagel allows that the outcomes/events in his formulation can simply be actions.[65] But such a formulation invites evaluation of my actions as some among other outcomes to be promoted, outcomes to be evaluated as better or worse from the appropriate standpoint for such evaluations. If my actions are taken into account as events/outcomes or as constituents of events/outcomes, it is natural to take the fundamental standpoints for the evaluation of my actions to be the standpoints appropriate for the evaluation of the outcomes of which they are constituents. Such an incorporation of actions as constituents of the events/outcomes to be promoted thus maintains the paradoxicality of impartial agent-relative reasons.

The interjection of events/outcomes to be promoted into Nagel's formulation of practical reasons, such that reasons do not count directly in favor of actions, but in favor of events/outcomes which the rational

[63] "It is hard to understand how there could be such a thing. One would expect that reasons stemming from the interests of others would be neutral and not relative" (Nagel 1986, p. 178). And again: "their paradoxical flavor tempts one to think that the whole thing is a kind of moral illusion" (ibid., p. 179). Yet Nagel is clear that such reasons are not intuitively puzzling, but "formally puzzling." Mine is an attempt to identify the component of Nagel's formal framework that renders these intuitive reasons formally puzzling, and to provide grounds for rejecting this component.

[64] Nagel emphasizes precisely this point (1986, pp. 178–80).

[65] "A can be an act, event, circumstance, state of affairs, and perhaps other things as well" (Nagel 1970, p. 47).

agent is then taken to have reasons to promote or prevent, threatens to exclude interpersonal reasons by fiat. But there is nothing to recommend such a formulation, and we have seen that there is much that counts against it. Taking seriously that practical reasons are reasons "to do" seems most naturally to involve taking Rs to count for and against actions, not for and against outcomes that are then to be promoted or prevented through action. The latter formulation arbitrarily excludes apparently relevant reasons, reasons that Nagel himself recognizes as relevant.

Reasons for acting, for performing some A, appear in some cases to be partial ("But I could be seriously injured!"), in other cases impartial and impersonal ("But that would prevent serious injuries!"), and in other cases, as Nagel himself insists, impartial and interpersonal ("But I would have to injure someone!"). Reasons of each of these three sorts appear to be relevant for distinguishing certain of the Rs that are relevant to "judgment about what one will have reason to do,"[66] evaluations of actions as better or worse. But only reasons of the first two types are relevant for distinguishing certain of the Rs that are relevant to judgment about better or worse events/outcomes. Because Nagel's 'outcome promotion' formulation effectively limits fundamental reasons to these two types, relevant interpersonal reasons for action come to seem paradoxical.

The relevance of the interpersonal conception cannot be derived (at least not directly) through appeal to the relevance of the impersonal conception—this is the root of the apparent paradox. But the impersonal conception does appear to play a central role in the articulation of certain interpersonal reasons. If, for example, we have not merely interpersonal claims not to be interfered with (e.g. not to be harmed), but interpersonal claims in addition for assistance in preventing such interference by others, such claims for assistance will compete (Should I assist these three, or those five?), and it will be necessary to have recourse to the impersonal standpoint to articulate the resulting interpersonal reasons in a way that takes into account the strength of such competing claims. If one course of action will allow me to address the needs of five people, and another exclusive course of action will allow me to address the needs of three people, then I might have a decisive interpersonal reason to perform the first course of action, and my reason will be that such a course of action will result in more needs

---

[66] Ibid., p. 64.

being met overall. On such an account, such good impersonal-involving reasons are interpersonal reasons that require recourse to the impersonal conception for their articulation.

I have argued that Nagel's characterization of practical reasons in terms of the promotion of outcomes can invite an interpretation upon which evaluation of actions as reasonable proceeds through evaluation of outcomes. Impartial agent-relative reasons come to seem paradoxical on such a characterization. If this characterization is modified and simplified in a way suggested by Nagel's own account, and reasons for acting are taken to count for and against actions directly, not for and against events/outcomes that can be promoted or prevented through action, the formal air of paradox surrounding interpersonal reasons dissipates. An agent p can cite a reason R, for example that it will involve his having to harm some person, as a reason not to push the person out of his way. This is not a reason for p to prevent a pushing the person out of the way from happening (by, as it happens, p), but a reason for p not to push the person—not to act in this way.[67]

So far arguments have been made that it is implausible, even on Nagel's own terms, to take practical reason to be fundamentally impersonal, whether or not it is plausible to take theoretical reason to be fundamentally impersonal. If practical reason is fundamentally impartial, and many practical reasons are fundamentally agent-relative, the interpersonal conception of impartiality, which does not rule out such agent-relative reason, seems a far better candidate than the impersonal conception, which rules out fundamentally agent-relative reasons ex ante. Consideration of the contrasting directions of fit that distinguish the theoretical and practical spheres, however, suggests something more—a rationale for this contrast which suggests both why the central conception of impartiality for theoretical reason is impersonal, and why the central conception of impartiality appropriate to practical reason is interpersonal.

We share one world, but the distinct directions of fit toward that world characteristic of the two spheres suggest that impartial evaluation will take fundamentally different forms in the two spheres. Beliefs have what is characterized as a mind-to-world direction of fit—the aim of belief is to fit the world that we share. Action has a world-to-mind direction of fit—the

---

[67] It may be possible to accommodate such reasons within Nagel's own event/outcome formulation. But if so this only shows that the formal air of paradox can be dissolved within his formulation as well, even without recourse to the simpler, modified formulation.

aim of action is to alter the world that we share to fit with the agent's reasons and desires.[68] In the theoretical sphere the direction of fit is from a world that we share to separate minds; in the practical sphere the direction of fit is from separate minds to a world that we share. In the theoretical sphere each mind strives to achieve a fit between the believer-neutral world we share and the beliefs that it holds; in the practical sphere each mind strives to achieve a fit between her largely agent-relative reasons and desires and the world that she shares with others. Compelling theoretical reasons to believe are reasons for me to take some belief of mine to be a good fit with the world that I share with each of you; good practical reasons are reasons for me to take some action of mine, some alteration by me of the world, to be good. Because each separate believer strives to represent the same world accurately, a good fit or mapping of this shared world for one believer is, ceteris paribus, a good fit for any other believer as well. Our practice of asserting reflects this fact.[69] I am typically prepared to assert what I take myself to have compelling reasons to believe, and in so doing to put it forward as appropriate for you to believe as well. Others take themselves, ceteris paribus, to have compelling reasons to believe what I assert. The good reasons that entitle me to assert are good reasons, ceteris paribus, for any other person to believe what I assert to be the case. The direction of fit characteristic of the theoretical sphere thus leads us to expect that reasons for one person to believe typically entitle anyone else to believe as well—they function believer-neutrally. The practices reflecting our theoretical reasoning operate from a standpoint that is both impartial and impersonal. I am just one among other believers equally real who occupy positions in our shared world. Access to theoretical reasons is often relative to one's position, but theoretical reasons typically are not: compelling reasons for one believer to take some aspect of the world that we share to be a certain way are typically reasons for anyone else to take that aspect of their shared world to be the same way.

Whereas we each aim in the theoretical sphere to fit our beliefs to the world that we share, in the practical sphere, by contrast, we each aim to fit the world that we share to our respective reasons and desires. Because the desires of each agent are largely relative to that agent, each aims to bring about different alterations of the world they share. As Robert Brandom has

---

[68] See G. E. M. Anscombe (2000), Michael Smith (1994, pp. 111–19), and Stephen Darwall (2004, pp. 157ff.) for accounts of the contrasting directions of fit in the theoretical and practical spheres.

[69] See the accounts of assertion put forward by Brandom (1994) and Kukla and Lance (2008).

pointed out, my compelling reasons to believe that the airport is to the west of Pittsburgh are good reasons, ceteris paribus, for you to believe it as well, and when I assert that the airport is to the west of Pittsburgh I put it forward as something appropriate for you to believe. But my decisive reasons to go to the Pittsburgh airport are not reasons for you to go as well, even ceteris paribus.[70] That I ought to go does not suggest that you ought to go, or even that you ought to bring it about that I go. When I claim that I ought to go, I do not put this proposed course of action forward as one that you ought to perform as well. Unlike theoretical reasons, good practical reasons are not typically neutral among believers/agents. This is not to say that such practical reasons are not often, or even always, impartial. The point is that whereas our aim in the theoretical sphere is to fit our beliefs to the believer-neutral truth of states of affairs (the world), our fundamental aim in the practical sphere is not in the same way guided by the agent-neutral goodness of states of affairs. The substantive aim of belief is truth,[71] and truth may well be a believer-neutral value of states of affairs. But although the substantive aim of action is goodness, goodness in the relevant sense, whether or not it is impartial, is not in this sense agent-neutral. It is not the agent-neutral goodness of states of affairs that is the substantive aim of action, but the agent-relative goodness of the actions.

In the theoretical sphere, then, we aim to fit our beliefs to the world that we share. In the practical sphere, by contrast, we aim to fit the world that we share to our agent-relative desires through action. We have seen that the direction of fit distinctive of the theoretical sphere results in its being the case that the conception of impartiality appropriate to achieving our aim as believers is believer-neutral impersonality. But the direction of fit characteristic of the practical sphere results in its being particularly ill-suited to such an agent-neutral conception of impartiality. Whereas from the theoretical direction the world is like a painted canvas that we each try to represent accurately, from the practical direction the world is like a shared canvas upon which each of us paints various pictures, aware that every brushstroke that one of us makes upon this shared canvas effects and is effected by the strokes of each other person. The direction of fit distinctive of the practical sphere thus suggests an agent-relative rather than a believer-neutral standpoint, but impartiality can be achieved from an

---

[70] Brandom (1994, p. 239).   [71] See Darwall (2006, p. 279, following Velleman).

agent-relative standpoint if it is structured by robust equal concern for each and every other agent, a recognition by each person of each other person's equal claim to act on her own agent-relative reasons, and in so acting to alter the world that we share. Such an impartial standpoint for evaluating the agent-relative reasons agents have to alter the world that we share will result in sufficient impartial reasons for an agent to act only if she has taken into account the equal claims of each other agent to act in the articulation of her own agent-relative reasons for action. The result of such impartial justification from an agent-relative standpoint of equal concern will be not only that the agent in question has sufficient agent-relative reasons from the impartial standpoint to perform the action in question, but that each other agent has (defeasible) impartial agent-relative reasons not to interfere with her action. Such impartial reasons establish that the action in question is one that an agent has sufficient reasons to perform by taking the equal standing of each and every other person into account. Other agents have impartial reasons not to interfere with such an action that an agent has sufficient impartial reasons to perform, and such interference, in the absence of other reasons, fails to show equal concern for the agent in question. To provide sufficient reasons to you from such an impartial practical standpoint for my acting in some way is at the same time to demonstrate that you have reasons from such an impartial practical standpoint not to interfere with my action. Such agent-relative limitations upon impartial reasons that others have to interfere will thus be correlates of sufficient agent-relative reasons for acting from such an impartial standpoint.

The impartial practical standpoint suggested by the distinct direction of fit characteristic of the practical sphere, from which an agent takes into account the equal claims of each person to act for agent-relative reasons in establishing her own agent-relative entitlement to act, has all of the markers of the interpersonal rather than the impersonal conception of impartiality. It is (1) a standpoint of equal concern from which no agent is more important than any other, a standpoint which generates not just (2) agent-relative reasons for action, but in addition (3) agent-relative claims against others; moreover, (4) the reasons in question are fundamentally reasons for some particular agents to do and avoid doing certain things, not reasons to promote or prevent certain states of affairs evaluated agent-neutrally.

To have such impartial reasons to act is to have claims upon others not to interfere with one's action, because such reasons are generated from an interpersonal standpoint of equal concern that takes into account the impartial claims of each other person. In our previous example Alice is understood as having such a claim upon me that I not interfere with her, in this case by killing her. This is an impartial claim that Alice has on any person, including Bob and Carol. Her independent moral significance as a distinct agent manifests itself as a claim that limits Ted's impartially justifiable actions, a claim that she has on each other person from a standpoint of equal concern. Her claim to act without being killed obligates each other person not to kill her. Ted's impartial reason for not killing her is thus not just that she would be killed but that Ted would be killing her, and Ted, like everyone else, has an interpersonal reason not to do so. Whatever reasons Ted has based in the impersonal badness of killings happening must thus be taken into account alongside Alice's independent claim from such an interpersonal standpoint not to be killed.

I have suggested that the distinctive directions of fit characteristic of the theoretical and practical spheres invite impersonal, agent-neutral impartial evaluation in the theoretical case, and interpersonal, agent-relative impartial evaluation in the practical case. The practical sphere requires an impartial standpoint for adjudicating the proposed alterations of our shared world by agents acting for largely agent-relative reasons, such that the equal claims of each other agent to act for agent-relative reasons are taken into account. Just as the impersonal structure of theoretical impartiality is reflected in our practice of assertion, so too the interpersonal structure of practical impartiality is reflected in our linguistic practices. To put forward my belief in the form of an assertion is to put it forward as something that I am entitled to, and as something that you should be committed to. To put forward some proposed course of action as one that I ought to perform, or should perform, is to put it forward as an action that I am obligated to perform, and as an action that I have a claim on you to permit me to perform. What I assert, I put forward as something that I am entitled to believe, and that you are obligated to believe; what I claim that I ought to do, I put forward as something I am obligated to do (that I have decisive reasons to do),[72] and that you have (defeasible) reasons to let me do. The relevant impartial standpoints are each reflected in practices

---

[72] See, for example, Parfit's (2008, ch. 1) discussion of the "decisive-reason-implying" sense of "ought".

that presuppose claims upon others, but in the theoretical case these are agent-neutral claims upon each person to believe what I have impartial reasons to believe, while in the practical case these are agent-relative claims upon each person to permit me to do what I have decisive impartial reasons to do. My recognition that you ought to believe is reflected, ceteris paribus, in a recognition that I ought to believe as well for the same reasons. My recognition that you ought to act, by contrast, is reflected in a recognition that I have impartial reasons to permit you to act—to avoid interference with your action. My recognition that you have compelling reasons to believe that your friend is misguided is typically recognition that I have compelling reasons to believe your friend is misguided. My recognition that you have decisive reasons to talk to your friend is not typically recognition that I have decisive reasons to talk to your friend, but it is typically recognition that I have reasons not to interfere with the action that you have decisive reasons to perform. To determine that Smith ought to act in some way is typically to determine at the same time that you have reasons not to interfere with his doing so, and that he has a claim upon each person against any such interference—precisely the relationship characteristic of an interpersonal standpoint of equal concern.

In the practical sphere the impartial reasons that I provide to you in support of some course of action of mine, from a standpoint of robust equal concern, are reasons both for *my* (rather than anyone else's) acting, and my actually *acting*—my actually altering the world that we share in the relevant respects.[73] Moreover, impartial reasons for my action are reasons that are provided to *you* from a standpoint that takes into account your equal claim to alter the world in pursuit of your own aims. From a standpoint that recognizes the equal claim that each of us has to alter the shared canvas upon which we all paint, I only have sufficient reasons to alter the world in some way if in so acting I take into account each other person's claims to make such alterations as well. Each alteration by me of our shared world changes the world that you have an equal claim to alter through action, and in so doing potentially violates your claims. Sufficient impartial practical reasons would appear to involve the demonstration that an action on the agent's part is to the best of her knowledge an exercise

---

[73] See on this point Korsgaard's (2008, pp. 12–13) discussion of the essential efficaciousness of practical reason.

of her own claim that does not violate the corresponding claims of other agents. If such an action is supported by such impartial reasons as an exercise of her agency, moreover, then interference with such an action by other agents is, ceteris paribus, a violation of her claims.

Robert Brandom's metaphor of the ticket taker is thus particularly apt as a characterization of impartial practical reasons.[74] To demonstrate to you my sufficient or decisive impartial reasons to act is to demonstrate to you my rational authority to act from a standpoint that is impartial between us. The offering of such impartial reasons is thus analogous to my purchase of a valid ticket from you. Just as the ticket authorizes my entrance to you, sufficient or decisive impartial reasons authorize my action to you. Moreover, just as my valid ticket makes a claim upon you, obligating you to permit me (at least) to enter, my sufficient or decisive impartial reasons make a claim upon you (at least) to let me act. My purchase of the ticket does not authorize you to bring about my entrance; it authorizes me to enter, and obligates you to allow me to do so. Similarly, my impartial reasons for my action do not provide you with reasons to bring about the state of affairs that will result from my action, they provide sufficient reasons for my acting, and in so doing obligate others to let me do so. The ticket taker metaphor is suggestive in yet another way. Certain tickets may only allow me to enter, but not to have some particular seat. If I have such a ticket, I have a claim upon you not to prevent me from entering, but no claim to prevent you from taking my preferred seat first. Even in such cases the terms of admission limit the means you can undertake to prevent me (e.g. you may not prevent me from getting to the seat first by tackling me). Only certain actions on my part can be undertaken without violating the terms of your admission, and only if I secure the seat in accordance with those terms am I entitled to it, and are you then obligated to let me have it. Similarly, reasons can be sufficient for me to attempt to land a job or take a jump shot (you cannot legitimately prevent me from applying or from playing), but I may not have a claim to make the shot or get the job. You may have decisive reasons, in light of my legitimate claims and your own, not to prevent me from playing or from applying, but you may have sufficient reasons to block my shot and land the job for yourself, or at least to attempt to do so. Even here, my legitimate

---

[74] Brandom (1994, p. 161).

interpersonal claims will produce limits on the steps that you are entitled to take to prevent me (e.g. no cheating, poisoning, or slandering one's competition).

I have argued that the distinct direction of fit towards our shared world that is characteristic of the practical sphere suggests an impartial standpoint that is fundamentally interpersonal rather than impersonal. The interpersonal reasons that result do not purport to be reasons based in impersonal evaluation of states of affairs. They are impartial grounds for some person, some particular "me," to act that, because they take into account the claim that each other agent has to act from a standpoint of equal concern, impartially obligate each other person to permit me to perform the act in question. This interpersonal conception of impartiality has already been shown to be superior on intuitive grounds to the impersonal alternative for the impartial evaluation of actions. The point here is that considerations of direction of fit suggest that its structure is appropriate to impartial practical evaluation of actions, just as such considerations suggests that a believer-neutral, impersonal standpoint is appropriate to the impartial evaluation of beliefs.

I have already suggested that a central role for agent-neutral, impersonal reasons can be reconciled to such an account upon which the interpersonal view from each particular point of view is taken to be the fundamental impartial standpoint in the practical sphere. Indeed, such an approach not only suggests a role for impersonal reasons, it suggests roughly the role that they seem, intuitively, to have. If Alice has interpersonal claims upon other agents not to interfere with her, for example not to kill her, lie to her, steal from her, or violate her personal security, and such claims are a function of the basic recognition of her independent moral significance from an interpersonal standpoint of equal concern, it seems a natural corollary of such interpersonal claims, generated from such a standpoint, that she will also have an additional interpersonal claim on each person to prevent such claims from being violated; that is, to prevent someone from killing her. If there are multiple such interpersonal claims of varying strengths that agents have upon another agent, say Ted, it will be necessary for him to have recourse to an impersonal standpoint to determine the most effective course of action for meeting these claims. The result will be a reason to perform the action that prevents more rather than less, and more severe rather than less severe, violations from happening. Such interpersonal reasons essentially involve the impersonal standpoint in their articulation—they are impersonally articulated interpersonal reasons. Moreover, Ted's reason for performing such an action—the fact that he will cite as counting in favor of the action—will be that it prevents more and worse rights violations from happening. Crucially, such an impersonally articulated interpersonal reason is merely one interpersonal reason alongside the interpersonal reasons each person has not to kill, violate personal security, etc. Indeed, it is an impersonally articulated interpersonal reason that presupposes such interpersonal reasons not to kill, and does not presume to supplant them. If the interpersonal reasons that it presupposes are of sufficient weight, it will be wrong to perform the action that prevents the most rights violations from happening—there will be an agent-centered restriction. Similarly, if Ted's own legitimate claims to pursue his own plans and projects are of sufficient weight, and they do not unduly interfere with the interpersonal claims of others, he will not be morally required from an interpersonal standpoint of equal concern to perform the action that prevents the most rights violations. He will be morally permitted, from the interpersonal standpoint, not to perform the action that brings about the best overall outcome.

I have suggested that the apparent case suggested by Nagel's theoretical/practical parallel that the impersonal conception is fundamental to the impartial evaluation of actions rests upon a mistake. From the claim that the fundamental impartial conception in the theoretical sphere is an impersonal believer-neutral evaluation of states of affairs (as true), it is inferred by analogy that the fundamental impartial conception in the practical sphere is an agent-neutral evaluation of states of affairs as good. Such an inference leads to the focus upon one subclass of practical reasons, impersonal involving reasons to promote certain overall outcomes, as the only truly impartial practical reasons, and to an inability to see the role played by good non-impersonal reasons, including impartial, interpersonal reasons.

Nagel's tempting inference leads us first to identify good practical reasons, then to adopt a higher-order impersonal standpoint towards those reasons, then to put forward the resulting impersonal-involving reasons as the only impartial practical reasons; reasons that, unsurprisingly, persistently conflict with the good reasons that we have. The resulting view is counter-intuitive and rife with deep tensions. Such problems are avoided if the conception of impartiality fundamental to practical evaluation of actions is not the impersonal conception. It has become apparent that the relevant comparisons with the theoretical sphere not only do not support such an identification, they tell against it, and in favor of recognizing interpersonality as the conception of impartiality fundamental to practical reason.

7.5 Impartial Reasons and the Impartiality of Reason

The distinct directions of fit characteristic of the practical and theoretical spheres suggest that it is an agent-relative, interpersonal conception of impartiality that fundamentally structures impartial practical reason, just as a believer-neutral, impersonal conception of impartiality fundamentally structures impartial theoretical reason. But Nagel claims something more in the theoretical case, that objective theoretical reasons are impartial theoretical reasons, hence that the conception of impartiality that structures impartial theoretical reason structures objective theoretical reason simpliciter as well. Nagel invokes a supposed parallel with the theoretical sphere to suggest that all good objective practical reasons as well are impartial practical reasons, hence that the conception of impartiality fundamentally structuring impartial practical reason structures objective practical reasoning simpliciter. Because he takes the conception of impartiality that structures impartial evaluation in each sphere to be the agent/believer-neutral impersonal standpoint, he initially takes such a parallel to suggest that all objectively good practical reasons are, or are ultimately grounded in, good impersonal practical reasons.

I have already suggested that one side of this alleged parallel, the theoretical side, finds wide acceptance. Objectively good reasons to believe are widely recognized as good impartial reasons to believe, and because the conception of impartiality fundamental to the theoretical sphere is impersonal believer-neutral impartiality that aims at the believer-neutral truth of states of affairs, objectively good reasons to believe are recognized as being good believer-neutral reasons to believe. Thus, there is wide acceptance of both the fundamental impartiality of good theoretical reasons, and the fundamental believer-neutrality of theoretical impartiality. But the practical side of this parallel fares less well. Many philosophers follow Nagel in taking the conception of impartiality fundamental to the practical sphere to be impersonal, agent-neutral impartiality, but this commitment is difficult to reconcile with the position that all objectively good reasons to act are good impartial reasons to act—with the fundamental impartiality of practical reason. The reason, a reason Nagel himself recognizes as legitimate in *The View From Nowhere*, is that among objectively good reasons for acting, at even the most fundamental level, are good agent-relative reasons. If practical impartiality is fundamentally agent-neutral and impersonal, but many good reasons are fundamentally agent-relative, then many objectively good reasons are not impartial reasons. The agent-neutral, impersonal conception of impartiality cannot allow agent-relative reasons to play the role that they do as objectively good reasons for acting. The tension that plagues Nagel's account in *The View From Nowhere* is precisely that agent-relative reasons are recognized as objectively good reasons for acting at even the most fundamental level, but objectivity is taken to require impartiality, and practical impartiality is identified, at least at the fundamental level, with impersonality.[75] Other philosophers resolve this tension by accepting that agent-relative reasons play a fundamental role in objective practical reason, and rejecting Nagel's claim that practical reason is fundamentally impartial.

For any approach that seeks to establish the rational authority of moral requirements, however, the cost of such a rejection is high. The central obstacle to establishing the rational authority of moral requirements is that we often appear to have good agent-relative, non-impersonal reasons to act. If practical impartiality is understood to be fundamentally impersonal, then because morality is impartial, such agent-relative reasons, in virtue of being non-impersonal, are partial. The apparent partiality of such objectively good reasons, reasons that often appear to outweigh whatever impersonal reasons we have, provides a fundamental obstacle to establishing the rational authority of moral requirements. If, however, practical impartiality is not understood as fundamentally impersonal, but as interpersonal, then the agent-relativity of certain objectively good reasons to act is no obstacle to recognizing their impartiality. Such good agent-relative reasons could be in the relevant sense impartial, and the central obstacle to recognizing the rational authority of moral requirements would be removed.

It is thus useful to highlight our previous distinction between two components of Nagel's parallel between the theoretical and practical spheres.

---

[75] See also the opening chapters of Nagel (1991), in which this point is made even more explicitly.

The first is that in each case good reasons are fundamentally impartial reasons, the second is that the fundamental conception of impartiality in each sphere is impersonality. It is the two components taken together than cannot be reconciled to the recognition that there are good agent-relative practical reasons. To maintain the second is to reject the first, and this rejection raises significant obstacles to establishing the rational authority of moral requirements. But we have already seen that there are good reasons to reject the second, and to recognize that the fundamental conception of impartiality in the practical sphere is interpersonality, not impersonality. This removes the standard obstacle to accepting the first component of Nagel's parallel, the component that would pave the way, if it could be defended, for establishing the rational authority of moral requirements.

It seems clear that if the fundamental standpoints from which objectively good reasons come into view are the partial standpoint for the evaluation of outcomes (as better or worse for me) and the impersonal standpoint for the evaluation of outcomes (as better overall), then (1) objectively good reasons of the former sort are not impartial, and (2) any role for the interpersonal conception of impartiality must somehow be grounded in such reasons provided by the evaluation of outcomes as better and better for me. An alternative possibility, however, is that accounts which take the partial and impersonal standpoints for the evaluation of outcomes to be fundamental, and take the interpersonal evaluation of actions to be constructed upon or derived from such fundamental standpoints, view the practical sphere as in a camera obscura. The inverse of this approach is one upon which the structure within which all objectively good practical reasons come into view is fundamentally interpersonal, and upon which the partial and impersonal standpoints for the evaluation of states of affairs, properly understood, play essential roles in the articulation of what are properly understood as in the relevant sense interpersonal (hence, impartial) reasons for determining what it is better or worse to do.

Here, then, is a fundamental contrast: between approaches that ground the rational evaluation of actions in the partial and/or impersonal evaluation of outcomes, and alternative approaches that take the interpersonal evaluation of actions to be fundamental and the partial and impersonal evaluation of outcomes to play essential roles in the articulation of what are all fundamentally interpersonal reasons. Each of these contrasting approaches includes a role for all three standpoints.[76] But the former approach allows for good reasons that are not impartial, and recognizes reasons from two fundamental and apparently incommensurable standpoints. Because one of these standpoints is, on this approach, partial, it confronts daunting obstacles to establishing the rational authority of impartial moral requirements. The latter approach maintains that all good practical reasons, including good agent-relative reasons, are in the relevant sense impartial, and maintains that all good practical reasons, even those articulated through appeal to the partial and impersonal standpoints, are fundamentally interpersonal reasons. Such an approach eliminates the central obstacle to recognition of the rational authority of moral requirements.

But can the interpersonal standpoint be called upon to play such a fundamental role? Can it account for traditional interpersonal reasons, impersonal reasons, and Nagel's subjective, partial reasons in such a way that these are all properly understood as fundamentally interpersonal reasons? The case of traditional interpersonal reasons is most straightforward. If practical reason has a fundamentally interpersonal structure, then it is structured by an equal concern by each person for each other person. Each person has an independent rational significance that is reflected explicitly in reasons that others have not to interfere with them, and in claims that each person has not to be interfered with by any other person. Such a standpoint would appear to support paradigmatic interpersonal reasons, reasons corresponding to the traditional perfect duties not to, for example, lie, steal from, and physically harm other persons.

Such an inversion of the traditional consequentialist account of practical reason also allows for certain paradigmatic impersonal reasons. These will be interpersonal reasons that involve recourse to the impersonal standpoint for their articulation—impersonally articulated interpersonal reasons. If, from the interpersonal standpoint, agents have not just claims against the interference of others but claims upon the assistance of others (for example, a Kantian requirement of mutual aid), and the nature and strength of these claims must be assessed and compared in the very process of articulating

---

[76] Principles that invoke the interpersonal conception of impartiality are typically seen as somehow constructed out of the interaction of the more fundamental partial and impersonal standpoints by those who take these two standpoints to be fundamental. Thus Sidgwick's intuitive morality and Mill's principles of justice deploy such an interpersonal impartial standpoint in practice, but purport to construct the role for this interpersonal conception out of the more fundamental partial and impersonal standpoints.

such reasons, then such facts as that some course of action will benefit more people, a determination made through recourse to the impersonal standpoint, can provide decisive impersonally articulated (but nonetheless interpersonal) reasons to act one way rather than another. Such interpersonal claims of assistance will involve the impersonal ranking of states of affairs for their articulation, and the better states of affairs, thus understood, will be the states of affairs that the agent has stronger interpersonal reasons of the relevant sort (e.g. those grounded in claims of assistance, for example, rather than claims against interference) to perform. Such an account can thus recognize certain reasons that are essentially articulated from the impersonal standpoint, facts about better and worse states of affairs that count in favor of or against proposed courses of action.

The approach which takes the interpersonal standpoint for the evaluation of actions to be fundamental can thus account for traditional interpersonal reasons that are explicitly agent-relative and impartial, and for interpersonal reasons that are essentially articulated through recourse to an agent-neutral, impersonal standpoint for the evaluation of states of affairs. The central challenge, however, is whether such an account of practical reasons as having a fundamentally interpersonal structure can accommodate what we have been characterizing as partial reasons (Nagel's subjective, autonomous reasons). Such reasons are not explicitly interpersonal nor are they essentially impersonally articulated; indeed, they are precisely the class of agent-relative reasons, for example that the action in question will further my career, improve my looks, add to my stamp collection, enhance my team's performance, or refine my jump shot, that presents such difficulties for any view upon which the impersonal conception of impartiality is taken to be the fundamental conception for the practical sphere. The question is whether an account that takes such interpersonality to fundamentally structure the practical sphere generally can provide a plausible account of the central and fundamental role that appears to be played by such partial reasons.

Here certain insights developed by Barbara Herman in a series of recent papers are suggestive. Herman points out that the desires of "mature human agents"

normally contain, in addition to a conception of an object, a conception of the object's value—for itself, as determined by its fit with others things valued, and as its satisfaction . . . comports with the principles of practical reason. We might say that desires so conceived have been brought within the scope of reason.[77]

Indeed, as T. M. Scanlon and many others have pointed out, bare dispositions shorn of any such conception of the object's value do not even "fit very well with what we ordinarily mean by desire."[78] Although many such desires "assail us," as it were, prior to reflection, they are nonetheless propositional attitudes within the scope of reason, attitudes that contain conceptions of their value.[79] The suggestion is that for mature rational agents the relevant preconceptual experiences typically flow into the scope of practical reason by default through what Herman characterizes as a deliberative field. Such a deliberative field normalizes preconceptual experiences within the interpersonally structured space of practical reason, much as an agent's perceptual field is often taken to normalize preconceptual experiences with the impersonally structured space of theoretical reason.

If the space of practical reasons has a fundamentally interpersonal structure, then desires normalized into the scope of reasons through such a structure will be constituted in part by valuations of their objects that are already normalized to the interpersonal structure of practical reason. The conceptions of value contained within such desires, although not explicitly interpersonal, are, in effect, implicitly interpersonal: they present the desired action as rational within a space of reasons that is interpersonally structured. To have such a desire is thus typically for the agent to take herself have a good reason to act, where such good reasons have already been normalized within the interpersonal structure of practical reason. The suggestion, then, is that for those who take the practical sphere to be fundamentally structured by such an interpersonal dimension, good partial reasons are just such implicitly interpersonal reasons, reasons that have been normalized within the interpersonally structured space of practical reason. Such attitudes are constituted in part by rational commitments to the goodness of the actions towards which they dispose agents, hence such rational commitments are defeasible in the face of explicitly interpersonal and impersonally-articulated considerations that oppose them.

---

[77] Herman (2007, p. 17). See also Hurley (2001) for a discussion of Herman's account and of possible variations upon it.

[78] Scanlon (1998, p. 38).

[79] See Hurley (2007) for a critical assessment of the various accounts of such containment that have been offered, and the development of an alternative account.

Although Herman is a Kantian, variants upon such a strategy for taking the interpersonal standpoint to fundamentally structure practical reason are available to philosophers with very different meta-ethical commitments.[80] Such a general strategy provides at least the outlines of an account of how an approach that takes the interpersonal standpoint to fundamentally structure the practical sphere can account for the fundamental roles that explicitly interpersonal reasons, impersonal reasons, and partial, subjective reasons appear to have within that structure.[81]

Let me emphasize that what I have offered above is merely the outlines of an account of *how* an impartially structured sphere of practical reason could account for impersonal and partial as well as explicitly interpersonal reasons. I have not provided an argument *that* the sphere of practical reasons is so structured, or an argument that partial and impersonal reasons are properly understood as articulated within and normalized to such a structure. The task of providing such an argument lies beyond the scope of my present argument. It is important to emphasize, however, that these two fundamentally different approaches each recognize roles for the interpersonal, partial, and impersonal standpoints. The partial/impersonal approach generates an account of interpersonal reasons from an account upon which fundamental reasons are partial and impersonal; the interpersonal approach takes the interpersonal standpoint to be fundamental, and generates an account of impersonal reasons as articulations of certain of these interpersonal reasons, and of partial reasons as implicitly interpersonal in virtue of being normalized within this interpersonal structure. The interpersonal approach builds an account of the roles of the other two standpoints out of the fundamental role played by the interpersonal standpoint. It suggests the outlines of accounts both of the fundamental role of reasons of all

---

[80] For example, such a strategy could be maintained by philosophers who reject the claim, often maintained by Kantians, that any such implicitly interpersonal reasons can all, at least in principle, be derived from explicitly interpersonal principles or maxims.

[81] Such an account of partial or subjective reasons in the practical sphere, moreover, parallels accounts that have been offered of perceptual beliefs in the theoretical sphere. Beliefs are understood as attitudes that contain conceptions of their objects as true, just as desires are understood as attitudes that contain conceptions of their objects as good. In the case of perceptual beliefs, beliefs that assail us prior to reflection, the account suggests that the relevant experiences flow "by a sort of default" through an inferentially articulated perceptual field into perceptual beliefs. Because such perceptual beliefs, even though they assail us prior to reflection, are actualizations "of capacities of a kind, the conceptual, whose paradigmatic mode of actualization is the exercise of freedom that judging is," they are "answerable to criticism in the light of rationally relevant considerations" (McDowell 1998, p. 434. See also McDowell 1994, pp. 5–13).

three sorts, and of the relationship among reasons of these different sorts. In addition, it holds out the prospect for an account of the basis for comparability of reasons of these various sorts. The partial/impersonal approach constructs an account of the role of one of these standpoints through appeal to two others that are taken to be fundamental. This approach, because it takes two different standpoints to provide fundamental reasons, confronts enormous difficulties, highlighted by Sidgwick and Parfit, in its attempt to account for the comparability of any such reasons; moreover, it confronts difficulties in accounting for the relationships among these various sorts of reasons. It also confronts significant obstacles to any effort to establish the rational authority of impartial moral requirements. The interpersonal approach, which takes interpersonality to be the fundamental practical conception of impartiality, and takes partial reasons to be good reasons precisely in virtue of being normalized to the fundamentally interpersonal space of practical reasons, is ideally suited to establish the rational authority of impartial moral requirements. "Partial" reasons, on such an account, are properly understood to be implicitly interpersonal reasons. They are not reasons from a fundamentally non-impartial foundation; they are good agent-relative reasons to act precisely in virtue of being normalized through the agent's deliberative field into the interpersonally structured space of reasons. Such reasons do not take us beyond impartiality, hence they are no threat to the rational authority of impartial requirements. Morality, on such an account, identifies a particular subset of the set of impartial reasons comprised of explicitly interpersonal reasons and impersonally-articulated interpersonal reasons, reasons that are typically decisive in cases of conflict with other merely implicitly impartial reasons.

Morality is impartial. But on such an account all good practical reasons for acting are impartial reasons. Moral reasons would not be distinguished on such an account by their impartiality. Rather, the impartial standpoint appropriate for identifying good reasons would also be the standpoint appropriate for identifying certain impartial principles, and/or certain impartial grounds for action, that provide a distinctive and typically decisive moral subset of this set of impartial reasons.

There is no fundamental conflict between good non-impersonal and impartial reasons on such an account because the standpoint of practical reason simpliciter is the interpersonal impartial standpoint, and good non-impersonal reasons will be those non-impersonal reasons that count in favor of a course of action within such an interpersonally structured standpoint. Such non-impersonal reasons for me to act are (defeasible) reasons for you not to interfere with my action. On such an account, any good reasons are reasons from a robust standpoint of equal concern, hence they are reasons that, in entitling me to act, make (defeasible) claims upon you to let me act.

Up to this point the arguments offered against consequentialism have focused almost exclusively upon standard act consequentialism. But most contemporary consequentialists are not standard act consequentialists. In the final chapter I will demonstrate that the arguments developed up to this point against standard act consequentialism also provide grounds for resisting moves to non-standard variants upon standard act consequentialism, including indirect act consequentialism, rule consequentialism, evaluator-relative consequentialism, and non-foundational normative consequentialism.

8

Generalizing to Other Forms of Consequentialism

8.1 Introduction

The argument up to this point has developed as a challenge to one particular, if paradigmatic, form of consequentialism, which I have characterized as standard act consequentialism. On such a consequentialist theory, I have shown, moral requirements lack rational authority. Indeed, the view presupposes that agents often have at least sufficient agent-relative reasons to act in the very articulation of an agent-neutral ranking of overall states of affairs. The moral requirement to bring about such agent-neutrally ranked states of affairs will frequently fail to coincide with what such an impersonal evaluation presupposes, in its very articulation, that we have sufficient or decisive reasons to do.

Nor is this absence of rational authority for consequentialist moral requirements counter-balanced by a set of arguments for the consequentialist theory of moral standards (CMS). The apparent force of many arguments for such a theory of moral standards, I have argued, is illusory, drawing upon systematic misappropriations of intuitions linking rightness of actions and goodness of actions, and treating them as intuitions concerning rightness of actions and goodness of overall states of affairs. Moreover, because the impersonal standpoint is plausibly adopted toward intrinsic non-impersonal moral values such as justice, rights, robust autonomy, and respect for persons as ends in themselves, its very deployment undermines not just the claim that it is a moral standpoint with rational authority, but the claim that it is the fundamental standpoint of morality at all. In Chapters 6 and 7 I argued that a rationale for consequentialism that appeals to the impartiality of morality does not provide support for the theory; indeed, that attempts to salvage the rational authority of morality by recognizing the independent rational significance of the personal point of view as reflected in its independent moral significance lead naturally to an alternative conception of impartiality, an interpersonal rather than an impersonal conception of equal concern. Such a conception, unlike the impersonal conception, can allow for both agent-centered permissions and agent-centered restrictions, and is not beset by the fundamental obstacles that confront any attempt by an act consequentialist to provide an account of the rational authority of moral requirements.

I suggested in the first two chapters that this argument against standard act consequentialism, when allowed to run its course, would provide the resources to demonstrate the shortcomings of other forms of consequentialism as well. In this chapter I attempt to cash in this promissory note. I cannot take up every variation upon standard act consequentialism, nor can I provide arguments against the particular variations that I do take up that are as detailed as those presented in the first seven chapters against standard act consequentialism. But I will take up many of the central variations upon standard act consequentialism and demonstrate that the arguments developed in the preceding seven chapters against the paradigmatic form of consequentialism tell against these other varieties as well.

In the next section I will briefly lay out several variants upon standard act consequentialism. In Section 8.3 I will demonstrate that the arguments developed in earlier chapters tell as well against evaluator-relative forms of consequentialism. In Section 8.4 I will take up indirect act consequentialism and forms of consequentialism that shift the direct focus of the theory from actions to rules or motives. I will demonstrate in Section 8.5 that the arguments developed in earlier chapters also provide resources for responses to recent arguments for consequentialist normative principles that are built upon non-consequentialist foundations.

8.2 Variations upon Standard Act Consequentialism

The traditional form of consequentialism upon which we have focused up to this point is act (as opposed to, for example, rule or motive) consequentialism, direct (as opposed to indirect) act consequentialism, agent-neutral/impersonal (as opposed to evaluator-relative) direct act consequentialism, and foundational as well as normative (as opposed to just normative) impersonal direct act consequentialism. What I have characterized as standard act consequentialism can thus also be characterized as foundational impersonal direct act consequentialism. Variations upon this standard form of consequentialism depart from its foundational aspect, its impersonal aspect, its direct aspect, and/or its focus upon acts rather than, for example, rules or motives. I will briefly elaborate upon each of these variations in turn.

To characterize the traditional form of consequentialism as act rather than motive or rule consequentialism is to suggest that the justificatory focus is directly upon the actions that bring about the best overall consequences, and at most indirectly upon rules or motives the inculcation of which might facilitate the performance of the right actions. But variants can shift the direct justificatory focus instead to the rightness of the rules and motives the inculcation of which will bring about the best overall consequences. On such variants, which shift the direct focus from acts to rules or motives, actions are taken to be right only insofar as they are, for example, in accordance with the right rules, regardless of whether or not such particular actions themselves bring about the best consequences.

To characterize standard act consequentialism as direct, by contrast, is to emphasize that it takes moral deliberation to aim directly at bringing about the best overall consequences, rather than taking moral deliberation to aim directly at obeying certain rules, or pursuing certain goals, or honoring certain commitments as an indirect strategy for performing the actions that will bring about the best overall consequences. The justificatory focal point of indirect act consequentialism, in contrast with rule or motive consequentialism, is still directly upon actions, and right actions are those that bring about the best overall consequences, but the appropriate deliberative strategy is taken to be one that aims directly at something other than the best overall consequences in order to achieve right action by indirection.

The states of affairs that it is taken to be right to promote are evaluated on the standard act consequentialist approach from an agent-neutral, impersonal standpoint. But evaluator-relative variants hold that states of affairs should instead be evaluated from a standpoint that is relative to the particular agent/evaluator. Such evaluator-relative variants maintain that an action is morally right just in case it promotes the best state of affairs, but maintain that the evaluation of states of affairs as better and worse is appropriately undertaken from an evaluator-relative rather than an agent-neutral standpoint.

Finally, the traditional theory does not merely justify a dominant role for consequentialist normative principles in our moral evaluation of actions, it justifies these principles through appeal to consequentialist moral foundations, foundations appealing to the impersonal value of resulting states of affairs. But a dominant role for consequentialist normative principles could in principle be established through appeal to non-consequentialist moral foundations, for example through appeal to a Rawlsian process of reflective equilibrium, or to contractarian or Kantian grounds. Such variants upon standard act consequentialism will reject consequentialism at the foundational level, but defend a dominant role for consequentialist normative principles in the moral evaluation of actions through appeal to non-consequentialist foundations.

For the traditional approach, then, the focal point is action, deliberation typically aims directly at bringing about the best outcome, such an outcome is determined from an agent-neutral, impersonal standpoint, and consequentialist normative moral principles are grounded in the appeal to consequentialist foundations. The main variations that I will consider either (1) maintain that the consequences it is right to promote are properly evaluated from a standpoint relative to the evaluator, (2) maintain the traditional justificatory focus upon acts, but adopt indirect deliberative strategies that do not aim at bringing about the best overall states of affairs, (3) switch the direct justificatory focus of the theory from actions to, for example, rules or motives, or (4) defend consequentialist normative principles, but through appeal to non-consequentialist justificatory foundations.

8.3 Evaluator-Relative Consequentialism

Evaluator-relative consequentialists maintain that if consequentialism is understood not as requiring the act that promotes agent-neutral value, but merely as requiring the act that promotes value, where such value promotion need not be understood impersonally, many of the traditional objections to traditional foundational act consequentialism can be avoided.[1]

---

[1] See, for example, Amartya Sen (1983, 1993), Douglas Portmore (2001), Michael Smith (2003), and James Dreier (1993) for sympathetic explorations of evaluator-relative consequentialism. For an insightful critique, see Mark Schroeder (2007).

The result is still taken by its advocates to be a form of foundational act consequentialism, but a consequentialism freed from the requirement to evaluate the value of the states of affairs to be promoted impersonally. Such a form of consequentialism, for example, can recognize agent-relative factors as playing a role in the evaluation of consequences, hence can allow both for agent-centered restrictions and for something like agent-centered permissions. Thus, Douglas Portmore suggests that such an evaluator-relative consequentialism can plausibly maintain that "from the agent's position the state of affairs in which she commits murder for the sake of preventing the five others from committing murder is worse than the one where she refrains from commiting murder and allows the five others to each commit murder."[2] Many of the central features that have been taken by both consequentialists and their critics to set consequentialism apart from ordinary morality, features such as the rejection of agent-centered restrictions, turn out not to be features of consequentialism generally, but of agent-neutral consequentialism in particular.

If such a position is recognized as consequentialist, then it may be thought that it is not consequentialism, but agent-neutral consequentialism, that has been our real target from the outset. Of course it is precisely agent-neutral consequentialism that most consequentialists have defended, hence the evaluator-relative consequentialist can join in certain of the arguments that have been presented in the preceding chapters for rejecting such a theory. But it is precisely agent-neutrality that many such consequentialists take to be an essential feature of consequentialist moral theory properly understood. On their view, the evaluator-relative option is not an alternative within consequentialism, but an alternative to consequentialism.[3]

Any dispute between the fundamentally interpersonal conception of the moral evaluation of actions that I have developed here and that developed by the evaluator-relative consequentialist thus may seem to be minor, and the dispute with agent-neutral consequentialists concerning whether or not the evaluator-relative version is in fact consequentialist might seem largely semantic. But the substantive rejection of central aspects of traditional consequentialism by the evaluator-relative consequentialist, at both the foundational and normative level, is quite real. For the

---

[2] Portmore (2001, p. 371).
[3] See Portmore (ibid., pp. 265–8) for a discussion of this debate.

evaluator-relative consequentialist morality may well often require the agent not to bring about the best consequences evaluated impersonally, and may well often not morally require the agent to bring about the best impersonal consequences when the costs to her are too great. The evaluator-relative consequentialist is thus no threat to many of the most central arguments that I have deployed up to this point against traditional act consequentialism, and may well seem to be an ally.

Yet there are several reasons, I would suggest, to prefer the traditional understanding of consequentialism as agent-neutral, and to resist the appeal of evaluator-relative consequentialism. First, the agent in Portmore's case seems to fall prey to a mis-description when she frames it in the terms put forward by the evaluator-relative consequentialist. It is not the case that her killing one person is a worse outcome, a worse thing to happen, than the five people being killed. It rather seems to be the case both that it will be a worse thing to happen, a worse outcome, if the five are killed, and that the action necessary to avoid the worse outcome, that the agent will have to kill someone, is morally unacceptable.[4] It is not that Nagel and agent-neutral consequentialists are mistaken when they maintain that what happens as a result will be worse—that it is a mistake to evaluate the goodness and bad-ness of outcomes from an agent-neutral perspective. It will be a worse thing to happen. Rather, the point is that it is nonetheless wrong to do what will prevent the worse thing from happening because the alternative will require the agent to do harm, and such an action is worse from the relevant impartial agent-relative standpoint. The agent's killing is unacceptable not because the resulting state of affairs is a worse thing to happen (evaluator-relatively or evaluator-neutrally), but because the victim has a claim on her not to act in the way that will bring about such an outcome, or, in Portmore's terms, because "agents bear a special responsibility for their own actions."[5]

This naturally suggests a second reason to be leery of evaluator-relative consequentialism. For consequentialists the claim has never been simply that the outcomes of right actions are in some sense better, whether or not "better" is understood agent-neutrally, but that the goodness or badness of states of affairs provides a rationale for the rightness or

---

[4] See Schroeder (2007, sec. IIIB) for a similar objection. His argument for the conclusion that evaluator-relative consequentialism "does not plausibly tell us what ordinary speakers of English have meant by the sentence stating consequentialism all along" (p. 282) is particularly relevant.

[5] Portmore (2001, p. 271).

wrongness of actions, a rationale based in the value of states of affairs.[6] But in the foregoing case the claim that the outcome is bad is based in what Portmore characterizes as the special responsibility of each agent, or what I have characterized as the interpersonal claims that each agent has upon each other agent. It is this non-impersonal, interpersonal claim that explains why the resulting state of affairs is revealed as in Portmore's sense worse. In general, such non-impersonal evaluations of states of affairs that dictate agent-centered restrictions must be explained through appeal to interpersonal moral reasons, but this is to explain the evaluator-relative badness of states of affairs through appeal to moral reasons to do and not to do certain things, not vice versa. It can of course simply be stipulated that a bad state of affairs is a state of affairs that results from actions that an agent has decisive moral reasons not to perform. But such a stipulation does not seem plausible as a characterization of our evaluation of states of affairs, and the resulting view does not seem to be, even in the most extended sense, consequentialist. It is the goodness of states of affairs that provides the rationale, on any recognizably consequentialist view, for the rightness of actions. But this does not appear to be a feature of any evaluator-relative option that can account for standard agent-centered restrictions.

Moreover, such evaluator-relative consequentialism appears to result in an implausible account of agent-centered permissions. For the agent-neutral consequentialist the agent is always morally required to bring about the best overall outcome. Alternative views side with ordinary morality against such an account, maintaining that when the costs to the agent are sufficiently high sometimes she is not morally required to bring about the best overall outcome. But neither, they hold, is the agent morally required to pursue personal projects rather than the best outcome. Both traditional consequentialists and their critics agree that whether or not the agent is permitted to pursue her own projects at the expense of the best impersonal outcome, she is not morally required to do so. Whether or not she is permitted to buy the CD or go off on the romantic weekend rather than donating the money to Oxfam, she is not morally required to buy the CD or go off on the romantic weekend rather than donating the money to Oxfam. It is not wrong to donate the money to Oxfam in such cases; the

---

[6] See also Schoeder's claim that what is attractive about consequentialism is "that it explains facts about what people ought to do in terms of facts about what is good," (2007, p. 287), and his subsequent arguments that evaluator-relative consequentialism loses this attractive feature.

question is only whether or not it is wrong to pursue certain other courses of action instead. But evaluator-relative consequentialism appears to suggest that it is morally wrong to donate the money to Oxfam, and that the agent is not just morally permitted but morally required to take the romantic weekend holiday. If costs to the agent figure in the evaluator-relative assessment of the best state of affairs, and the agent is morally required to do what is best, then the agent is morally required to buy the CD or take the vacation unless she is morally required not to. Such costs have impersonal moral significance, and they have independent rational significance. Critics of traditional consequentialism maintain that the independent rational significance of such costs is reflected in moral significance that they have independent of their impersonal significance. But they are not moral costs such that, if they are sufficiently great, the agent is morally required to avoid them.[7] By incorporating such costs into the determination of the evaluator-relative state of affairs, and morally requiring the agent to bring about the best state of affairs thus determined, evaluator-relative consequentialism does appear to morally require the agent to take the vacation or go to the ballpark instead of donating to Oxfam or working the weekend for Habitat for Humanity, and such a result seems implausible.[8]

Finally, we have seen that the intuitive link is not between right action and good states of affairs, whether understood agent-neutrally or not, but between right actions and good actions, where the latter are determined through appeal to good reasons for acting.[9] There appear to be clear senses of best outcome, determined impersonally, and best action, determined through appeal to the best reasons for acting. Evaluator-relative consequentialism points to legitimate considerations: that it is appropriate to appeal to facts in the moral and rational evaluation of actions that support agent-centered restrictions upon bringing about the best overall outcome. But it appeals to these considerations to gerrymander the clear impersonal sense of better and worse outcomes so that it can do the

---

[7] Recall the discussion of Scheffler and agent-centered permissions in Chapter 6.

[8] Such moral requirements could be avoided if the relevant evaluator-neutral and evaluator-relative considerations were taken to be incommensurable with each other. But on such a view there might often not be either a best, or even (among options) a better outcome.

[9] Portmore takes the fundamental intuition to be not that it is never wrong to do what's best, to perform the better action rather than the worse one, but the consequentialist interpretation of this intuition, that it is "never wrong to bring about the best available state of affairs" (2001, p. 372). But the implausibility of such an interpretation was established in Chapter 5.

work that is appropriately done through appeal to evaluations of better and worse courses of action. A more plausible strategy, I would suggest, is to recognize the legitimacy of the considerations, but, in light of the arguments presented in Chapters 5–7, to resist the contortions. The result will not be evaluator-relative consequentialism, but an evaluator-relative alternative to consequentialism.

Perhaps such concerns can be addressed by the evaluator-relative consequentialist. If so, as I suggested above, the result will not be a challenge to most of the criticisms offered in earlier chapters, but a claim that they are grounds for rejecting agent-neutral forms of consequentialism, forms that have traditionally been taken to exhaust moral consequentialism. For the reasons outlined above, however, my own suspicion is that such arguments are best understood not as leading us to evaluator-relative consequentialism, but as leading us away from anything recognizable as consequentialism.

8.4 Indirect Act Consequentialism and Rule vs. Act Consequentialism

Indirect Act Consequentialism

It has long been argued that agents aiming at their own happiness or pleasure are confronted with a paradox—if they aim in deliberation at the end of maximal pleasure or happiness they will achieve less pleasure or happiness than they would if their aim in the context of deliberation is something other than overall pleasure or happiness. As Peter Railton and Eric Wiland have argued, a similar threat of paradox confronts standard act consequentialists as well. Agents who aim in deliberation at the goal of bringing about the best overall state of affairs seem to be less effective in achieving this goal than are agents who recognize other ends as intrinsically valuable or adhere to certain rules regardless of consequences. Indirect hedonists and consequentialists have argued, however, that the appearance of paradox can be avoided if a careful distinction is made between the context of deliberation about what agents are rationally or morally required to do and the context of moral and rational justification of actions.[10]

---

[10] Railton (1988) presents and defends a form of indirect act consequetialism. Wiland (2007) presents and criticizes various forms of indirect act consequentialism. Wiland points out that there are different

Hedonism and consequentialism can avoid the threatened paradox by indirection. Hedonist or consequentialist deliberation will recognize the intrinsic non-impersonal value of rules, plans, projects, and commitments, but the indirect result of such direct recognition of intrinsic value in deliberative contexts will be the performance of actions that bring about the greatest happiness for the individual or the greatest overall happiness, that is, the performance of the actions that are justified as morally right because they promote the best overall state of affairs.

Such an indirect strategy might be thought to provide the standard act consequentialist with the necessary tools to avoid the tensions in our normative triad. Within the context of deliberation consequentialism may well come to resemble more closely the ordinary morality that does, intuitively, have rational authority. Hence it might be thought that indirect act consequentialism can consistently appeal to our ordinary intuitions about the rational authority of moral requirements, since moral requirements, in the context of indirect consequentialist deliberation, may well align closely with such ordinary moral requirements. Such an indirect variation upon act consequentialism may as a result seem to hold out the prospect of at least minimizing the tension in our initial triad.

Eric Wiland and others have raised powerful objections against such indirect forms of act consequentialism.[11] But the arguments developed in preceding chapters generate a new set of objections. To see why, it will help to reintroduce the example from Chapter 1 of Carl the card-carrying consequentialist. Carl is an act consequentialist, thereby embracing the third member of our original triad (CMS), and he recognizes that he has fundamentally non-impersonal reasons, thereby embracing the second member of the triad (NIR). For simplicity, we will assume that he is a utilitarian consequentialist who takes the right action to maximize overall happiness, and takes the rational action to maximize his happiness. Let us assume, moreover, that an indirect strategy is best for acting in the way that maximizes overall happiness—acting rightly—and that an indirect strategy is best for acting in the way that maximizes his happiness—acting rationally. Insofar as Carl functions as a rational agent, then, he will

degrees of indirection adopted by consequentialists, and different obstacles that confront accounts that occupy various points along this scale.

[11] Wiland (2007, pp. 275–301).

adopt the deliberative strategies that will lead to rational actions, actions that maximize his own happiness. If the deliberative strategies that lead to actions maximizing his own happiness differ from the deliberative strategies that lead to actions maximizing overall happiness, then Carl, insofar as he is rational, will pursue the first set of deliberative strategies rather than the second, and many (perhaps even all) of his actions will be wrong. They will be actions that to the maximal extent realize his own happiness, but may only rarely in fact be the actions that maximize overall happiness—the right actions. The diagnosis provided in the first seven chapters shows that the appeal to indirection does not avoid the fundamental tension within consequentialism, it merely transposes this tension into a different—indirect—key. If it turns out, for example, that the best indirect strategy for maximizing one's own happiness in most circumstances is a constrained maximization strategy of the sort advocated by Hobbesians, then Carl, insofar as he is rational, will adopt an indirect deliberative strategy that functions like Hobbesian morality. As a *rational* consequentialist Carl will accept Hobbesian moral standards as providing the appropriate framework within which to deliberate, but as a rational *consequentialist* he will also identify many if not most of these actions as wrong. The consequentialist moral wrongness of such actions will simply have no relevance for Carl in either the justificatory or deliberative contexts that he will occupy as a rational agent. The problems with Carl's account generalize—it is the indirect strategies for acting rationally rather than rightly that will be adopted by indirect consequentialists. For the consequentialist the context of justification, or practical reason, contains fundamentally non-impersonal reasons, but the context of moral justification is impersonal through and through. Indirect pursuit of fundamental aims of reason will incorporate and reflect these fundamental non-impersonal reasons, hence it seems implausible that it will result in indirect pursuit of the best overall states of affairs. The result of such a pursuit of indirection for Carl would seem to be just what Bernard Williams predicted—the marginalization of consequentialist morality within what even such rational consequentialists recognize as the relevant justificatory and deliberative contexts.

The arguments developed in Chapters 4 and 6 raise additional difficulties for indirect act consequentialism. If overall states of affairs are appropriately evaluated by adopting an impersonal standpoint towards what is appropriately recognized as valuable from the standpoints of individual persons, and persons appropriately recognize myriad non-impersonal values, including certain non-impersonal moral values, then the impersonal standpoint does not even provide the context of moral justification, much less the contexts of justification or deliberation simpliciter. This is because on such an account whatever impersonally articulated moral considerations are relevant to the moral evaluation of actions are, ex hypothesi, only some among other non-impersonal morally relevant considerations. An indirect strategy that promotes action in pursuit of the best impersonal states of affairs will not be morally justifiable, on such an account, because it will only be responsive to some (impersonal) morally relevant considerations to the exclusion of other (non-impersonal) morally relevant considerations.[12]

Rule Consequentialism

An indirect variant upon act focused consequentialism is problematic, but many variants upon consequentialism shift its primary focus in justificatory contexts from acts to rules or motives. The direct justificatory focus of such variations in both justificatory and deliberative contexts is upon rules or motives rather than acts. Whether or not an act promotes the best overall

---

[12] What if the consequentialist rejects pluralism in the justificatory context and reserves it for the deliberative context alone? Here a new set of difficulties emerges. Wiland and others have shown that in order to avoid the collapse back into direct act consequentialism such an indirect consequentialism must recognize certain plans, projects, and commitments as having non-impersonal value. Among these commitments are likely to be certain moral commitments to non-impersonal values. Within such deliberative contexts that recognize non-impersonal values it will be necessary to take impersonal considerations into account—no one save the minimalist Hobbesian denies this (Kagan 1989, chs 1 and 2). Such overall outcomes will be evaluated by adopting an impersonal standpoint towards what we recognize as non-impersonally valuable, and determining the actions that most effectively promote such outcomes overall. But such impersonal evaluation, in such deliberative contexts, will presuppose the relevance of non-impersonal values with non-impersonal rationales. Moreover, it will presuppose that the impersonal standpoint is not the moral standpoint, since impersonal considerations, ex hypothesi, are only some of the considerations relevant in the determination of what it is right or wrong to do in such contexts, and the very process of determining the best overall outcome in such contexts presupposes that this is the case. Let us assume that acting rightly within this deliberative context does maximize overall happiness, or utility, or well-being. It is no longer clear how such an agent can take the standpoint of overall happiness as providing the relevant context of justification, whether or not what he takes to be right action in deliberative contexts maximizes overall happiness. Even if such an agent takes the impersonal standpoint to provide the context of justification, he takes the impersonal standpoint to be adopted properly towards non-impersonal moral values, and we have already seen that recognition of such non-impersonal values is at odds with recognizing the impersonal standpoint as providing the relevant context of justification. The deliberative context provides an account of the impersonal standpoint upon which it is adopted towards non-impersonal moral values with non-impersonal rationales, hence upon which it is mistaken to appeal to the impersonal standpoint as grounding the context of moral justification.

state of affairs, it is the right action to perform on such an account if it is in accordance with the morally right rules or is produced by the morally right motives, the rules or motives inculcation of which will promote the best overall state of affairs. In what follows I will focus primarily upon rule focused consequentialism.

One enduring source of the appeal of such consequentialist approaches that shift the justificatory focal point from acts to rules or motives is that forms of consequentialism with such alternative focal points are thought to result in standards for right action that are more in line with ordinary morality. If it is intuitive that ordinary moral requirements and prohibitions have rational authority, and rule or motive consequentialist moral standards align more closely with these ordinary moral requirements, then such versions of consequentialism may in this central respect be better positioned to establish the rational authority of their moral standards than act consequentialism has proven to be, other problems with such theories notwithstanding. Thus, it may seem to be a strength of such theories that they at least deflect the full force of our original triad.

But many contemporary advocates of rule consequentialism reject consequentialism at the foundational level, appealing to non-impersonal considerations at the foundational level of moral justification in an attempt to defend the adoption of consequentialist moral rules at the normative level. I will postpone consideration of such non-foundational rule consequen-tialist accounts to Section 8.5, in which such non-foundational variants upon consequentialism will be taken up as a group.[13] This widespread move to non-foundational defenses of rule consequentialism, however, is a response to powerful objections to forms of foundational consequential-ism that shift the direct focus from acts to rules or motives, objections deployed with brutal effectiveness by consequentialist sympathizers them-selves.[14] Whatever the difficulties confronting a consequentialism that only directly evaluates acts through appeal to overall consequences, a founda-tional consequentialism that only directly evaluates rules through appeal to overall consequences, and indirectly evaluates actions as right or wrong

---

[13] Brad Hooker and Derek Parfit provide two very different arguments for forms of normative rule consequentialism from non-consequentialist foundations. Their arguments will be taken up in Section 8.5.

[14] See, for example, the arguments against versions of consequentialism that shift the direct focus away from acts that have been offered by Peter Railton (1988), Tim Mulgan (2001), Pettit and Smith (2000), and Shelly Kagan (2000).

insofar as they accord with such rules, brings a host of new difficulties in its wake. One is the very problem that has been raised with devastating effectiveness by Scheffler and Kagan against attempts to justify agent-centered restrictions through appeal to the badness of resulting states of affairs.[15] If the rationale for keeping promises is provided by the appeal to the impersonal badness of breaking them, they argue, such a rationale will not support agent-centered restrictions upon breaking promises; indeed, it will support breaking a promise whenever, for example, doing so can prevent two equally damaging breakings of promises. Such an impersonal rationale for keeping a promise in typical cases becomes a rationale for breaking them in precisely those cases in which agent-centered restrictions intuitively apply. Similarly, if the rationale for the rightness of certain rules is that doing so will promote the best overall states of affairs, the rationale for following such rules in typical cases will be a rationale for violating them in cases in which a better overall state of affairs results from doing so. Agent-centered restrictions upon the morality of breaking promises come to seem paradoxical from an impersonal standpoint, but so too do rule-centered restrictions upon the morality of acting to promote the best overall state of affairs. If breaking the rule in this case will lead to the best overall outcome, am I not at least morally permitted to do so? We have seen that the Kagan/Scheffler objection can be avoided if the rationale for such restrictions is interpersonal rather than impersonal. But no such alternative is open to foundational rule consequentialism, since ex hypothesi the fundamental rationale on such an approach is impersonal.

Of course on many such forms of rule or motive consequentialism what is taken to be right is not just following such rules but internalizing them. On such versions of foundational rule rather than act consequentialism I simply cannot break the rule or resist the motive in such cases because I have internalized it. Such internalized rules or motives, however, function as psychological constraints on an agent's ability to act in ways that will bring about the best overall state of affairs in particular cases. I have internalized certain psychological constraints against breaking rules because this is the set of constraints that, if widely internalized, will promote the best overall state of affairs. But in certain cases the constraint prevents me from performing the act that will bring about the best overall state of affairs.

---

[15] These arguments have been taken up earlier in Chapters 3 and 6.

In such cases the failure of such a psychological mechanism would lead to a better state of affairs as determined by the very rationale for the adoption of the mechanism. Indeed, in such cases the rationale for resisting such a psychological disposition when possible is supplied by the very impersonal standpoint that leads to its internalization. The agent has an impersonal value-based rationale for struggling to overcome the mechanism in such cases that she has an impersonal value-based rationale to internalize. If the action dictated by the relevant rule or motive is right, then such an agent would seem to have an impersonal value-based rationale for struggling to do what is wrong. As Pettit and Smith argue, if the agent in such a case manages to resist the internalized mechanism, and acts in a way that brings about the best resulting state of affairs, "a consequentialist should surely think that there is therefore much to rejoice about, and little to regret."[16] It seems implausible on such a view to continue to maintain that the impersonally justified action in violation of the rule is on any viable foundational consequentialist view morally wrong.

The diagnosis in Chapter 5 helps in many cases to clarify the force of other objections to such focal variants upon act consequentialism. The standard rationales for consequentialism draw upon the intuitive link between what it is right to do and what is best—between rightness as a property of actions and goodness. Rule consequentialism attempts to avoid the problems with the rational authority of act consequentialist requirements, but it also loses the support of the standard rationales, which appeal to the direct intuitive linkage between the evaluation of actions as right or wrong and the evaluation of states of affairs as good or bad.

Foundational forms of rule consequentialism, then, are problematic even on the foundational consequentialist's own terms. But the criticisms developed in the previous three chapters render moot this debate concerning which focal point is appropriate for direct foundational impersonal moral assessment. Our initial focus upon problems with the rational authority of act consequentialist moral requirements opened the door for fundamental challenges to the appeal to the impersonal standpoint as the foundation for morality—in Brad Hooker's words, to "the thesis that what yields the best consequences is morally best."[17] The impersonal standpoint is not

---

[16] Pettit and Smith (2000, p. 126).
[17] Hooker (2000b, p. 222).

plausible as a candidate either for the foundations of the moral evaluation of actions or for the foundations of the rational evaluation of actions. The suggestion that it plays either role is counter-intuitive, and alleged rationales for setting aside such intuitions turn either upon misappropriations of the linkage between rightness and goodness as properties of actions, or upon misguided parallels between the theoretical and practical spheres, or upon the appeal (in the moral case) to the impartiality of moral evaluation, which appears to be better understood as fundamentally interpersonal rather than impersonal. The agent-neutral impersonal conception of impartiality is not an attractive foundation upon which to construct a plausible theory of rationally authoritative moral reasons, or even a plausible theory of moral standards alone. These arguments against a foundational role for the impersonal conception of impartiality are simply not addressed by shifting the focal point of impersonal evaluation from actions to rules or motives.

I have argued that the force of many of the rationales for foundational act consequentialism is lost if the focus is shifted from actions to rules or motives. Moreover, the fundamental objection that has arisen in previous chapters is to the claim that an impersonal value-based rationale can provide a plausible foundation for either a theory of moral standards or a theory of moral reasons, and this objection is effective regardless of what is or is not put forward as the candidate for direct evaluation through appeal to such a rationale. Such considerations taken together suggest that there is little promise in the move to alternative foundational focal points. It is this second point, that the impersonal conception of impartiality cannot provide the foundation for a plausible theory of moral evaluation, that also tells most forcefully against any move to global consequentialism. The "global consequentialism" developed by Smith and Pettit draws upon the plausible view that there are many "evaluands", including acts, rules, and motives, that are appropriate objects of direct impersonal evaluation. It certainly seems right that we can directly evaluate most anything, including sets of motives, systems of rules, and actions, in terms of their conduciveness to realizing better or worse states of affairs. Smith and Pettit also make the wholly sound point that focus on direct evaluation of rules, motives, or any other focal point rather than upon actions, in short foundational rule or motive consequentialism, is particularly implausible. But the global consequentialist does not just evaluate various focal points in terms of their contribution to the overall good. She claims in addition that such acts, rules, and motives are morally right, where "the right X" is understood as "the best X," and "the best X, in turn, is that which maximizes overall value."[18] Thus, the global consequentialist argues that not only can we directly evaluate any such focal point from the impersonal standpoint, but that the actions, rules, and motives most highly evaluated from such a standpoint are the morally best actions, rules, and motives, and in the appropriate sense the morally right actions, rules, and motives.

The view seems intuitively right as an account of the deployment of the impersonal standpoint in evaluation—anything can be directly evaluated from the impersonal standpoint. But the global consequentialism that results from identifying impersonality as the conception of impartiality fundamental to morality would appear to fall prey to each of the challenges that has been raised in preceding chapters towards foundational act consequentialism, since they are challenges to the plausibility of the appeal to the impersonal conception of impartiality as the foundation for morality, challenges that are effective regardless of the number and nature of the focal points that are directly impersonally evaluated. In light of the independent rational significance of the personal point of view, it appears that rational agents not only have good reasons not to perform the right action thus understood, but good reasons as well not to inculcate the right motives, internalize the right rules, etc. Indeed, rational agents may well have decisive reasons not to inculcate such motives and internalize such reasons. Moreover, the rationales for taking the impersonal standpoint, contrary to intuition, to be foundational for morality have been undermined. We have seen that the intuitive linkage is not between what it is right to do and the best overall state of affairs, but between what it is right to do and what it is best to do. What is missing is any basis for the identification of what it is best to do with what promotes the impersonal value of states of affairs. Indeed, there appear to be compelling reasons for resisting any such identification.[19]

---

[18] Pettit and Smith (2000, p. 121).

[19] Many of these reasons were presented in Chapters 5 and 7. It is noteworthy that the arguments in Pettit and Smith (2000) can plausibly be read as having a conditional form, establishing that if the impersonal standpoint is the foundational standpoint for moral evaluation, each focal point is appropriately recognized as a candidate for direct moral evaluation. On this reading, the argument is not that this form of consequentialism is defensible, but that if consequentialism is defensible, this is the form that it will take.

The story is quite different if the arguments Pettit and Smith offer for global consequentialism are wedded to the arguments offered elsewhere by Pettit that the rational attitude towards value is promotion.[20] But we have already seen in Chapter 5, and again in the discussion of Nagel's arguments in Chapter 7, that such a rationale for a consequentialist theory of moral reasons is not plausible as presented. The rational attitude towards certain values, such as the goodness of actions and the rightness of actions, is performance, not promotion. The rational response is to do the right or good action, not to promote its being done. Nor can the appeal to overall value of outcomes be the rationale for determining what it is good or right to do, since we have good fundamental non-impersonal reasons for acting that are also relevant to the determination of what it is better or worse to do, reasons that are often sufficient—good enough—for rational agents not to bring about the best overall state of affairs. Moreover, because impersonal-involving reasons are at most some of the reasons among others that are relevant in the determination of what it is better or worse (and right or wrong, if moral requirements have rational authority) to do, what appears to be necessary is a rationale that can account for why, and if so to what extent, consideration of the best overall states of affairs is relevant to the determination of what it is better to do and right to do. What appears to be necessary, in short, is a rationale for the role of impersonal-involving reasons in the evaluation of actions as better or worse and right or wrong, a rationale that bases the evaluation of overall states of affairs as better and worse in the evaluation of actions as better and worse. I suggested in Chapter 7 that an approach to practical evaluation that takes an interpersonal conception to be fundamental has the resources to provide such a rationale. But such an approach takes us beyond foundational consequentialism in any form.

8.5 Non-foundational Consequentialism

The variants taken up in the previous section share with standard act consequentialism the conviction that the ultimate foundation for morality is provided by the appeal to the impersonal value of states of affairs. Judgments of the rightness and wrongness of acts appeal to the best state of affairs and/or

---

[20] See Pettit (2000).

the rules, motives, etc. the internalization of which will bring about the best state of affairs, and the foundational rationale for such moral evaluations of actions is such an appeal to the value of states of affairs. A growing number of philosophers reject the claim that the foundational rationale for moral evaluations of actions is provided by the appeal to the impersonal value of states of affairs, but continue to defend some form of consequentialism at the normative level. Such approaches can take ultimate foundations for normative moral principles to be provided by something other than impersonal value, for example by appeal to hypothetical consent from a fair standpoint, or to reasons that no one could reasonably reject, or to reflective equilibrium among general and particular moral intuitions, or to respecting persons as ends and not means only. They argue, however, that such non-impersonal foundations justify the adoption of consequentialist principles or rules for the moral evaluation of actions at the normative level. It will be consequentialist normative principles that will be adopted by hypothetical consent from a fair standpoint, for example, or consequentialist rules that will be adopted through appeal to reflective equilibrium.

The possibility for and potential appeal of such non-foundational forms of normative consequentialism is highlighted by Rawls,[21] who argues that we should adopt the principles of justice that would be the result of a hypothetical agreement from an original position that is fair. It is open to a consequentialist to accept these contractualist foundations, but argue that it is the principle of average utility that would be chosen from such a standpoint. Indeed, Rawls recognizes the initial appeal of just such a position, and the force of his arguments that the principle of average utility would not be chosen from his original position is far from clear. The moral foundations of such an account are contractarian rather than consequentialist, but the principle of justice that is justified through appeal to such non-consequentialist foundations may turn out nonetheless to be a consequentialist principle of justice. Rawls' argument is limited to political morality, and to an argument for the principles of justice governing the basic structure of a just society, but an argument similar in form could readily be given for morality generally. Thus, although T. M. Scanlon rejected philosophical (foundational) utilitarianism in favor of philosophical contractualism in "Contractualism and Utilitarianism,"

---

[21] Rawls (1971).

concluding that the proper foundation for an account of moral right and wrong is provided not through appeal to overall well-being but to principles that are supported by reasons no one could reasonably reject,[22] he also allowed that such philosophical contractualism could nonetheless result in normative consequentialism, for example if the principles that no one could reasonably reject are dominated by impersonal principles.[23] If the overarching principle that no one could reasonably reject turned out, for example, to be the principle of average utility, the resulting view would be a consequentialist normative ethical theory with contractualist foundations. The consequentialist who defends such a view concedes the foundational battle as part of a strategy for winning the normative war. When we ask what it is right to do, it is one of the variants of consequentialism, on such an account, that provides the correct answer.

Such non-foundational arguments for forms of normative consequentialism have become extremely influential, and comprise some of the most interesting work currently being done in normative ethics. They have striking advantages, for example the ability to acknowledge non-consequentialist intuitions and non-impersonal intrinsic moral values even (indeed especially) at the most foundational level. They can also draw upon non-impersonal sources of rational authority, again even at the most foundational level. Such arguments are of radically different kinds, reflecting the very different foundations upon which they can be built. In what follows I will limit myself to some general remarks demonstrating that the arguments in Chapters 1–7 generate a presumption against the success of any such non-foundational arguments for consequentialism. I will then apply these general arguments to specific versions of non-foundational consequentialism that have been put forward by Brad Hooker, David Cummiskey, and Derek Parfit. The richness of these views does not allow for full engagement with any of them, and the variety of the foundations upon which they draw does not allow for general arguments against them. It must suffice to identify the places in their respective arguments at which the arguments developed up to this point appear to provide resources for challenging the claims that the different foundational approaches in question will lead to some form of normative consequentialism.

---

[22] Scanlon (1982).

[23] Ibid., sec. III. Scanlon proceeds to offer considerations that he believes demonstrate that philosophical contractualism will not support normative utilitarianism/consequentialism.

The account that has emerged over the course of the last several chapters raises a strong presumption against any such non-foundational argument for normative consequentialism. Arguments for non-foundational consequentialism often appeal to broad claims about reasonableness, fairness, moral intuitions, or respect for persons, and suggest that the normative ethical principles supported by such non-consequentialist foundations are consequentialist principles. On such accounts, to act on reasons that no one could reasonably reject, or to treat others fairly, or to respect persons as ends, is to act either in accordance with certain impersonal principles, or in accordance with certain principles the internalization of which will lead to better overall consequences.

But we have seen that appeals to such non-impersonal moral values and/or such a non-impersonal but impartial standpoint of evaluation appear to dictate agent-centered restrictions and agent-centered permissions. Moreover, they presuppose the relevance of an interpersonal conception of impartiality at the most foundational level of moral justification, hence of certain agent-relative impartial principles of equal concern. Any view upon which impersonal normative principles are taken to dominate at the normative level would appear to be in tension with such recognition of non-impersonal moral values and of the foundational relevance of an interpersonal conception of impartiality.

In what follows I will argue that although in each of the cases I consider the argument for normative consequentialism purports to appeal to non-consequentialist foundations, it in fact continues to rely upon appeal to the consequentialist's impersonal conception of impartiality at the foundational level. Normative consequentialist principles are the outputs of these arguments, I suggest, only because consequentialist commitments continue to enter in at various points as part of the foundational input. When these accounts are purged of such foundational consequentialist commitments, I will show that in each case the argument for consequentialist normative principles is called into question.

Hooker

I will first consider Brad Hooker's non-foundationalist argument for rule consequentialism. Hooker is clear that he is rejecting any foundationalist argument for rule consequentialism that involves a "pre-commitment to a consequentialist framework" in favor of an argument that "does not start from consequentialist premises."[24] His argument deploys a version of the reflective equilibrium method developed by John Rawls, arguing that "rule consequentialism does a better job of according with our considered moral convictions, at all levels of generality, than any other moral theory."[25] A central criterion to which he appeals is impartiality: "a moral theory that is fundamentally impartial seems to have a decisive advantage over its rivals."[26] His view is that rule consequentialism fares very well in the face of these criteria. It meets the impartiality criterion because it invokes "the familiar idea that we should try to live by the moral code whose communal acceptance would, as far as we can tell, have the best consequences, impartially considered."[27] Moreover, the "Rossian rules" about which we are most confident in ethics, rules such as "don't steal," "keep your promises," and "Don't kill or physically injure the innocent," accord well with a rule consequentialist principle. The particular Rossian rules fit, the general criterion of impartiality is satisfied—the rule consequentialist principle can seem promising as the outcome of such a reflective equilibrium process.

But I have argued that the conception of impartiality to which Hooker and other consequentialists appeal, the agent-neutral impersonal conception that he takes to be most natural, is neither natural, at least as the fundamental practical conception of free and equal moral concern, nor even the most attractive. Rather, it is the interpersonal conception of impartiality that reflects the structure of practical as opposed to theoretical objectivity, appears to be presupposed as more basic by the operation of the impersonal standpoint, and appears much more likely to generate moral principles with claims to rational authority. Such an interpersonal conception of impartiality does not at all support rule consequentialism; moreover, it gives rise directly to the agent-centered "Rossian rules" that Hooker finds so attractive without the problematic intermediary of rule consequentialism.

Hooker's reflective equilibrium invokes the consequentialist's impersonal conception of impartiality as the most "natural," and appeals to Rossian agent-centered principles as providing an adequacy criterion. It is not surprising that the appeal to such moral rules and the impersonal conception

---

[24] Hooker (2000*b*, p. 222).   [25] Ibid., p. 222.

[26] Ibid., p. 229. See also Hooker's (2000*a*) extensive discussion of impartiality, in particular his discussion of "Impartiality in Justification" (ibid., pp. 25–9).

[27] Hooker (2000*b*, p. 226).

of impartiality supports rule consequentialism as the best approach. But I have provided grounds for rejecting the claim that impersonality is the fundamental conception of impartiality for the moral evaluation of actions, and the alternative interpersonal conception of impartiality can provide straightforward rationales for both Rossian rules (restrictions) and the intuitive agent-centered permissions that bedevil rule consequentialist accounts. Nor is preference for assistance to the worst off problematic for the interpersonal conception of impartiality, as Hooker recognizes that it is for the impersonal conception.[28] Whether or not the impersonal conception results in identification of such preferences as biased, they are precisely the sorts of preferences that emerge as impartial and unbiased from most approaches that recognize the interpersonal conception as morally fundamental (Hobbesian variants excepted).

Cummiskey

David Cummiskey and Derek Parfit offer two quite different strategies for grounding versions of normative consequentialism in what they take to be broadly Kantian rather than consequentialist foundations. These are extraordinarily rich accounts, and I do not pretend to do them justice here. In each case I will instead point out aspects of their arguments for normative consequentialism that come to seem problematic within the framework provided in preceding chapters. Central to Cummiskey's argument is his claim that Kant's categorical imperative is most plausibly understood as generating a fundamental normative "requirement to maximally promote the conditions necessary for the flourishing of rational nature and happiness."[29] This is a consequentialist normative theory, Cummisky maintains, because it "requires the promotion of the good, without including any agent-centered constraints on the maximization of the good."[30] The second formulation of Kant's categorical imperative, the requirement to treat each person always as an end-in-themselves and never as a means only, is pivotal for Cummiskey's purposes.[31] Yet on what would seem to be the most straightforward interpretation of this imperative, the interpretation that appears to have been accepted by Kant himself, it would seem to rule out Cummiskey's fundamental normative principle. A "requirement to

---

[28] Hooker (2000b, 228–9).   [29] Cummiskey (1996, p. 98).   [30] Ibid., p. 88.
[31] Kant (1997, sec. II).

maximally promote the conditions necessary for the flourishing of rational nature and happiness" would seem to require the agent to treat not only herself but all other agents only as means to this overarching end, hence to conflict straightforwardly with the Kantian requirement never to treat persons as means only.

Cummiskey offers an alternative interpretation of the Kantian imperative, however, that would reconcile it to his fundamental normative principle. On this alternative interpretation the prohibition against treating agents as means only is a prohibition against treating agents as means only to my subjective ends, for example to my pursuit of my own happiness.[32] Treating them as means to the satisfaction of the maximizing goal, by contrast, is just what it is on this alternative interpretation to treat such agents as ends in themselves. Why, however, accept such an interpretation, upon which the prohibition against treating rational agents as means only is properly understood as a requirement to treat individual rational agents as means to an impersonal goal?

Cummiskey's case for this interpretation emphasizes the impartiality of the Kantian requirement, and suggests that the most plausible understanding of this impartiality supports his alternative to the straightforward interpretation. On such an interpretation the "equal value of all rational beings" is best understood as suggesting that "all rational beings are equally significant in deciding what to do,"[33] and this impartial recognition of rational nature as "a value for any rational agent"[34] is contrasted with the egoist's view that each person's happiness is a good only for that person. Egoistic, partial recognition is recognition as good for me, impartial, agent-neutral recognition is recognition as good simpliciter, such that "each agent has a reason to treat the rational agency of any other agent as an end."[35] The categorical imperative requires impartiality, Cummiskey puts forward the impersonal conception of impartiality as the most plausible conception for this purpose, and this impersonal conception results in a normative requirement to promote the conditions for the exercise of rational nature overall.

Kant himself takes it to be the case the his categorical imperative generates prohibitions upon the rightness of action in accordance with Cummiskey's

---

[32] Cummiskey (1996, p. 89).   [33] Ibid., p. 89.   [34] Ibid., p. 88.
[35] Ibid., p. 88.

principle, and we have seen that such a principle is in considerable tension with the most straightforward reading of the imperative, upon which it prohibits treating rational agents only as means to ends, whether personal or impersonal. Kant's own understanding of the implications of his principle and the straightforward interpretation that supports it can be vindicated, however, only if there is an alternative to Cummiskey's interpretation of the impartiality appropriate to the imperative that generates agent-centered restrictions in the sorts of cases Kant seems to have in mind. We have already seen that the interpersonal conception of impartiality is just such a conception. If the choice is between partiality and impersonal impartiality, the Cummiskey interpretation of the imperative seems difficult to avoid. If the choice is between the impersonal and interpersonal conceptions of impartiality, the interpersonal conception appears to provide a plausible alternative that supports the straightforward interpretation of the categorical imperative and vindicates Kant's own understanding of its implications.

On this alternative happiness comes into view as a lower-order value from the partial standpoint of each person, and we recognize in addition certain impartial but impersonally articulated reasons to promote happiness overall. Rational nature comes into view as a lower-order value from the interpersonal standpoint. We have lower-order partial reasons to pursue our own happiness, and higher-order reasons to promote happiness overall. We have lower-order interpersonal reasons to treat people as ends and never as means only, and higher-order reasons to promote the conditions for such treatment overall. But these lower-order interpersonal reasons are agent-relative moral reasons, reasons that are presupposed in the articulation of whatever higher-order moral reasons agents have in addition. Such lower-order interpersonal moral reasons will generate the agent-centered restrictions that Kant himself takes to follow from the preferred interpretation of the second formulation of his categorical imperative. I have already argued for the advantages of an approach that takes the interpersonal rather than the impersonal conception of impartiality as fundamental to the moral evaluation of actions. An interpretation of Kantian moral foundations that adopts such an interpersonal conception, an interpretation that fits with the most natural (and Kant's own) interpretation of the categorical imperative, will not support Kantian consequentialism.

It can come to seem puzzling how else the value of rational nature can come on the scene as an appropriate candidate for higher-order promotion except as a lower-order non-impersonal moral value. There is no rationale for such a value from the agent's own partial standpoint, nor does the impersonal conception of impartiality provide such a rationale. Rather, the impersonal standpoint is a higher-order standpoint that takes up happiness and rational nature as values in the articulation of certain relevant reasons, and the intrinsic value of rational nature as a lower-order value to be taken up in impersonal evaluation appears to be most plausibly understood as presupposing an interpersonal conception of impartiality. My suggestion is that Cummiskey's interpretation of Kant elides the role that the interpersonal standpoint plays in establishing rational nature as a lower-order moral value.[36]

Parfit

Perhaps the most systematic effort to provide a non-consequentialist foundation for a form of consequentialism has been provided by Derek Parfit. Full engagement with Parfit's argument on behalf of the interpersonal alternative as it has been developed here would require a book in its own right—my remarks will thus be restricted to providing the bare outlines of such engagement between his arguments and my own.[37] Parfit argues that "Kantian Contractualism implies Rule Consequentialism."[38] Such a view, Parfit argues, "does not have any premise that assumes the truth

---

[36] Additional problems arise for such a Kantian account that does not recognize a fundamental role for the interpersonal conception of impartiality. Crucial to Cummiskey's articulation of his higher-order decisive reasons, for example, is the determination of each agent's "self-chosen conception of the good" and "rationally chosen ends" (ibid., p. 99). But such Kantian consequentialist agents have decisive higher-order reasons to promote the conditions for pursuing conceptions of the good and to "promote the happiness of others" (ibid., p. 98). For such agents, however, their dominant rationally chosen ends will just be these consequentialist higher-order ends, e.g. the promotion of the conditions for the pursuit by agents of their rationally chosen ends, where the ends of all such agents will also be dominated by the promotion of the conditions for the pursuit by agents of their rationally chosen ends. Unless agents have other fundamental rationally chosen lower-order ends, it is not even clear what the content of these higher-order ends could be. The account appears to presuppose a standpoint of practical reason and deliberation from which rational agents determine their lower-order rationally chosen ends, but also holds that the fundamental rational ends of such agents are the higher-order ends of promoting the conditions for the pursuit of such lower-order ends. Such higher-order ends threaten to pre-empt and supplant the rational ends that they appear to presuppose in their very articulation. I argued in the previous chapter that an account which recognizes that the fundamental conception of impartiality for practical rational evaluation is interpersonal rather than impersonal has resources to avoid such difficulties.

[37] In particular, although he argues against many specific challenges to his Deontic Beliefs Restriction in the text and in Appendix D, I will not have the space to demonstrate that my own challenge is not, properly understood, a target of most of these arguments, and has the resources to deflect others.

[38] Parfit (2008, p. 342). This and all subsequent quotations by permission of the author.

of Consequentialism," but "implies its Consequentialist conclusion."[39] In particular, his is not a foundational consequentialist view because although the resulting "view is Consequentialist in its claims about which are the *principles* we ought to follow, it is not Consequentialist . . . in its claims about *why* we ought to follow these principles."[40]

The relevant part of Parfit's Kantian Contractualist argument for rule consequentialism begins with what he characterizes as the Kantian Contractualist Formula, that "everyone ought to follow the principles that everyone could rationally will to be universal laws."[41] But the argument from this formula to a version of rule consequentialism only succeeds if contractualism must properly recognize what Parfit characterizes as a deontic beliefs restriction, according to which contractualists cannot consistently appeal to "the wrongness of any of the acts that we are considering."[42] This is because if we claim, as the contractualist does, that "acts are wrong when any principle permitting them would fail some Kantian or Contractualist test," we cannot also claim that "principles would fail this test when and because the acts they permit are wrong."[43] It is illicit bootstrapping to ground an account of morality in the appeal to reasons that are themselves provided by appeal to moral beliefs.

If impersonal reasons are in some cases outweighed by relevant conflicting deontic reasons, then it will not be the "optimific principles" of the rule consequentialist whose universal acceptance everyone would have sufficient reasons to choose, and contractualist foundations will not support rule consequentialist normative principles. The recognition of such deontic reasons by the contractualist would, Parfit allows, support a Harmful Means Principle[44] that would generate moral restrictions upon acting in accordance with rule consequentialist principles. But the source of such countervailing reasons that appear to constrain impersonal considerations, he maintains, must be intuitive deontic beliefs about wrongness, and contractualism itself precludes appeal to any such moral beliefs to support the reasons upon which a contractualist account of morality is based.

It is helpful to see why Parfit believes that a similar charge of illicit bootstrapping is not warranted against the appeal by contractualists to impersonal (his telic) as opposed to interpersonal (his deontic) reasons.

---

[39] Parfit (2008, p. 335).   [40] Ibid., p. 348.   [41] Ibid., p. 340.
[42] Ibid., p. 299.   [43] Ibid., p. 304.   [44] Ibid., p. 303.

Facts, Parfit suggests, give us reasons.[45] He focuses primarily upon two groups of reasons that we have for acting, those "provided by facts about what would be good for us," what would result in good outcomes from some agent's own partial point of view, and reasons provided by facts about what would be "impersonally good,"[46] what would result in the best outcome from the impersonal point of view. That more harms would occur, for example, is a fact about what would be worse overall that provides me with a reason to act to prevent such an outcome. We do typically have intuitive moral beliefs that failure to act in extreme cases of this sort is wrong. But no illicit bootstrapping upon such moral intuitions occurs because the fact that more harms would occur provides us with a reason not in virtue of the intuitive wrongness of failing to do so, but as a fact about what outcome would be impersonally good or bad. The act is morally wrong because the outcome—that in fact more harms would occur—is worse. It is the fact about what would be impersonally good, that more harms would occur, that provides us with a fundamental reason, without any appeal to the intuitive moral belief that it is morally right to act to prevent such harms.

In the case of deontic reasons a different fact, that I would have to harm someone, is introduced as apparently providing us with a reason, albeit in this case a reason not to perform the action that will prevent more harms from occurring. But such apparent reasons are not provided by facts about what would be good for us,[47] nor are they provided by facts about what would be impersonally good. Parfit takes the only viable alternative to be that such a reason is provided by a fact, that I would have to harm someone, about what it would be wrong to do, and such an appeal to intuitive moral beliefs about wrong actions to provide reasons would involve the Kantian Contractualist in illicit bootstrapping.

A crucial assumption in this argument, however, is that deontic (our interpersonal) reasons, because they are not provided by facts about good impersonal outcomes or good outcomes for some particular person, must be provided by facts about what we intuitively take to be morally wrong. The assumption is that if these reasons are not provided by facts about the goodness of outcomes, they must be provided by facts about the wrongness

---

[45] Parfit (2008, ch. 1).   [46] Ibid., pp. 50 and 52.
[47] Cases can readily be constructed in which performing such a harmful act will promote outcomes that are very good for the agent in question.

of actions. But many reasons appear to be provided by facts not about the wrongness of action or about the goodness of outcomes, but about the goodness of actions, and such facts can provide deontic reasons without any illicit bootstrapping. In addition to facts about what would be good outcomes for us, facts that are relevant from the partial point of view (that I would be harmed), and facts about what would be good outcomes overall, facts that are relevant from the impersonal point of view (that more people would be harmed), there are facts about what would be good or bad actions, facts that are relevant from the interpersonal point of view (that I would have to harm someone). The fact that I would have to harm someone does not purport to provide a reason as a fact about what would be good for me or good overall, but as a fact about what it would be good to do, a fact that counts in favor of acting not within the context of the partial or impersonal evaluation of outcomes, but within the context of the interpersonal evaluation of actions as better or worse.

Of course the fact that I would have to do harm correlates with the intuition that so acting is wrong, but this feature of deontic reasons is a point of similarity to rather than contrast with the relevant telic reasons, since the fact that more harms would be done correlates with the intuition that failure to act to prevent such harms from occurring is morally wrong. Both correlate with intuitive beliefs about moral wrongness, but the first reason is a fact about what it would be impartially (interpersonally) good to do, and the second reason is a fact about what would be an impartially (interpersonally) good state of affairs. The fact about what it would be interpersonally good to do, not the intuitive moral rightness of the action, provides us with a non-bootstrapping reason, just as the fact about the best impersonal outcome provides us with a non-bootstrapping reason, not the intuitive moral rightness of action in accordance with such reasons.

Only if grounds were provided to exclude such reasons that are provided by facts about what it would be interpersonally good to do would the charge of illicit bootstrapping gain any traction, but at no point does Parfit appear to provide an argument to support such exclusion. Intuitively wrong actions supported by impersonal reasons, reasons about good impersonal outcomes, are readily countenanced, but intuitively wrong actions supported by interpersonal reasons, reasons about interpersonally good actions, are not. Facts relevant from the standpoint of the impartial (impersonal) evaluation of outcomes as better or worse are recognized as reasons, but facts relevant from the standpoint of the impartial (interpersonal) evaluation of actions as better or worse are not. But no grounds are provided for recognizing the one set of apparently relevant facts as providing reasons and not the other. As a result there is no basis for the charge of illicit bootstrapping in either case. Good deontic reasons can support some form of harmful means principle without bootstrapping, hence Kantian contractualist foundations can support a harmful means principle that rules out normative consequentialism.

In failing to allow any role for interpersonal reasons at the fundamental level, Parfit reflects a central feature of Sidgwick's account, the account which serves Parfit in many respects as the point of departure for the development of his own account of practical reason. But the aspects of Sidgwick's account that are hostile to recognition of such a fundamental role for deontic reasons about what it is better or worse to do are precisely the aspects that Parfit most clearly rejects. Sidgwick maintains that the only foundational reasons are those provided by facts about states of affairs that are good for us or good overall, and that there is no standpoint from which these reasons are comparable: if partial and impersonal reasons dictate alternative courses of action, there is no standpoint from which the rational agent can adjudicate among these conflicting reasons by assigning them appropriate weights. Such an account does exclude a fundamental role for reasons provided by facts about what it would be interpersonally good to do.

But Parfit rightly distances his own account from the very aspects of Sidgwick's account that support such an exclusion.[48] Although he is clear that many of our reasons are provided by facts about what outcomes would be good overall or good for us, he does not limit relevant reasons to facts of these sorts. Moreover, Parfit rejects Sidgwick's claim that partial and impersonal telic reasons are not at all comparable, maintaining instead that the standpoint of the person as a rational agent not only recognizes the independent rational significance of partial and impersonal telic reasons, but deploys standards for adjudication among such potentially conflicting reasons in the determination of what the agent has sufficient or decisive reasons to do. For the rational person, Parfit recognizes, sufficiently compelling impersonal reasons will be decisive in conflicts with partial reasons.[49] These are not impersonal standards or partial standards—they are rational standards for the proper adjudication of conflicts between

---

[48] See Parfit's (2008, ch. 6, sec. 16) discussion.   [49] See ibid., p. 124.

reasons provided by facts about outcomes evaluated impersonally and partially.

Once Sidgwick's reduction of the standpoint of the person as rational agent to the partial and impersonal standpoints is accepted, conflicts between the reasons provided by these standpoints cannot be adjudicated because there is no standpoint outside of each from which to rationally adjudicate these conflicting claims. Partial reasons are decisive from the partial standpoint, impersonal reasons are decisive from the impersonal standpoint, and there is no standpoint from which to adjudicate among such potentially competing claims. But Parfit moves beyond this reduction and the imcomparability that it entails, recognizing the standpoint of the rational person as deploying standards for adjudicating conflicting claims provided by facts about outcomes that are good for me and good overall. There is no longer any reason for the rational person thus understood not to recognize in addition competing reasons provided by facts about what it would be interpersonally good to do. Unlike Sidgwick's, Parfit's account provides no basis for excluding fundamental reasons provided by facts other than facts about what outcome is best or best for me. And unlike Sidgwick's, Parfit's account allows that the standpoint of the rational person involves standards for the appropriate adjudication of conflicting reasons from various standpoints. The very aspects of Sidgwick's account that appear to preclude recognition of the fact that I would have to harm someone as a fundamental deontic reason are the aspects that Parfit rejects.

Other aspects of Parfit's account, such as his objective, value-based (as opposed to subjective, desire-based) account of reasons and what I will characterize as his outcome-based account of desires, may seem to provide grounds for hostility to recognition of fundamental deontic reasons. But the former, I will argue, provides no such grounds, and the latter, although it does provide such grounds, is beset with the same problems that we have already revealed with Nagel's outcome-based account of reasons (Chapter 7).

Central to his value-based, objective account of reasons is his claim that reasons are provided by facts.[50] These are often facts about states of affairs that will result, and such states of affairs, it may be thought, are appropriately evaluated from the standpoints appropriate for the evaluation of states of

---

[50] The value-based account of reasons is developed in Parfit (2008, ch. 2).

affairs rather than actions, that is from the partial and impersonal standpoints. But I have already provided arguments in Chapter 5 demonstrating that commitment to such a value-based, objective account of reasons is simply not an obstacle to recognition of a fundamental role for interpersonal reasons. Parfit's own account serves only to reinforce these arguments. Reasons are provided by facts that count for or against various courses of action. Such an account allows that certain of these reasons can be provided by facts about good outcomes considered impersonally, and others can be provided by facts about good outcomes considered partially. But it can also allow that certain of these reasons are provided by facts about good actions considered interpersonally. The fact that I would have to harm someone can provide me with an interpersonal reason not to do so, just as the facts that I would be harmed or more people would be harmed overall provide me with impersonal or partial reasons to act in other ways. The rational agent, on Parfit's account, takes into account all such relevant facts that count in favor of or against various courses of action, whether the reasons they provide are partial, impersonal, or interpersonal. In itself, then, a value-based, objective account of reasons is no obstacle to recognition of a fundamental role for interpersonal, deontic reasons. Indeed, it provides a framework within which it becomes clear how certain appeals to facts—that I would have to do harm—can provide fundamental deontic reasons just as other appeals to facts—that more harms would happen—can provide telic reasons.

What I am characterizing as Parfit's outcome-based account of desire can also invite an interpretation upon which it blocks recognition of fundamental deontic reasons. He characterizes desire in the wide sense as "any state of being motivated, or of wanting something to happen and being to some degree disposed to make it happen, if we can."[51] More specifically, "All desires have objects . . . these objects are all events in the wide sense that also covers acts, processes, and states of affairs." To want is thus to "want some event to occur,"[52] and among such events that we may want to occur may be actions of ours.

Such an account of desires as aiming in every case at the promo-tion of outcomes—events the occurrence of which we are motivated to promote—naturally takes appropriate reasons for desiring to be reasons

---

[51] Ibid., p. 53.   [52] Ibid., p. 53 (both quotations).

to promote or prevent such events/outcomes. Such reasons to promote or prevent outcomes, and the corresponding desires to which they give rise, will emerge within the standpoints for the evaluation of outcomes, the partial and impersonal standpoints. The interpersonal standpoint, by contrast, is a standpoint for the evaluation of actions, a standpoint that generates reasons and corresponding desires to act in certain ways, not to promote the occurrence of certain events. This outcome-based account of desires suggested by Parfit's formulation is familiar from the previous chapter; it is Nagel's outcome-based account of practical reasons transposed into an account of the desires to which such outcome-based reasons give rise.[53] If all reasons are taken to be reasons for the promotion of outcomes, as Nagel's account suggests, then insofar as we are rational our desires will aim at the promotion of the events/outcomes supported by such reasons. The standpoints for identifying such reasons, and the desires to which they give rise, will be the standpoints for evaluating outcomes, the partial and impersonal standpoints. Because the interpersonal standpoint is not such a standpoint for the evaluation of outcomes, and the facts that it identifies as reasons are not reasons for the promotion of outcomes (but for the performance of actions), it, and the facts that it identifies as reasons, can play no fundamental role on such outcome-based accounts of practical reasons and desires that reflect them.

But I have already shown that such an outcome-based account of reasons is problematic, and begs important questions against the opponent of consequentialism. These problems carry over to an outcome-based account of desires. The arguments in Chapter 7 demonstrated that Nagel's outcome-based account of reasons, upon which reasons are facts that count in favor of the promotion of events, is less plausible than an action-based account of reasons, upon which reasons are facts that count in favor of acting some way rather than another. The desires to which such reasons give rise involve in the first instance motivation to act as reason dictates. Practical reasons are reasons to act, and in rational agents they give rise to corresponding desires to do what we have such reasons to do.

---

[53] Nor, as I suggested in the discussion of Nagel, does it address the difficulties to include the agent's own actions, as both Parfit and Nagel do, among the events to be evaluated. See, on this point, Richard Moran's argument, following Anscombe, that my actions cannot be viewed by me, like yours, as "just part of the passing show" (2001, p. 32), as possible occurrences to be promoted or prevented.

Interpersonal reasons are not among the reasons that are relevant in the evaluation of outcomes as better or worse, but they do appear to be among the reasons that are relevant in the evaluation of actions as better or worse. An account of practical reason and desire that identifies all such reasons, and the attitudes to which they give rise, as reasons and corresponding desires to promote outcomes excludes interpersonal reasons at the fundamental level by fiat. But there is no reason to accept such an identification, and, as I argued in the previous chapter, ample reason to question it. If, by contrast, practical reasons are recognized as facts that count in favor of acting, and desires are recognized as involving motivations to act that are appropriately sensitive, in a rational agent, to such reasons, then, facts about what it is interpersonally good to do can play a fundamental role alongside facts about partially or impersonally good outcomes in the rational evaluation of actions and the corresponding desires to do what we have such reasons to do.

It may be mistaken to interpret Parfit's account of desires as in the preceding sense outcome-based. If it is not in this sense outcome-based, then the account presents no obstacle to the recognition of deontic reasons without bootstrapping. If it is outcome-based in the above sense, the reasons for challenging Nagel's outcome-based account of practical reason are reasons for challenging such an outcome-based account of the desires generated in rational agents by the recognition of such reasons. The result is a plausible alternative conception of desire that does not restrict desires to dispositions to promote things that can happen (outcomes) for reasons, hence that allows room for the recognition of deontic reasons without bootstrapping. Both Sidgwick's and Nagel's accounts of practical reason presuppose that good reasons at the fundamental level are reasons that count in favor of good outcomes, hence that the rational evaluation of actions is based in the evaluation of outcomes as better or worse. My suggestion is that in adopting central components of their accounts Parfit has brought with them this presupposition, and with it the consequentialist conviction that the only impartiality that plays a fundamental role in practical reason is impersonal impartiality. When this consequentialist commitment is deployed in Parfit's allegedly non-consequentialist foundations, it is not surprising that the result is normative consequentialism. Nor is it surprising that such contractualist foundations for morality, once purged of this consequentialist commitment, no longer support normative consequentialism.

8.6 Conclusion

If the foundations proposed for normative ethics invoke only an impersonal conception of impartiality, it is hardly surprising that some form of normative consequentialism will result. If only such an impersonal conception is brought into reflective equilibrium (Hooker), or is deployed in the interpretation of Kant's categorical imperative (Cummiskey), or only facts that are relevant from such an impersonal conception are allowed to count for the contractarian as non-bootstrapping reasons (Parfit), the impartiality fundamental to morality will be impersonal impartiality, and some version of consequentialism at the normative level is difficult to avoid.

I have argued, however, that such a privileging of the impersonal conception of impartiality in morality is the product of a set of mutually reinforcing mistakes. If the impersonal conception of impartiality were the only viable candidate for the conception of impartiality fundamental to morality and practicality, some variation upon consequentialism might nonetheless hold the field by default. But I demonstrated in the previous two chapters that an alternative conception of impartiality is readily available; indeed, that such an interpersonal conception comes into view through a consistent application of the very liberation strategy that Scheffler deploys as a component of his arguments that there is no such fundamental alternative moral conception. This interpersonal conception takes the independent rational significance of the personal point of view of each rational agent to be reflected in moral significance of each agent's personal point of view for each agent, significance that is independent of whatever impersonal moral significance it has. Consequentialists recognize the independent rational significance of the personal point of view, and recognize what it would be for such independent rational significance of each agent's point of view to be reflected in its independent moral significance for that agent. Only a misapplication of Scheffler's rationale, I suggest, stands in the way of recognizing what it would be for such independent rational significance of each agent's point of view to be reflected in its independent moral significance not just for himself but for each other agent.

I argued in Chapters 6 and 7 that an account of the moral evaluation of actions that is fundamentally structured by such an interpersonal conception of impartiality can account straightforwardly for both agent-centered restrictions and agent-centered permissions. The arguments in Chapter 7 establish that its prospects for accounting for both the rational authority of moral requirements (RAMS) and the moral authority of rational requirements (MARS) are far superior to those of its impersonally structured counterpart.

The characterization of this alternative interpersonal conception that I have offered is highly schematic. My efforts have focused upon demonstrating how such an interpersonal conception of impartiality comes into view as a coherent and natural response to the intractable difficulties that plague the consequentialist alternative. I have also suggested why such an interpersonal conception of impartiality is better suited than its impersonal counterpart to the space of practical reasons, with its direction of fit from many separate minds to one shared world. Yet both Hobbesian and Kantian theories of right action can plausibly be understood as having such a fundamentally interpersonal structure, and these are dramatically different moral theories that ground the appeal to the interpersonal conception in very different ways.[54]

In addition, I have left underdeveloped any account of the relationship between a fundamentally interpersonal theory of right action and any particular account of practical reason, hence of good, better, and best actions. At the end of Chapter 7 I took up Nagel's suggestion that the objectivity of practical reason and deliberation presupposes the fundamental impartiality of practical reason. I suggested that an account which takes practical reason to have a fundamentally interpersonal structure offers the prospect for a simple and elegant theory of moral reasons that accounts for the fundamental roles of partial reasons, essentially impersonally articulated reasons, and explicitly impersonal reasons, and provides in addition the resources for adjudicating conflicts among such reasons. But such an outline of an account, however attractive, is not an argument for such an account, nor have I offered an argument in support of Nagel's claim that practical reason is fundamentally impartial. A Hobbesian, for example, can accept many of the arguments that I have offered for the fundamental interpersonality of the moral evaluation of right actions, but offer a rationale for his particular minimalist articulation of such an interpersonal

---

[54] The point here is not in any way to privilege Hobbesian and Kantians options, but to emphasize, in citing these two very distinct accounts that are nonetheless both fundamental interpersonal in structure, the range of possible alternatives.

conception that is grounded in practical reason understood as fundamentally partial.

My own view is that although Nagel does not provide a persuasive argument for the claim that the objectivity of practical reasons presupposes the impartiality of practical reason, such a claim can be vindicated, and the conception of impartiality required to vindicate this claim is the interpersonal conception. Christine Korsgaard takes Kant to argue that a vicious regress of practical justification can only be avoided if some reasons are unconditionally justified. On her reading, Kant argues that such unconditional justification can only be provided if practical reason has what I have been characterizing as a fundamentally interpersonal form or structure; indeed, if such an interpersonal structure is fundamental to the very constitution of rational agency.[55]

I believe that a successful argument along these lines can be made, but such a claim must take the form at this point of a large promissory note. Nothing that I have argued so far definitively rules out a fundamentally interpersonal account of right action grounded in a Hobbesian account of partial practical reason in favor of a such an account of right action that is grounded in a more Kantian account of practical reason as fundamentally impartial and interpersonal. What I believe that I have shown, however, is that the temptation to recoil from the complexities of such daunting challenges towards what is often viewed as the relative simplicity and elegance of a consequentialist alternative is a snare and a delusion. Consequentialism, we have seen, does not avoid any of the challenges confronting such alternative accounts. Rather, it relocates them off-stage through a set of subtle misinterpretations and misguided parallels with the theoretical sphere. I have demonstrated that such misguided parallels between the theoretical and practical spheres have led consequentialists to misappropriate certain general intuitions concerning rightness and goodness. The impersonal standpoint is relevant to the articulation of only some of the reasons that are appropriately taken into account in the determination of what it is better or worse, and right or wrong, to do. This misappropriation leads the consequentialist to treat impersonality instead as the fundamental standpoint of moral evaluation, and, through appeal to RAMS, of rational evaluation

---

[55] For her argument that Kant's own argument is best understood as having this form, see Korsgaard (2007). See also Lectures 3 and 4 in Korsgaard (1996). I have explored aspects of such an argument in Hurley (2000 and 2007).

as well. The theory mistakes a higher-order standpoint that comprehends the lower-order reasons of persons for a standpoint of comprehensive reasons. By usurping the role of the rational evaluation of actions as better or worse, and supplanting it with the impersonally structured evaluation of the goodness of overall states of affairs, the consequentialist precludes plausible accounts not only of right action and the rational authority of moral requirements, but, ironically, of the impersonal evaluation of states of affairs and the important but circumscribed role that such impersonal evaluation plays in the moral and rational evaluation of actions.

I have made the case on many grounds for the superiority of theories of moral reasons that take an interpersonal rather than an impersonal conception of impartiality to be fundamental to the evaluation of actions as morally right or wrong. Although these arguments have not made the case for the superiority of one of these interpersonally structured theories in particular, they have, I suggest, taken us beyond consequentialism in the quest for such a theory.

References

Anderson, E. (1993). *Value in Ethics and Economics* (Cambridge: Harvard University Press).

Anscombe, G. E. M. (2000). *Intention*, 2nd edn (Cambridge: Harvard University Press).

Aristotle (1999). *Nicomachean Ethics*, 2nd edn (Indianapolis: Hackett Publishing).

Ashford, E. (2003). "The Demandingness of Scanlon's Contractualism," *Ethics* 113, 273–302.

Brand-Ballard, J. (2004). "Contractualism and Deontic Restrictions," *Ethics* 114, pp. 269–300.

Brandom, R. (1994). *Making it Explicit* (Cambridge: Harvard University Press).

Brink, D. (1997). "Kantian Rationalism . . .," in Cullity, G. and Gaut, B. (eds), *Ethics and Practical Reason* (New York: Oxford University Press), pp. 255–92.

Burge, T. (2003). "Perceptual Entitlement," *Philosophy and Phenomenological Research*, LXVII, pp. 503–48.

Chisholm, R. (1977). *Theory of Knowledge*, 2nd edn (Englewood Cliffs: Prentice Hall).

Copp, D. (1997). "The Ring of Gyges: Overridingness and the Unity of Reason," *Social Philosophy and Policy* 14, pp. 86–106.

Cummiskey, D. (1996). *Kantian Consequentialism* (Oxford: Oxford University Press).

Darwall, S. (1986). "Agent-centered Restrictions From the Inside Out," *Philosophical Studies* 69, pp. 291–319.

——(1995). *The British Moralists and the Internal Ought: 1640–1740* (Cambridge: Cambridge University Press).

——(1998). *Philosophical Ethics* (Boulder: Westview Press).

——(2004). "Respect and the Second-Person Standpoint," *Proceedings and Addresses of the American Philosophical Association* 78, pp. 43–60.

——(2006). *The Second-Person Standpoint* (Cambridge: Harvard University Press).

Davidson, D. (1980). "How is Weakness of the Will Possible?," in Davidson, D., *Essays on Actions & Events* (Oxford: Clarendon Press), pp. 21–42.

Donagan, A. (1977). *The Theory of Morality* (Chicago: University of Chicago Press).

Dreier, J. (1993). "Structures of Normative Theories," *The Monist* 76, pp. 22–40.

Fischer, J. and Ravizza, M. (1992). *Ethics: Problems and Principles* (Orlando: Harcourt Brace Jovanovich).

Foot, P. (1978). "The Problem of Abortion and the Doctrine of the Double Effect," reprinted in Foot, P., *Virtues and Vices* (Oxford: Basil Blackwell).

—— (1988). "Utilitarianism and the Virtues," in Scheffler, S. (ed.), *Consequentialism and its Critics* (Oxford: Oxford University Press).

—— (2001). *Natural Goodness* (Oxford: Clarendon Press).

Gaus, G. (1990). *Value and Justification* (Cambridge: Cambridge University Press).

Gauthier, D. (1986). *Morals By Agreement* (Oxford: Oxford University Press).

Gert, J. (2004). *Brute Rationality* (Cambridge: Cambridge University Press).

Gibbard, A. (1990). *Wise Choices, Apt Feelings* (Cambridge: Harvard University Press).

Hare, R. M. (1981). *Moral Thinking* (Oxford: Clarendon Press).

Harsanyi, J. (1976). "Ethics in Terms of Hypothetical Imperatives," in Harsanyi, J., *Essays on Ethics, Social Behavior, and Scientific Explanation* (London: D. Reidel), pp. 24–36.

Herman, B. (1993). *The Practice of Moral Judgment* (Cambridge: Harvard University Press).

—— (2007). "Making Room for Character," in Herman, B., *Moral Literacy* (Cambridge: Harvard University Press).

Hobbes, T. (1994). *Leviathan*, ed. E. Curley (Indianapolis: Hackett Publishing).

Hooker, B. (2000a). *Ideal Code, Real World* (Oxford: Clarendon Press).

—— (2000b). "Reflective Equilibrium and Rule Consequentialism," in Hooker, B., Mason, E., and Miller, D. (eds), *Morality, Rules, and Consequences* (Lanham: Rowman & Littlefield), pp. 222–38.

Hurley, P. (1993). "Scheffler's Argument for Deontology," *Pacific Philosophical Quarterly* 74, pp. 118–34.

—— (1995). "Getting Our Options Clear: A Closer Look at Agent-Centered Options," *Philosophical Studies* 78, pp. 163–88.

—— (1997). "Agent-centered Restrictions: Clearing the Air of Paradox," *Ethics* 108, pp. 120–46.

—— (2000). "Sellars's Ethics: Variations on Kantian Themes," *Philosophical Studies* 101, pp. 291–324.

—— (2001). "A Kantian Account of Desire-based Justification," *Philosophers' Imprint* 1, pp. 1–16.

—— (2003). "Fairness and Beneficence," *Ethics* 113, pp. 841–64.

—— (2006). "Does Consequentialism Make Too Many Demands, or None at All?" *Ethics* 116, pp. 680–706.

—— (2007). "Desire, Judgment, and Reason: Exploring the Path Not Taken," *The Journal of Ethics* 11, pp. 437–63.

Kagan, S. (1989). *The Limits of Morality* (Oxford: Clarendon Press).

Kagan, S. (1998). *Normative Ethics* (Boulder: Westview).

—— (2000). "Evaluative Focal Points," in Hooker, B., Mason, E., and Miller, D. (eds), *Morality, Rules, and Consequences* (Lanham: Rowman & Littlefield), pp. 134–55.

Kamm, F. M. (1996). *Morality, Mortality Vol. II* (New York: Oxford University Press).

Kant, I. (1997). *Groundwork of the Metaphysics of Morals*, ed. Mary Gregor (Cambridge: Cambridge University Press).

Korsgaard, C. (1996a). *The Sources of Normativity* (Cambridge: Cambridge University Press).

—— (1996b). *Creating the Kingdom of Ends* (New York: Cambridge University Press).

—— (2007). "Autonomy and the Second Person Within: A Commentary on Stephen Darwall's *The Second-Person Standpoint*," *Ethics* 118, pp. 8–23.

—— (2008). *The Constitution of Agency: Essays on Practical Reason and Moral Psychology* (New York: Oxford University Press).

Kukla, R. and Lance, M. (2008). *'Yo!' and 'Lo!': The Pragmatic Topography of the Space of Reasons* (Cambridge: Harvard University Press).

Kumar, R. (1999). "Defending the Moral Moderate: Contractualism and Common Sense," *Philosophy and Public Affairs* 28, pp. 275–309.

—— (2003). "Reasonable Reasons in Contractualist Moral Argument," *Ethics* 114, pp. 6–37.

McDowell, J. (1994). *Mind and World* (Harvard: Harvard University Press).

—— (1995). "Might There Be External Reasons?' in Altham, J. and Harrison, R. (eds), *World, Mind, and Ethics* (Cambridge: Cambridge University Press), pp. 68–85.

—— (1998). "Having the World in View," *The Journal of Philosophy* 95, 431–92.

McNaughton, D. and Rawling, P. (1991). "Agent-Relativity and the Doing–Happening Distinction," *Philosophical Studies* 63, pp. 167–95.

Mill, J. S. (2001). *Utilitarianism* (Indianapolis: Hackett).

Millgram, E. (2000). "Mill's Proof of the Principle of Utility," *Ethics* 110, pp. 282–310.

Moran, R. (2001). *Authority and Estrangement* (Princeton: Princeton University Press).

Mulgan, T. (2001). *The Demands of Consequentialism* (Oxford: Oxford University Press).

Murphy, L. (2000). *Moral Demands in Nonideal Theory* (Oxford: Oxford University Press).

Nagel, T. (1970). *The Possibility of Altruism* (Princeton: Princeton University Press).

—— (1986). *The View From Nowhere* (Oxford: Oxford University Press).

—— (1991). *Equality and Partiality* (Oxford: Oxford University Press).

—— (2002). *Concealment and Exposure* (New York: Oxford University Press).

Nietzsche, F. (1967). *On The Genealogy of Morals*, trans. W. Kaufman (New York: Vintage Books).

Norcross, A. (2006). "Reasons Without Demands: Rethinking Rightness," in Dreier, J. (ed.), *Contemporary Debates in Moral Theory* (Oxford: Blackwell), pp. 38–53.

—— and Howard-Snyder, F. (1993). "A Consequentialist Case for Rejecting the Right," *The Journal of Philosophical Research* 18, pp. 109–25.

Nozick, R. (1974). *Anarchy, State, and Utopia* (New York: Basic Books).

O'Neill, O. (1989). *Constructions of Reason* (Cambridge: Cambridge University Press).

Parfit, D. (1984). *Reasons and Persons* (Oxford: Clarendon Press).

—— (2004). "What We Could Rationally Will," in Peterson, G. (ed.), *The Tanner Lectures on Human Values, Vol. 4* (Salt Lake City: The University of Utah Press).

—— (2008). "On What Matters," unpublished manuscript, draft of August 9.

Pettit, P. (1993a). *The Common Mind* (New York: Oxford University Press).

—— (1993b). "Consequentialism," in Singer, P. (ed.), *A Companion to Ethics* (Oxford: Blackwell), pp. 230–40.

—— (2000). "Non-consequentialism and Universalizability," *The Philosophical Quarterly* 50, pp. 175–90.

—— and Smith, M. (2000). "Global Consequentialism," in Hooker, B., Mason, E., and Miller, D. E. (eds), *Morality, Rules, and Consequences* (Lanham: Rowman & Littlefield), pp. 121–33.

Phillips, D. (1998). "Sidgwick, Dualism, and Indeterminacy in Practical Reason," *History of Philosophy Quarterly* 15, pp. 57–78.

Portmore, D. (2001). "Can an Act-Consequentialist Theory Be Agent-Relative?" *American Philosophical Quarterly* 38, pp. 363–77.

Posner, R. (1981). *The Economics of Justice* (Cambridge: Harvard University Press).

Putnam, H. (1981). *Reason, Truth and History* (New York: Cambridge University Press).

—— (1990). "Objectivity and the Science/Ethics Distinction," in Putnam, H., *Realism With a Human Face* (Cambridge: Harvard University Press).

—— (1992). *Renewing Philosophy* (Cambridge: Harvard University Press).

Quinn, W. (1993). "Actions, Intentions, and Consequences," in Quinn, W., *Morality and Action* (Cambridge: Cambridge University Press), pp. 175–93.

Railton, P. (1988). "Alienation, Consequentiaism, and the Demands of Morality," in Scheffler, S. (ed.), *Consequentialism and Its Critics* (Oxford: Oxford University Press).

—— (2003). *"Facts, Values, and Norms* (Cambridge: Cambridge University Press).

Rawls, J. (1971). *A Theory of Justice* (Cambridge: Harvard University Press).

Richardson, H. (2001). "The Stupidity of the Cost–Benefit Standard," in Adler, M. and Posner, E. (eds), *Cost–Benefit Analysis* (Chicago: Chicago University Press), pp. 135–68.

Ridge, M., "Agent-Neutral vs Agent-Relative Reasons," *Stanford Encyclopedia of Philosophy* (Summer 2006 Edition), Edward Zalta (ed.), <http://plato. stanford.edu/entries/reasons-agent/>

Ripstein, A. (1999). *Equality, Responsibility, and the Law* (Cambridge: Cambridge University Press).

Sayre-McCord, G. (2001). "Mill's 'Proof' of the Principle of Utility," *Social Philosophy and Policy* 18, pp. 330–60.

Scanlon, T. M. (1982). "Contractualism and Utilitarianism," in Sen, A. and Williams, B. (eds), *Utilitarianism and Beyond* (Cambridge: Cambridge University Press), pp. 103–28.

—— (1998). *What We Owe to Each Other* (Cambridge: Harvard University Press).

—— (2008). *Moral Dimensions* (Cambridge: Belknap Press of Harvard University Press).

Scheffler, S. (1982). *The Rejection of Consequentialism* (Oxford: Oxford University Press).

—— (ed.) (1988). *Consequentialism and Its Critics* (Oxford: Oxford University Press).

—— (1992a). *Human Morality* (Oxford: Oxford University Press).

—— (1992b). "Prerogatives Without Restrictions," *Philosophical Perspectives* 6, pp. 377–97.

—— (2004). "Doing and Allowing," *Ethics* 114, pp. 215–39.

Schroeder, M. (2007). "Teleology, Agent-Relative Value, and 'Good'*," *Ethics* 117, pp. 265–95.

Sen, A. (1983). "Evaluator Relativity and Consequential Evaluation," *Philosophy and Public Affairs* 12, pp. 113–32.

—— (1985). "Well-Being, Agency, and Freedom," *The Journal of Philosophy* 82, pp. 169–221.

—— (1993). "Positional Objectivity," *Philosophy and Public Affairs* 22, pp. 126–45.

—— (2001). "The Discipline of Cost–Benefit Analysis," in Adler, M. and Posner, E. (eds), *Cost–Benefit Analysis* (Chicago: Chicago University Press), pp. 95–116.

Sidgwick, H. (1981). *The Methods of Ethics* (Indianapolis: Hackett).

Singer, P. (1993). *Practical Ethics*, 2nd edn (Cambridge: Cambridge University Press).

Slote, M. (1984). "Satisficing Consequentialism," *Proceedings of the Aristotelean Society*, supplementary vol. 58, pp. 165–76.

Smart, J. J. C. and Williams, B. (1973). *Utilitarianism: For and Against* (Cambridge: Cambridge University Press).

Smith, M. (1994). *The Moral Problem* (Oxford: Blackwell).

—— (2003). "Neutral and Relative Value after Moore," *Ethics* 113, pp. 576–98.

Strawson, P. (1971). "Truth," in Strawson, P., *Logico-Linguistic Papers* (London: Methuen).

—— (2003). "Freedom and Resentment," reprinted in Gary Watson's *Free Will*, 2nd edn (Oxford: Oxford University Press), pp. 72–93.

Thompson, J. J. (2008). "Turning the Trolley," *Philosophy & Public Affairs*, 36, pp. 359–74.

Velleman, J. D. (2000). *The Possibility of Practical Reason* (Oxford: Clarendon Press).

Wallace, J. (2006). *Normativity and the Will* (Oxford: Clarendon Press).

Watson, G. (2004a). "Free Agency," in Watson, G., *Agency and Answerability* (Oxford: Clarendon Press), pp. 13–32.

—— (2004b). "The Work of the Will," in Watson, G., *Agency and Answerability* (Oxford: Clarendon Press), pp. 123–57.

Wiland, E. (2007). "How Indirect Can Indirect Utilitarianism Be?" *Philosophy and Phenomenological Research* 75, pp. 275–301.

—— (1981). *Moral Luck* (Cambridge: Cambridge University Press).

—— (1985). *Ethics and the Limits of Philosophy* (Cambridge: Harvard University Press).

—— (1995). *Making Sense of Humanity* (Cambridge: Cambridge University Press).

Wolf, S. (1982). "Moral Saints," *The Journal of Philosophy*, pp. 419–39.

Wood, A. (1999). *Kant's Ethical Thought* (Cambridge: Cambridge University Press).

Index